Venice

Cities of the Imagination

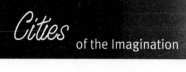

Cities of the Imagination

Venice

A cultural and literary companion

Martin Garrett

Signal
Books
Oxford

First published in 2001 by
Signal Books Limited
9 Park End Street
Oxford
OX1 1HH

A catalogue record for this book is available from the British Library.

ISBN 1-902669-28-2 Cloth
ISBN 1-902669-29-0 Paper

Line Drawings by Nicki Averill
Photographs by Andrew Esson
Cover Design: Baseline Arts
Typesetting: WorldView Publishing Services
Cover images: Andrew Esson; Pictorial Press Ltd.; The Royal Collection
© 2001 Her Majesty Queen Elizabeth II

Printed in Canada

Contents

Foreword

"It is a great pleasure to write the word," wrote Henry James of Venice, "but I am not sure there is not a certain impudence in pretending to add anything to it." Such an admonition from the master of pudeur, not to mention the double negative, is enough to give pause to any presumptive journalist, essayist, or in this case prefacer.

Is there anything to add? "Venice has been painted and described many thousands of times," James continues, "and of all the cities of the world is the easiest to visit without going there." These words were first published in *Century Magazine* almost 120 years ago, in November 1882. If they were true then, how much more true must they be today?

"Painted and described:" from amateur aquarellists to the artists he calls "the Tintoret and the Veronese," from Ruskin's "queer late-coming prose" to the observations of James's own "sentimental tourist," these two terms still appear to many people to exhaust the possibilities of interaction with Venice. But I think there is something to add, even at this late date. It is, quite simply, a personal stereo.

Thirty years before James's essay, Robert Browning wrote *A Toccata of Galuppi's*. "Poor Browning"—Shaw's epithet, based on the poet's ill-advised line comparing Rossini and Verdi—managed to get almost everything wrong here too, from the composer's Christian name to the non-existent toccata (Galuppi's keyboard works are actually sonatas, but that would have sounded too modern) to the idea of the fusty old fogey being ignored and patronized by the gay young things of his day (a native of the lace-making island of Burano, Galuppi was one of the most popular and successful musicians of the eighteenth century, whose fame as a keyboard virtuoso, among other things, was such that Catherine the Great invited him to tour Russia).

The astonishing thing is that Browning had heard of Galuppi at all. An inveterate haunter of flea-markets, he may well have come across some of his printed music there, as he did the volume which was later to form the basis of *The Ring and the Book*. It is very unlikely that he ever heard any of Galuppi's music performed, still less that of earlier

Venetian composers. But while we can't visit the Venice which James or Ruskin or Browning knew, we do have a key denied to them for imaginatively unlocking the experience of living in the city at the height of its glory. That key is the music which for them was not just unplayed, but literally unplayable.

It is worth stressing that this is a very recent development. I remember listening, back in the sixties, to a performance of the Monteverdi Vespers of 1610 and wincing at the painful attempt of the cornett players to tackle the runs in the Magnificat. At the same period, Giovanni Gabrieli's sonatas were played, if at all, as clumsy show-pieces for modern brass ensemble. Now both composers' works are practically middle-of-the-road Early Music concert fare, thanks to a new generation of virtuoso instrumentalists who can play anything written for the cornett, sackbut, dulcian, and all the other weird and wonderful voices in the Renaissance band, to a dedicated number of singers who have cultivated the techniques necessary to sing the vocal lines to such music, and to the musicologists who have combed libraries all over Europe and produced modern performance editions of these "lost" masterpieces.

This is not the place to expatiate further on the riches of Venetian music; and there are in any case excellent works on the subject available. What I have in mind is a piece of practical advice. Before you go, explore the recorded repertoire and make a few compilation tapes. Unless you have an invitation to stay in a palazzo, I would suggest that you concentrate on the vocal and notionally religious music. (Most secular music—sonatas, concerti, and solo cantatas—was performed in private spaces.) Public performances were normally given either in one of the city's Confraternities or in the Basilica of San Marco—which, it is worth remembering, had no more standing from an ecclesiastical point of view that that of the Doge's private chapel, exactly like those which can be seen in many English country houses. (By deliberate contrast, the cathedral of San Pietro di Castello, a sad vacant monstrosity with all the charm of a Victorian railway terminus on a failed branch line, is to be found tucked away on a desolate islet in the industrial fringes of the city, a clear retort by the Venetians to the pretensions of Rome and the papacy; there was a very real chance at one point that the Republic might have sided with the Protestant cause in the on-going religious Cold War.)

Such "public" music can be best understood and listened to as a straightforwardly brash and shameless display of the power, glory and splendor of *la serenissima*, for which the religious text and even God himself served merely as a pretext. You will find it at the height of its confidence in the various reconstructions recorded by the Gabrieli Consort and Players directed by Paul McCreesh, and in its dulcet decadence in the series of recordings of Vivaldi's church music by the King's Consort under Robert King. Notice especially the dark, sumptuous tones of the Gabrieli, and the ever-present sound of water to be heard throughout the Vivaldi pieces, most notably in the slower movements, where it serves as a perpetual *ostinato* reminiscent of the lapping of the lagoon.

Having taped your selected extracts, you must become a creature of the night. Leave your hotel after dark, turn on the music, take the second right and third left, and then get lost. Venice is one of the safest cities in the world, and you will eventually spot one of the nocturnal *vaporetti* which keep circulating all night long. Hop on, see the city from the water, then try and find your way back on foot. You will have the place virtually to yourself—the greatest luxury it has to offer—and if the sounds pouring into your ears do not put you into a very intense personal and private communion with the ghosts of Browning's "dear, dead women" and men, then for you I feel nothing but pity.

Capping this experience with the slow movement of Mahler's Fifth Symphony, on the basis that Visconti used it for his film of Thomas Mann's novelette set in the city, would be an error of taste. Mahler's Adagietto was explicitly intended as a love song to his wife Alma, should not be played at funereal pace, and has nothing whatsoever to do with either death or Venice. My own suggestion would be the first movement of Stravinsky's ballet *Orpheus*, with its elliptical memories of Vivaldian string *ostinatos*, woodwind and brass interjections like an appearance by the ghost of Gabrieli, and a final unresolved progression which seems to spell out the words "Now what?" Brief, poignant and inconclusive, it is a perfect musical farewell to the city which the composer loved above all others. He is buried on the cemetery island of San Michele, a quiet refuge in which to spend the touristic rush hours reading Martin Garrett's excellent guidebook, and perhaps Italo Calvino's *Invisible Cities*, a sort of fictional Baedeker to Venice. Soon night will fall, and the invisible city will once again come to resonant life.

Michael Dibdin

Preface

There is no substitute for going to Venice. The experience can, however, be enhanced by reading about the place. You can profitably read the long history of the Venetian republic. More poetically you can, say, wander in Henry James' Venice until it becomes part of your own. On second and subsequent visits, of course, the impression combines memory, reading, and the extraordinary new encounter. Consciously or not, we try the medieval chroniclers' Venice, Ruskin's, Ian McEwan's— or Carpaccio's or Canaletto's—against our own; we follow some of the contours of their city, speak, as it were, with some of their cadences.

This book provides a guide to the buildings and art of Venice. By including also a history of the city and accounts of its literature, theater, music, festivities, and food, it seeks to help readers develop the understanding and enjoyment of their own many and various Venices. (A final chapter covers some of the other exciting places within easy traveling distance.)

I should like to thank John Edmondson for his interest and encouragement, James Ferguson for his helpful suggestions, and Helen, Philip, and Edmund for their continuing support.

Martin Garrett

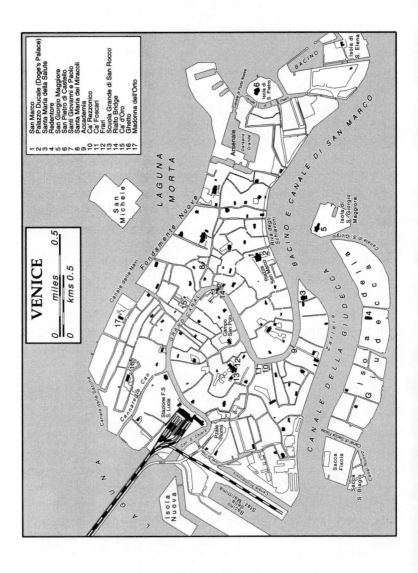

INTRODUCTION

Land and Water

Guidebooks often issue stern reminders to visitors that they should not think they can go everywhere in Venice by boat. The speaker of Robert Browning's *A Toccata of Galuppi's*, who thinks "the sea's the street there," at least has an excuse for such culpable exaggeration, as he "was never out of England." In fact, there are not only streets of the more conventional sort, but several distinct species of them: the narrow *calle*; the *rio terà* created by filling in a *rio* or small canal; the covered or arched *sottoportego*; the broader *salizada* (originally a term used for the first medieval paved streets), the *fondamenta* running along a canal; the *riva* or wharf. And there are nineteenth-century developments like the long Strada Nuova, which runs from near the station to the Rialto bridge, or the broad Via Garibaldi in eastern Venice (once a canal) with its variety of bars, restaurants, shops, and morning fruit-stalls.

Near Via Garibaldi, the Public Gardens would probably surprise Browning's speaker even more. The gardens, and the other green areas around them, make up what looks like the forest to the right of the city that you see when approaching in a boat from the Lido. At one time there was a menagerie here, to which Browning himself, who knew Venice rather better than his *Toccata* character, came regularly in order to perform a very English duty. His friend Katharine de Kay Bronson remembered how the elderly poet and his sister, Sarianna

> *never failed to carry with them a store of cakes and fruits for the prisoned elephant, whose lonely fate was often pityingly alluded to by the poet, in whom a love of animals amounted to a passion. A large baboon, confined in what had once been a greenhouse, was also an object of special interest*

*to him. This beast fortunately excited no commiseration, being healthy and
content, and taking equal pleasure with the givers in his daily present of
dainty food. After saying "Good morning" and "Good appetite" to these
animals, he gave a passing salutation to a pair of beautiful gazelles...
then a glance to the pelicans, the ostriches, and the quaint kangaroos.*

The quaint kangaroos have gone, leaving a peaceful place of trees and
grass, often as quiet as when George Sand wandered here and could
find only only "a few grumbling old men, a few stupid smokers, and a
few bilious melancholics." Elegant Venetian ladies, she observed, were
too afraid of the heat—or the cold—and "civilized men seek, by
preference, places where they can meet the fair sex: the theater,
conversazioni, cafés, and the sheltered enclosure of the Piazzetta at seven
o'clock in the evening."

Not only are there streets and (some) gardens, but the streets
open up into small *corti* and *campielli* and larger *campi;* sometimes a
campo is busy, quite often it has a café or two, an antique shop
(Campo Bandiera e Moro), a pharmacy (Campo San Stin); many are
quiet, like much of Venice beyond the main tourist attractions,
places where a few neighbors sit and talk and the occasional child
charges by on a bicycle. Only Piazza San Marco is so large that it is
dignified with the title "piazza," and even here—as in few such
spaces outside Venice—the human voice dominates. (The Piazzetta
is the area between San Marco and the waterfront. There is also, to
the left of San Marco, Piazzetta Giovanni XXIII—the reforming
pope was a former patriarch of Venice—better known, for its lions in
red marble, as Piazzetta dei Leoncini.) And there is a plethora of
bridges linking the many islets that make up Venice, excellent
viewing-points for the smaller canals, the buildings that line them,
the delivery boats precariously laden with fruit, groceries, drink, and
building materials. Visitors not endowed with a very good sense of
direction and neither skilled nor imaginative as map-readers are
bound to get lost, to find that promising restaurants have
mysteriously disappeared when they attempt to retrace their steps of
a few minutes ago, unintentionally to re-acquaint themselves with
the lanes they tried to leave an hour ago. Signs for San Marco, the
Rialto, the station, and Piazzale Roma are thoughtfully provided,

and will often at least confirm that you are going the wrong way. As a tonic, and especially if you want to see the church of the Gesuati at once, walk down the straight Rio Terà Foscarini di Sant'Agnese, next to the Accademia galleries, and it will bring you rapidly, to your complete astonishment, to the Zattere waterfront.

Some people are better than others at following the "turn sharp left after the Ponte dei Perduti, proceed along the calle, now turn right at the *second* bridge across the rio and double back toward Sant'Antonio" form of advice. Prepared for all eventualities, however, some Victorian guides recommended walkers to take a compass with them. Venetians, too, can usually unhesitatingly tell you the way; they know, as the visitor stunned by beauty, blisters, and winding routes cannot, that this is a fairly small city. And, bearing this smallness of scale in mind, it is often well worth getting lost, finding the church you weren't looking for. Along the way, the advice of Augustus Hare, author of many late nineteenth- and early twentieth-century travel-guides, may profitably be followed. Under the page-heading "What to Do!" he counsels that: "Few occupations in spare time are more absorbing than to sit upon the creamy marble parapet of some quay in the shade, and to look up and down a canal of the better sort." Even canals which sound less well-connected will do; in the 1850s the French writer Théophile Gautier had found poetry in waterways lined with tumble-down houses where the water crept by, full of vegetable leftovers and straw from old mattresses.

Traveling by boat does also—provided too many turnip peelings don't float by—have much to recommend it. Once the gondola was a distinctive part of Venetian experience. In the seventeenth century it was, to the diarist John Evelyn, a "water coach"; almost as natural as the Thames boats of the time. Such coaches gracefully dot Venetian paintings from Carpaccio's fifteenth-century water scenes to Canaletto's regattas and canal-views. (The boat's cover or *felze* survived until the nineteenth century when, it seems, it became terminally unfashionable.) As the world beyond Venice became more industrialized, the gondola came to seem more exotic. J.M.W. Turner painted what John Ruskin described as "those azure, fathomless depths of crystal mystery, on which the swiftness of the poised gondola floats double... its scarlet draperies flashed from the kindling surface, and its bent oar breaking the radiant water into a dust of gold." Lord Byron hinted at other uses for gondolas in *Beppo* (1818): although they look funereal, indeed "just like a coffin clapt in a canoe," at least once you are under the cover, "none can make out what you say or do." Sometimes

> *round the theatres, a sable throng,*
> *They wait in their dusk livery of woe, —*
> *But not to them do woeful things belong,*
> *For sometimes they contain a deal of fun,*
> *Like mourning coaches when the funeral's done.*

Leaving their gondolas moored below, the wealthy, aristocratic, or foreign, visited each other's canal-side *palazzi* with ease. They stepped from gondolas in their pearls and furs to garnish the theaters and were patiently awaited by Byron's "sable throng." Ruskin, however, irritated his *gondolieri* by keeping them and their craft moored or circling for hours on end as he peered up at, and drew with minute attention, the doorways, moldings, or escutcheons of the crumbling palaces.

Now the status and function have changed: on the whole, only tourists hire gondolas, and for most people they have become prohibitively expensive. The consolation, however, is that it is perfectly exciting to travel, as most people do, by *vaporetto*—the efficient motorized water-bus. Originally it was powered by *vapore*, steam. The serious disadvantage of the modern version is that its wake and reverberations are damaging the fabric of the city. But anyone who does not live permanently in Venice is likely to find some charm in waiting at a bus-stop that is a swaying water-cabin and traveling— at least in good or tolerable weather conditions—on an airy bus with views of scenes not unlike the ones Turner and Ruskin created. And, as when walking, it is easy to lose the crowds, and pretend to yourself that you have merged with the locals, by traveling away for a time from the obvious sights.

A good way to get a sense of the shape and contours of the city is to take one of the *Giracittà* routes, whose long loop travels from San Marco along the Giudecca Canal, past docks and huge ferries bound for Greece, to Piazzale Roma and the station, then briefly onto the Grand Canal before pushing up the Cannaregio Canal, at first civilized and elegant (and, at this end, usefully supplied with food shops), but soon more austere as it prepares to issue into the northern lagoon. Here the boat rides through rougher waters, parallel with the long promenade of the Fondamente Nuove—rather bleak even in summer—moving in now and then for stops conveniently placed for northern parts of the city and especially for the churches of the Madonna dell'Orto, Santi Giovanni e Paolo, and the Gesuiti. The *campanili* of these and other churches punctuate the long view back; in another direction, on clear days, is the outline of the mountains on the mainland, a distant and different world. And now at last the boat rounds the eastern extreme of Venice and gradually returns to the beginning.

Part of the excitement of the Giracittà is simple wonder at being able to circumnavigate a city. There is the same sense of completeness when you see the whole of Venice, with the great silver snake of the Grand Canal dividing it, from the air or in an early map. The experience of proceeding along the Canal itself, after so many generations of amazed ambassadors, proud inhabitants, color-starved northerners and surprised skeptics, has a different quality. The number of palaces and other waterside sights is finite, but seems to expand at will with each fresh journey. In other words, there are many buildings on each side, much sculptural and decorative detail, many interesting or illegible plaques; the head cannot turn two ways at once. The light is always changing, the water reflecting it in myriad variety on the different textures of stone. Light-patterns were perhaps even more various in the late Middle Ages when palazzi windows were glazed with many small panes.

The vaporetto speeds and slows and stops and, briefly rolling backwards, moves off again. Heads of numerous nationalities obscure the palazzi and water-life distracts you from them: water-taxis and ambulances, police and *carabinieri* boats, firefighters, delivery-boats with stuttering outboard motors seemingly about to be sunk by the vaporetto.

In Venice even everyday things surprise the outsider. The sirens on the emergency service boats amaze people at first by sounding just like ones on land (but surrounded by no thrum of road traffic); a barge chugging across the lagoon carrying a lorry with turning cement-mixer seems surreal. Movements glimpsed in the palaces on the Grand Canal are endowed with poetry; a middle-aged woman sitting on a balcony, shielding her face from the sun, bored perhaps, becomes Rodin's thinker; for a moment one glimpses, in an upper room at Palazzo Barzizza, someone watering flowers with what becomes, in this setting, peculiar elegance and grace. Then at night some palaces recede into the blackness and others glow and display their rich interiors.

CHAPTER ONE

Historic Venice (I): Rise of a City State

Experts have concluded that Venice, although threatened by pollution and erosion, is not actually sinking. During Carnival-time and the summer, however, the city center looks as if it is subsiding under—certainly it is damaged by—thousands of people; there are often 80,000 visitors in a day, occasionally up to 150,000. There are queues outside San Marco, reduced only slightly when officials dourly turn back those they consider to be disrespectfully under-clad. On the Ponte della Paglia movement sometimes stops entirely as a crowd jostles to photograph the Bridge of Sighs, while tour-guides flail their colorful umbrellas in an attempt to keep their groups together. And somehow, on the crammed steps of the bridge, there is also space to demonstrate and sell mechanical toys: Mickey Mouse dancing, and prone soldiers machine-gunning, to the accompaniment of loud recorded music.

Music—the latest songs, usually in English of one sort or another—also explodes from the smaller cafés. In the Piazza ring-pulls fly and tourists feed the pigeons (which is illegal in other parts of the city). Friends call and laugh and dance. They buy gondoliers' straw hats, coral necklaces, flags, footballs shirts from around the world, postcards. In the shopping areas nearby, people mill about looking for more expensive purchases of jewelry, leather, hand-printed paper, silk, lace, glass, sweets, ice-cream. All this is very human. (The lack of cars and lorries makes it difficult to wax apocalyptic about the center for very long.) And central Venice has been almost this busy and equally materialistic for hundreds of years. Nevertheless, the crowds would, to say the least, have surprised the first Venetians. They came to these then remote islands to get away not from traffic and work, but from the likes of Attila the Hun.

Beginnings

Attila invaded Italy in AD 452. One of the places that suffered his attentions was Aquileia, a major city of the Roman province of Venetia et Histria. In *The History of the Decline and Fall of the Roman Empire* Edward Gibbon describes how Attila captured it, having assaulted its walls for several months "by a formidable train of battering rams, moveable turrets, and engines, that threw stones, darts, and fire." By the time he had finished with the city, "the succeeding generation could hardly discover the ruins of Aquileia." (On what has survived see pp. 213-4.) Once he had inflicted "this dreadful chastisement, Attila pursued his march; and as he passed, the cities of Altinum, Concordia, and Padua [also prosperous cities of the Veneto], were reduced into heaps of stones and ashes." The Huns stormed on to destroy or disrupt life throughout northern Italy.

Not surprisingly, some people preferred to seek "a safe, though obscure, refuge in the neighbouring islands" of what is now called the Venetian lagoon. Refugees had already come here to escape the Visigoths in 405–6, but had mostly been able to return home after the immediate crisis was over. (After the Huns there was much less to return to.) More than a hundred of these small islands, Gibbon goes on, "are separated by shallow water from the continent, and protected from the waves by several long strips of land, which admit the entrance of vessels through some secret and narrow channels." Here there were no rich pickings to tempt Visigoths, Huns, Vandals, and the like. And the area was not entirely foreign to most of the refugees, since the Veneti—the local tribe who, speaking a language similar to Latin, had easily assimilated with Rome—had always lived near rivers, channels, and marshes. Probably only a few fishermen lived on the lagoon before the exiles joined them, but the newcomers themselves must have included experienced fishermen. No doubt there were also people versed in extracting and trading in salt, the other staple industry of the early lagoon settlements. Another important sort of continuity with life on the mainland was the bringing over, during the gradual process of emigration that continued through the later fifth century, of fragments, precious, inscribed, decorated, from temples and other public buildings. These would contribute to the Venetians' sense of identity, their frequent later conception of themselves as the new Romans, and the taste for fine and varied marble that would make their city a by-word for splendor from the eleventh century onwards.

But such splendor was six centuries ahead. At first buildings were wooden and much trial and error must have gone into protecting them against flood and erosion. The best solution, it became clear, was to build on rafts or platforms supported by wooden piles driven down, closely packed together, into the island clay. Channels needed to be maintained and the first bridges between islets built. Fear of invasion no doubt remained. And, abundant though the fish and the salt were, some food still needed to be imported from the mainland. Wells were sunk (later decorative well-heads remain a feature of most *campi*) but were subject to salting by unusually high tides. Lack of fresh water remained a problem for many centuries: in 1494 Canon Pietro Cassola of Milan was surprised, amidst so much water, to see dried-up wells, cisterns for collecting rain, and boat-loads of water from the River Brenta expensively for sale. (By this time, of course, water was needed by a much larger population than in the time of the early settlers.) It was for wood, food, and water as well as for military and political reasons that Venice built a *terraferma* empire from the fifteenth century.

Consolidation and Independence

Yet within a hundred years, as warring tribes and factions continued to rampage about the mainland, the islanders had established a viable way of life. By 466 they were sufficiently well-organized for twelve groups of islands to agree to start electing annual tribunes to represent them. As the western Roman Empire fell apart the islanders managed the balancing trick which, in one version or another, their descendants would go on performing for much of the thousand-year history of the Venetian Republic: they kept on good terms with the "Barbarian" kings of Italy while remaining subjects of the Eastern or Byzantine Empire. Their effective independence from both these powers was guaranteed, besides, by the geography of the lagoon. By 523 they were already regarded as something of a special case, a breed of survivors—or at least it was clear that anyone relying on their cooperation had best flatter them judiciously. A letter is extant in which Cassiodorus, prefect under Theodoric the Ostrogoth (king of Italy 493–526), politely explains to the prefects of the lagoon that oil and grain need to be transported from Istria to Theodoric's capital, Ravenna. In the process he depicts a Venetian utopia, if one expressed in florid Latin which the practical people he salutes might have eschewed. John Julius Norwich's translates:

> *Pray show your devotion, therefore, by bringing them hither with all speed. For you possess many vessels in the region... Your ships need fear no angry gusts, since they may continually hug the shore. Often, with their hulls invisible, they seem to be moving across the fields. Sometimes you pull them with ropes, at others men help them along with their feet...*
>
> *For you live like sea-birds, with your homes dispersed, like the Cyclades, across the surface of the water. The solidity of the earth on which they rest is secured only by osier and wattle; yet you do not hesitate to oppose so frail a bulwark to the wildness of the sea. Your people have one great wealth—the fish which suffices for them all. Among you there is no difference between rich and poor; your food is the same, your houses are all alike. Envy, which rules the rest of the world, is unknown to you. All your energies are spent on your salt-fields; in them indeed lies your prosperity, and your power to purchase those things which you have not. For though there be men who have little need of gold, yet none live who desire not salt.*

At first the islanders' main centers of commerce and power were at Malamocco, on the long island between the lagoon and the Adriatic now called the Lido, and on Torcello. Malamocco, which faced the sea, was eventually swept away by an earthquake and tidal wave early in the twelfth century (the present village of the same name was subsequently established on the lagoon side of the island), while malaria and the silting-up of the river Sile in the later Middle Ages began Torcello's decline from thriving trade-station to the present near-deserted green retreat. But already by the eighth century these settlements were beginning to be superseded by the island cluster of Rivus Altus ("high bank"), or *rivo alto*, which became, as Rialto, the commercial heart of Venice.

The First Doges
The first doge (the Venetian form of the Latin *Dux* and Italian *Duce*—duke, leader), Orso, had his palace or castle at Malamocco. His election in 727 resulted from a temporary breach with Constantinople. When the literally iconoclastic Emperor Leo III denounced the use of icons and other images in churches, Italy was one of the provinces that refused to implement the policy. The Byzantine viceroy or Exarch, based in Ravenna, was murdered, the status of the pope as leader of western Christians was confirmed, and in Venice Orso came to power. But iconoclasm, in the west at least, was abandoned and good relations soon restored. Orso reasserted his loyalty to the emperor and was given the Greek title *hypatos*, consul, which became in effect his family's surname, *Ipato*. (Later Venetian legend had it that the first doge was elected in 697 and remained completely independent of Byzantium.)

Internal affairs proceeded less smoothly; several early doges were deposed or died violent deaths. The strongly pro-Byzantine Giovanni Galbaio (doge from 775) and his family were removed after murdering the spiritual head of the lagoon churches, the Patriarch of Grado, for refusing to do their bidding; he was hurled from the tower of his own palace. Doge Obelerio degli Antenori, elected in 804, was equally vigorous in his support of the new power in Europe, the Frankish Emperor Charlemagne, and equally high-handed. In 810 Obelerio and his brothers, hoping to subdue their enemies, called upon Pepin, son of Charlemagne, to occupy Venice. The Venetians, not even pausing until later to expel the dynasts, blocked the channel between the islands of Lido and Pellestrina with sharp stakes. Safe behind their barricade, they were able, metaphorically and perhaps literally, to thumb their noses at the Franks who, after six months' bombardment with stones and arrows, withdrew. Venice did, however, agree to pay Pepin tribute.

Subsequent negotiations between the two empires, finalized in the Ratisbon Treaty of 814, confirmed Venice as Byzantine but also continued the payment of tribute-money to the western empire, which in return gave up its claim to Venice. A peaceable conclusion had been reached. But the fighting on the outer islands persuaded the Venetians, under the new Doge Agnello Participazio (811–27), to move their capital from Malamocco to the safer Rialtine islands—the site of the present city. The events of 810 were also significant, Norwich argues persuasively, because the Venetians had shown themselves willing and able to fight for their independence. Whatever the old rivalries and jealousies, "in a moment of real crisis they were capable of seeing themselves not as men of Malamocco or Chioggia, of Jesolo or Pellestrina, but as Venetians." It was in this atmosphere of increased national consciousness that in 828 the body of St Mark was brought to Venice and in about 830 the first basilica of San Marco was begun to house it. The city which could acquire not merely the relics but the whole corpse of one of the four evangelists was guaranteed special status indeed.

Stability and Prosperity

By the tenth century the Venetians were trading extensively in Alexandria, Palestine, Syria, Byzantium and the Black Sea. Prosperity was increasing, largely unaffected by the internal feuding which continued periodically to erupt. More general stability does seem to have been achieved under Doge Pietro Orseolo II (991–1008), a capable ruler who, among much else, reconciled feuding parties, negotiated treaties with both the empires and with the Arabs of North Africa, relieved Byzantine Bari from another force of Arabs ("Saracens") and established himself as Duke of Dalmatia—or at least some of its major ports and coastal areas—in a triumphant expedition to the eastern Adriatic.

In 992 Byzantium granted Venice some of the privileges on which its subsequent domination of the Aegean and eastern Mediterranean were based: most importantly, customs dues payable by ships arriving in Constantinople were considerably reduced. Ninety years later a new *chrysobull* ("golden bull" or imperial decree) set aside for Venetian use a number of shops, houses and factories in Perama (a market area of Constantinople), exempted the Venetians now from all duties and taxes in Byzantine territory with the exception of Crete and Corfu, and established penalties for anyone with the temerity to withhold their rights. Similar privileges were given to the Venetians' rivals in the region, the Genoese and Pisans, but always later and rarely so comprehensively. And where quoting the chrysobull did not have the desired effect, Venice could, where necessary, enforce its will; in the years following 1119, when Emperor John II refused to renew the exemptions, the Venetians hinted at the need for their restoration by besieging Corfu and raiding other islands including Cephalonia, where they made off with the body of St. Donatus. (They installed it in the basilica on Murano, re-dedicated, as a result, as Santa Maria e Donato). In 1126 John took the hint and restored the rights. Another chrysobull reaffirmed them in 1147. By this time exemptions applied also to the trade-rich, well placed islands of Crete and Corfu.

For all this, however, relations between fading Byzantium and freshly glowing Venice could be difficult. Matters were complicated by the need to maintain positive contacts with the western empire and, where it was necessary or gainful, the Arabs, the Normans, and other "Latins," all vying at this time for Mediterranean influence, trade, or territory. Between 1147 and 1149, encouraged by the latest golden bull, the Venetians joined the Byzantines in laying siege to the Normans of Sicily who had captured Corfu. The allies eventually won the day but during the long siege squabbles and even violence had broken out between them. In the worst incident a group of Venetians, fired perhaps by alcohol, certainly by contempt for the Greeks and the divinity with which they insisted on hedging a king, seized the flagship of Emperor Manuel Komnenos. They proceeded, to the indescribable fury of the watching Greeks, to put up the gold-sewn imperial curtains, roll out the purple imperial carpets, and crown as emperor someone described by the chronicler Niketas Khoniates as a cursed "Ethiopian with black skin," intended for the dark-complexioned Manuel. According to Niketas, the emperor's first thought was to visit due punishment on these "barbarians," but he swallowed his pride to preserve the alliance. All the same, he "nourished anger in his heart like an ember beneath the ashes." Venice went on its way, exciting further Byzantine suspicions by signing agreements, in 1154, with the King of Sicily and the western emperor Frederick Barbarossa. The Sicilian agreement was renewed in 1175 but in 1167 Venice was a founder member of the Lombard League of north Italian cities opposed to Frederick. At last, in 1171, the "ember" was kindled when, after Venetians in Constantinople had smashed up the quarter newly allotted to their enemies the Genoese, Manuel suddenly ordered the mass arrest of all Venetians in his empire. Doge Vitale Michiel II mounted an expedition against the empire and got as far as Chios, but was driven back both by disease in the fleet and by Byzantine delaying tactics. On his return, the doge was stabbed to death by an angry citizen in Calle delle Rasse as he fled from the palace toward the convent of San Zaccaria.

Doge Michiel's peers, who had not sought his death but who had found him too little willing to consult them, took the opportunity to reform the constitution, beginning the long, very gradual limitation of ducal powers. Sebastiano Ziani, the first doge elected under the new dispensation, did much to restore Venetian fortunes by his skill in negotiating treaties, mainly with Sicily and, again, Frederick Barbarossa. This helped to persuade Manuel Komnenos of the imprudence of continuing to offend people with such potentially dangerous friends; most of the prisoners taken in 1171 were at last freed in 1179. And the powerful independent status of Venice was more emphatically asserted when, in 1177, it hosted the great gathering at which Pope Alexander III and Frederick Barbarossa were reconciled after their long and divisive schism.

Having acknowledged the spiritual and temporal authority of Alexander III in the presence of four cardinals at the Lido, and had his seventeen-year excommunication lifted, Frederick was accompanied by the doge, with much pageantry, to San Marco. There Alexander, enthroned, awaited the return of the prodigal (to whom he later, with the parable in mind, sent a fatted calf). Archbishops and canons led the emperor forward, he cast aside his red cloak, prostrated himself, and kissed the pontiff's feet and knees in ritual obeisance.

A lozenge of white marble before the central door of San Marco marks the spot where Frederick is said to have knelt. The basilica, which had already acquired essentially its modern form, was an appropriate setting for such important events. In many ways this third basilica on the site was Byzantine in style and inspiration, but by the eleventh and twelfth centuries this represented less a declaration of old loyalties than a confident assertion of the right of Venice to rank with, perhaps even replace, the "new Rome" of the Bosphorus. The Piazza and Piazzetta also, under Doge Ziani, took on much of their modern appearance: the canal which ran past San Marco was filled in, the whole area paved with brick, the surrounding houses colonnaded, the ducal palace extended, a wall along part of the waterfront demolished, and the two ancient columns erected in the Piazzetta. The columns, which had come back with Michiel's expedition to Greece, were later crowned by statues of the lion of St. Mark and St. Theodore and his crocodile. In other ways, too, the city was thriving and developing. Banks opened on the Rialto in the 1150s; some streets and campi were paved; some streets were even lit, long in advance of other European cities, by small oil-lamps.

Enrico Dandolo and the Fourth Crusade

In 1192 Enrico Dandolo was elected doge. He was in at least his mid-seventies and had been one of the envoys Michiel had (pointlessly, as it turned out) sent to Constantinople twenty years earlier. He was blind, possibly as a result of injury inflicted on him at that time, more likely in some other incident or battle. Certainly he was no friend of the Byzantines, whose capital he was primarily responsible for ransacking at the end of the so-called Fourth Crusade. Venice, not keen to spend money if there was no commercial or diplomatic advantage to be gained, had played a minimal part in the Third Crusade. Whether the Venetian role in the Fourth was astutely plotted from the outset or simply evolved with circumstances is uncertain.

The story begins with the arrival in the city, in 1201, of a delegation of six French noblemen seeking a fleet to take crusaders to Palestine or Egypt. They included Geoffroi de Villehardouin, Marshal of Champagne and chronicler. After careful deliberation (of the sort dangerously lacking in Vitale Michiel's day) the doge and Council made their offer: they would provide ships sufficient to transport 4,500 knights, their horses, their 9,000 squires, and 20,000 soldiers, on payment of 85,000 silver marks. Venice itself would also—"pour l'amour de Dieu" said Dandolo according to Villehardouin—contribute fifty armed galleys in exchange for half of any conquest "by sea or by land." The French knights agreed to these terms and, as was still constitutionally necessary for such major decisions, the doge called an *arengo* or assembly, at least in theory, of all male citizens, to grant approval. Villehardouin says that 10,000 people came to San Marco and, having heard mass and the Marshal's promise that they would take pity on captive Jerusalem and avenge the shame of Jesus Christ, thundered their consent so that the earth seemed to shake beneath them. A crusading army would assemble, and the cash would be produced, the following year.

In the event, as Dandolo and his advisers may well have expected, the French and German leaders of the intended expedition had difficulty raising so large an army and so much money. In June 1202 they had still raised only 50,000 marks. The Venetians, opportunistic as ever, now offered nevertheless to proceed on condition that the crusaders helped them, en route, to recapture their former colony of Zara. The new agreement was again publicly saluted in the basilica. From the pulpit Dandolo "asked" (the Council must already have decided the matter) to be allowed to take the cross himself. He was an old man, he said, weak, in need of rest but, he felt, the best available person to command the Venetian force. Probably his most valuable qualification for the job was his long experience of dealing with, and direct knowledge of, Constantinople. The people, moved to tears by the aged blind man's willingness to sacrifice himself for the holy cause, shouted their approval once again. The doge, himself weeping (according to Villehardouin), knelt before the high altar while a cross was sewn onto his large cotton hat, the better to be seen and followed by all. Many citizens did follow his lead, which helped to fill up the empty ships.

In November 1202 the fleet set off from Venice. From the beginning it was clear that the Venetians would play a dominant part. They were experts in seamanship and experts in self-presentation; Dandolo's own galley, painted vermilion, sailed out to the accompaniment of silver trumpets and timbrels. From the masts of his own and other ships, priests and their assistants sang the hymn *Veni Creator Spiritus*.

Pageantry and holiness soon gave way to savagery. Zara was sacked. From Rome Pope Innocent III fulminated against this diversion to fight fellow Christians instead of sailing against the infidel. For a time all the crusaders were excommunicated, as were Dandolo and Venice for a longer period. While wintering in Zara, the doge, Boniface of Montferrat, and the other leaders decided on a larger diversion. They would make for Constantinople in order to install as emperor the pretender Alexios, who joined them at Zara in the spring of 1203. Dandolo at least, and perhaps the others, must have foreseen rich pickings once they were in the ancient and richly adorned capital. Alexios promised privileges, large sums of money, and the submission of the Orthodox Church to the pope. The fleet reached the walls of Constantinople in June. Forces then advanced by land and water; the great iron chain across the Golden Horn was either loosed or broken through. The usurping Emperor Alexios III could offer little organized resistance, so depleted at this time were Byzantine forces, coffers, and confidence. The Venetians positioned ships along the walls on the sea side and set efficiently to work with scaling ladders, slings, mangonels, and battering-rams. They also used "flying bridges," platforms that swung out from the ships' fo'c'sles. The doge himself, in spite of his years and infirmity, played a vital part in egging the besiegers on. As the defenders rained down missiles he stood boldly, fully armed, on the prow of his galley by the banner of St. Mark. He insisted that the galley should be run ashore and himself leapt down with the others, with the banner still borne before him. This stung the crews of other galleys, hesitant until now, to do likewise. Soon, in spite of determined axe-work by the Varangian Guard—Scandinavian and English mercenaries in imperial service—towers began to be captured and defenses breached.

As the crusaders moved into the city, Alexios III moved rapidly out and was replaced by Isaac II, father of the much-promising pretender Alexios. At the crusaders' insistence the pretender was then made co-emperor as Alexios IV. Meanwhile the fleet waited, outside the city, for the extravagant promises to be fulfilled. The Venetians, with their knowledge of Byzantium, surely knew all along that this was impossible. The crusaders' relationship with their protégé rapidly declined and he was equally unpopular with his subjects who, perceiving him as ineffectual and foreign-dominated, eventually murdered him and probably did the same for his father. By March 1204, the way was clear for the seizure of the city and, it was decided, the whole Byzantine empire. Once the walls had again been breached, three days of terrible slaughter, rape, vandalism, and desecration followed. (Still the Pope protested impotently at this conclusion to his crusade.) Then the loot was distributed, three-eighths of it going to the Venetians. Some of their prizes, including the four famous bronze horses, went to adorn San Marco (see pp.62-3).

Venice gained much else from this episode. A committee of six Venetians and six "Franks" was appointed to elect a new non-Greek emperor, who turned out, unsurprisingly, to be the candidate Dandolo wanted, Baldwin of Flanders. The Venetian Tommaso Morosini became Patriarch, a Roman Catholic replacing the Orthodox incumbent; although Pope Innocent III at first demurred at the appointment, he soon gave in and, bowing to the realities of the situation, lifted the excommunication on the doge and Venice. The republic was awarded three-eighths both of Constantinople and of the empire, although most of this still had to be fought or negotiated for over the next few years. Venice carefully selected the ports and islands that would benefit Venetian commerce most. The Venetians relied probably both on their knowledge of these places and their partners' ignorance of them. Gains included the southern Greek ports of Modon (Methoni) and Coron (Koroni), Negroponte and parts of the island of the same name (ancient Euboia) and, most importantly, Crete. This island was not only itself a major producer of oil, wine, grain, and fruit, but an important staging-post on the route from Italy to Egypt and the Levant and a key to the control of the Aegean. It was not part of Venice's original allocation but was obtained, for 1,000 marks, from Boniface of Montferrat. Crete was to remain for several centuries the cornerstone of the Venetian sea-empire.

In June 1205 Dandolo died, aged about eighty-five or even ninety, in Constantinople. He was buried in Agia Sophia. He is honored as the most forceful and victorious of doges and sighed over as the leading spirit in a crusade of freebooting and murder that began hundreds of years of political instability in the former territories of the Byzantine empire. In the long term the way had been opened for the success of the Ottoman Turks, who would later do much to reduce the Mediterranean power of Venice.

Constitution and Conspiracy

At the victorious end of his life Enrico Dandolo could probably, had he so chosen, have been crowned emperor in Constantinople. (One unlikely tradition maintains that a proposal at least to transfer the Venetian capital there was defeated by a single providential vote.) But he did not, and his son Ranieri, vice-doge during his absence, made no attempt to continue the dynasty. Instead Ranieri supervised the election of a new doge (Pietro Ziani) in 1205, accepted the command of an expedition against still unsubjugated Crete, and was killed in action. "His name is not on the list of the doges," says F.C. Lane, "but should be on a list of those who established the tradition of behaviour which gave viability to the Venetian political system. In that system, the non-doges, those who gracefully accepted second place, are as important as those who fulfilled the highest office successfully."

While this is true one should bear in mind that the Venetians were very good, in later centuries, at propagating what has become known as the Myth of Venice: the ideal geographical situation, the perfectly balanced constitution, the perfect mix of monarchic, oligarchic, and (somewhat less plausibly) democratic elements, the long list of altruistic "non-doges." Cardinal Gasparo Contarini, one of the main Renaissance proponents of the myth, makes all these claims and altogether commends the "wisdom and virtue" of the ancestors who, as his Elizabethan translator Lewis Lewkenor has it:

> omitted nothing which might seem to pertain to the right institution of a commonwealth: for first they ordained the whole life and exercise of the citizens to the use and office of virtue, and always with greater regard and reckoning applied their minds to the maintenance of peace than to glory of wars: bending always their chiefest care to the preservation of civil concord and agreement among themselves, [while] not in the meantime neglecting warlike offices.

The system did work better than most and attracted due respect from outsiders as well as Venetians, but it rarely functioned as smoothly as the myth would have it: the noble families and larger clans inevitably wielded strong influence; there was antagonism between the old and new nobility; particularly in the sixteenth and seventeenth centuries there were cases of bribery and vote-fixing in the Great Council; and however well intentioned the system was, it was so complicated that administration and justice often moved painfully slowly and inefficiently.

The constitution of the republic evolved through gradual restriction, definition and delegation of the once monarchical power of the doge. In the mid-eleventh century, as the age of the dynastic doges ended, a group of *sapientes* acted as ducal advisers, able at least in theory to curb over-mighty tendencies. The advisers who assumed power at the assassination of Vitale Michiel II in 1172 introduced more formally "democratic" measures: a body which would elect the new doge was formally established for the first time, as was the subsequently important Great Council. Doges were later (from 1229) held to account—if often, again, only in theory—by the swearing of individualized *promissioni* or accession oaths. Later a committee was established to scrutinize their record in office and could, if necessary, impose fines on their heirs. This was only one of the many committees, and one of the many checks and balances, which helped to produce relative stability. Regulations prevented members of the same family from holding office at the same time. The Great Council elected, for sixteen-month terms, the three *Avvogadori di comun* (state attorneys) whose job was to police public officials and to prosecute any, however senior, who neglected or abused their position. As part of the same pattern the election of the doge became increasingly complicated; by the fourteenth century the electors emerged only after themselves being chosen by a mixture of committees electing other committees and, at several stages along the way, the drawing of lots.

The people doing all this policing and electing were, of course, noblemen. One of the surprises of Venetian history is how little resentment other social groups seem to have expressed at their exclusion from power. In the 1260s, unusually, there was some unrest in the trade guilds, which exercised much more power in some other Italian cities of the time. Measures taken in 1268 by Doge Lorenzo Tiepolo probably helped to minimize later discontent. The guilds were given greater autonomy and accorded a greater prominence in public ceremonial: an action not only tactful but of real significance in a city that delighted in any excuse for pageantry and saw its richness as a symbol of its greatness. At about the same time Tiepolo created the office, tenable only by citizens and elected by the Great Council, of Grand Chancellor. The chancellor, as head of the civil service, held a position of great influence even if not directly of power, and again the fact was publicly acknowledged: in many ceremonies he took priority over everyone but the doge. He was, moreover, paid a handsome salary, as were the senior chancellery secretaries. Lower-ranking administrators seem also to have been able to pursue fulfilling careers, and there were many government jobs for guards, boatmen, messengers, and the like.

When in 1509, with Venice seemingly about to be overwhelmed by its enemies (see below), citizens did complain unusually loudly about being expected to pay high taxes without being allowed any share in decision-making, the councilor Antonio Loredan met a large group of them in the Ducal Palace. He spoke plausibly to them about the advantages and esteem they enjoyed: how many of them held important offices, sometimes hereditary, usually more permanent than those held by the nobility; how heavily these temporary noble officers relied on their experienced clerks; how fortunate the citizens were compared with Loredan and his class who, custom dictated, had to spend lavishly on clothing, ceremonies and—he wisely put in—"games arranged for the people." Not everyone was persuaded by this, but enough people did agree for complaints not to issue in rebellion. (Another area in which non-patricians could gain fulfillment and respect was the *scuole* or religious confraternities: see Chapter 6.)

The *Maggior Consiglio* or Great Council held, technically at least, much of the power. For practical reasons in the thirteenth century it came to eclipse the old *arengo* or assembly of all the people. For the same reasons, as the state became richer, more populous, and more stretched overseas, most decision-making was further devolved to the Senate, about 120 strong, and above them to the *Quarantia* (the Forty, the chief court of appeal), the Ducal Council, and the still at least highly influential doge. But the Great Council retained a different sort of importance, since the way it was constituted played a considerable part in preventing the lesser nobility from feeling excluded from government. In 1297 the *serrata* (closing, locking) *del Maggior Consiglio* restricted membership to those already in the council over the preceding four years; soon afterwards, however, eligibility was extended to people (men only, of course) whose ancestors had been members. It has often been argued that factionalism among the nobility was made less likely because this system recognized the position not only of their leaders but even of those who lacked connections or were poor. (Poor noblemen, known as *barnabotti* because they tended to live in the parish of San Barnabà, became a common phenomenon only much later, in the seventeenth and eighteenth centuries when Venice was clearly in decline.) The numbers of the Great Council increased fivefold between 1297 and 1311, a growth that would soon necessitate the building of their grand new Sala del Maggior Consiglio in the Ducal Palace, a further public statement of the glory of the whole patriciate.

Naturally some patricians were not so easily satisfied, and the faction could not entirely be stamped out. The most ambitious attempted coup was led by Marco Querini and his son-in-law Bajamonte Tiepolo, members of noble families who had opposed Doge Pietro Gradenigo's complex intervention in the affairs of Ferrara, which had resulted in military humiliation, economic hardship and papal interdict. Venice and the pope had backed rival claimants to the marquisate of Ferrara, which was technically under papal rule. Incensed by this, by the traditional rivalry between the *case vecchie* and newer rich men like Gradenigo, and by various more personal grudges, the disaffected group conspired to seize power on June 15, 1310. They wanted to strike at the Ducal Palace both from the lagoon and from the Piazza. But while plans were being finalized, one of the conspirators, Marco Donato, changed sides and betrayed his fellows. Marco Querini arrived in the Piazza as planned only to find it full of armed men, including the doge's allies and Querini's enemies, the Dandolo. Querini was killed in the fighting. The group who were meant to attack from the lagoon, but who had been stopped from leaving the mainland by a storm, were attacked there, captured and executed. And as Bajamonte Tiepolo and his followers paused to regroup before riding into the Piazza, an old woman who happened to be using a pestle and mortar either hurled or accidentally dropped the mortar (or the pestle, say some) from a high window, killing the rebels' standard-bearer. A relief above the Sottoportego del Cappello, just before the clock-tower in the Piazza, commemorates her deed. In reward, the story goes, she asked only to have the rent on her house pegged and to be allowed to fly the flag of St. Mark from it on feast-days and the anniversary of the foiled rebellion.

Morale collapsed and the Tiepolo insurgents rushed back to the Rialto bridge, then made of wood, demolished it behind them, and shored up in Tiepolo's home *sestiere* of San Polo, where they could count on local support. Doge Gradenigo and his advisers, moving with a degree of forethought and restraint which few contemporary rulers would have shown, opted to banish the surviving ringleaders rather than fight it out and in the process further endanger the state. Continued faction-fighting would have been especially dangerous while the Ferrara affair was still unresolved.

Once the crisis was over, Tiepolo's house was demolished and that of the Querini converted into a slaughterhouse. The conspiracy also had a more lasting consequence since the Council of Ten was formed in reaction to it, at first simply in order to keep the exiled plotters under surveillance. In 1334 it was reconstituted as a permanent body with sweeping powers to investigate and suppress all attempts at factional activity, anything considered detrimental to the state. The "Ten" were in fact often a powerful seventeen: for voting purposes they were joined by the doge and his six councilors. In later generations their lack of accountability—even the *avvogadori* could not investigate them—and the secrecy of their proceedings helped to give them a reputation for arbitrary justice. Increasingly, too, members were drawn almost exclusively from the richest noble families. Some of the political power of the Ten was successfully legislated away in the sixteenth and seventeenth centuries, but their role in intelligence and criminal matters continued to grow. In 1539 the Ten created an equally feared group, the three State Inquisitors.

Members of the Ten were elected only for a year, and three of them became its *capi* or heads each month. They were unlikely to be able to use their position to mastermind a Tiepolo-style coup attempt. Almost the only patrician who was elected to his post for life was the doge, and one doge—although before he had been in office long—did make the attempt. Marin Falier, elected at the age of seventy-six in 1354, soon developed (or perhaps had long nourished) a fanatical hatred of younger members of his own class. What sparked his particular resentment, apparently, was the merely nominal punishment by the Forty of a young aristocrat who had deposited a mocking verse on the doge's throne. (The verse suggested, according to a later account, that he was a cuckold.) Falier, already seething, then heard complaints from other people about high-handed conduct by aristocrats. One of the most important non-patrician figures in Venice, the director of the Arsenale, Stefano Ghiazza, was one of the complainants and became one of the doge's collaborators in a plot to massacre the obnoxious young lords, having lured them into the Piazza, on the night of April 15, 1355, with a false report that a hostile Genoese fleet was approaching. According to the plan, Falier would then be installed as an absolute prince and Ghiazza, no doubt, would become his right-hand man. As with the Tiepolo plot forty-five years earlier, the conspirators were betrayed. (Here there were several informers.) The Ten investigated the facts and then consulted the *avvogadori* and other senior officials. Ten of the lesser conspirators were hanged at once. A Council of Thirty, comprising the Ten and twenty other senators, was appointed to try Falier. He had no defense to offer, admitted his guilt, and was beheaded on the morning of April 18. The system had worked; the betrayal of the plot could be put down to luck, but it also probably suggests the widespread Venetian loyalty to the republic. There were later attempts to modify the constitution, to weaken the Council of Ten, for instance, but not, until 1797, to overthrow it.

Trade and the Genoese Wars

Stability was provided also by the extraordinary success of Venetian commerce. From the early days of the republic there was profitable trade with Byzantium and Egypt. By the thirteenth century Venetian traders were active from the Middle East to England; after 1260 the Polo family and others even reached China. The spices that were much in demand for flavoring meat in Europe—nutmeg, cloves, coriander, cinnamon, ginger—were the mainstay of trade, bought in the markets of Alexandria, Acre, and other eastern Mediterranean ports, having been carried from India across the Arabian Sea to the Red Sea and on by camel through Arabia or Egypt. Many other goods were imported from the east, including silk, Cretan sugar and wine, raisins from the Ionian islands (mostly Venetian territory from the fourteenth or fifteenth century), Syrian wax, and Black Sea caviar. Venetian merchants carried these across the Alps on long-established routes to the growing cities of southern Germany and brought back German and Bohemian silver, copper and iron, and wool cloth from Flanders and England. So important was this trade that by 1228 Venice had provided German merchants with their own Fondaco dei Tedeschi, a building on the Grand Canal which combined warehousing, accommodation, and a trade center. The present building replaces the one that burned down in 1505.

Other routes were exploited: up the rivers of France from Marseille to the great trading fairs in Burgundy, Champagne, and beyond; to the Spanish ports; to the Black Sea, which the Byzantines had once tried jealously to reserve for themselves and where rivalry with the Genoese remained fierce. Timber was brought from the forests of Dalmatia and Istria, some grain from the Black Sea and more from Apulia and Sicily (then more fertile than now). And at the end of the thirteenth century the sea-route through the Straits of Gibraltar was opened up, making possible direct trade with England and Flanders. The most valuable items produced in or near Venice itself for export by these various routes were leather-work, dyed cloth, fine glassware from Murano, and salt from Chioggia. Less happily, slaves were traded without scruple. People, often Georgians and Armenians, were bought mostly in eastern Black Sea ports like Trebizond and sold in Venice. Most of them ended up in other northern Italian cities or in north Africa.

The Straits of Gibraltar voyage necessitated the development of more robust sea-going craft. The voyage itself was made feasible by the invention during the thirteenth century of more accurate methods of mapping, the mariner's compass and the stern rudder. By the early fourteenth century the Arsenale shipyards were producing high, broad but swift-moving triremes. These were manned by free citizens who were allowed to take a certain quantity of goods with them to trade in foreign markets. Only in the sixteenth century, when the Turkish wars put greater pressure on manpower, was most of the rowing done by slaves or offenders sentenced to the galleys. More prosperous investors benefited from the system of the *colleganza*, a partnership between a merchant captain who undertook the voyage itself and a more prosperous businessman who put up a larger share of the capital outlay.

Trade rivalry was the basis of the long drawn-out struggle for supremacy between the maritime republics of Venice and Genoa. Pisa, the third contender, began to concentrate its resources on the western Mediterranean from the early thirteenth century in the face of the rival republics' success in the Levant. The naval defeat of the Pisans by the Genoese at Meloria in 1284 permanently put them out of the running. In addition to minor skirmishes Venice and Genoa fought four major wars between 1255 and 1381. Fighting—in Palestine, the Black Sea, the Aegean, and sometimes dangerously nearer home—cost each city many thousands of men. Venetian ships inflicted massive defeats on the Genoese off Acre in 1258 and off Trapani in 1266, but a combination of corsair raids and diplomacy soon enabled Genoa to recover its influence. The Genoese made a particularly timely alliance with the Byzantine emperor in 1261, just before he expelled the Latins and re-established Greek rule in Constantinople. Off the island of Curzola (Korcula) in September 1298 the Venetians suffered a disastrous defeat at the hands of the outnumbered fleet of Oberto Doria, with as many as 9,000 men killed or wounded and 4,000 captured (including Marco Polo, who dictated his travels while in prison). But again the setback was surprisingly short-lived, due mainly to the formidable productivity of the Arsenale, which set to and rapidly built a hundred replacement galleys. To demonstrate exactly how uncowed the Venetians were, one of their captains, Domenico Schiavo, sailed coolly into Genoa harbor and struck a golden ducat— first minted in 1284, long to remain the symbol of Venetian wealth and dependability—on the mole.

For an interlude of over fifty years (1299–1350) a fragile peace between the republics was maintained. This coincided with a period of increasing Venetian wealth, substantial portions of which were spent on the embellishment of the city: work on a largely new Ducal Palace began in 1341, the great Franciscan church of the Frari was rebuilt in its present form from about 1330, the Dominicans' Santi Giovanni e Paolo from 1333.

For a time the progress of architecture and commerce was brought to a halt by the Black Death, which arrived with seamen from the east in 1348. According to most calculations, three-fifths of the population died. Yet it was not long before the survivors resumed not only their building, but their fighting. Genoese aggression in the Black Sea started a new war with the usual mixed fortunes on both sides. In February 1352 the Venetians suffered another major defeat in the Bosphorus, but in August 1353 the Venetian fleet under Nicolò Pisani, with their Aragonese allies, inflicted a similar pounding on the enemy off Sardinia; and then in November 1354 the Genoese captured all fifty-six of Pisani's ships in a surprise attack, while most of their crews were ashore at Portolongo in southern Greece. Again the exhausted powers made peace in 1355. This lasted for twenty-one years, until a dispute erupted over who should occupy the island of Tenedos. So began the "War of Chioggia," which came close to curtailing the proud history of the Venetian republic.

In 1379 Chioggia, the southernmost town on the lagoon, was captured and the end seemed near. But by a mixture of determination and luck Venice turned the tables on Pietro Doria's Genoese, sinking ships full of stones to blockade them into Chioggia. The aged Doge Andrea Contarini personally led the flotilla that performed the scuppering, contributing to Venetian morale by this echo of the days of the crusader doge. There was greater enthusiasm, however, for the newly appointed commander Vettor Pisani, whose idea this expedition was and who had just been released, by popular demand, from the prison to which he had been condemned after a recent naval defeat. Chioggia was eventually regained in June 1380. Pisani did not live long to join in the celebrations. He died of wounds after a skirmish off Apulia that August. Yet another peace was arranged in 1381. This time, as Genoa entered a long period of political and economic instability, the peace was more lasting.

If the Genoese threat was over at last, other difficulties remained. Trade was disrupted by the growing power of the Turks and especially by their capture of Constantinople in 1453. The Turkish wars continued to swallow up money and colonies. English and Dutch commerce expanded in the sixteenth century at Venetian expense and the old trade-routes were menaced when in 1499 Vasco da Gama opened up the sea-route around the Cape of Good Hope, enabling direct Portuguese access to India and its spices. (This had more direct effect on Venetian fortunes than even the voyages to America of Columbus and his successors.) But the decline was more gradual than expected. In 1423, in a speech delivered shortly before his death, Doge Tommaso Mocenigo could still point—accurately, modern historians have concluded—to a recent reduction of the national debt from ten to six million ducats, a gain of two million in interest on foreign trade, and a rent-roll of more than seven million; a million gold ducats and 200,000 silver were being minted annually. In the sixteenth century, in spite of Portuguese activities in India, the old spice-roads continued to function; to many the long sea-voyage round Africa seemed riskier. It was not until the seventeenth century, especially after the Dutch had achieved control of the Spice Islands, that this trade finally collapsed for Mediterranean merchants, and even then Venice remained a by no means negligible trader in other wares, helped by good commercial relations with the Ottoman empire.

CHAPTER TWO

Historic Venice (II): The Long Decline

At some point in the late Middle Ages or early Renaissance Venice began, slowly but inexorably, to decline from its apogee of power and self-confidence. The changing patterns of international trade, discussed in the last chapter, played some part in this. But many Venetians felt that the fatal mistake came when the Republic began to focus more on the Italian mainland than on the "gorgeous east," which, as Wordsworth put it, she once held in fee. Even today the Veneto feels very different from Venice, more Italian in many ways, more western, in its landscape, architecture, traditions, and contacts. Although the difference was culturally enriching, mainland politics were one of the factors that made life seem more complicated, less virginal, for Wordsworth's "maiden City, bright and free." Its position had never, we now realize, been quite so pure and simple. And its decline cannot solely have resulted from the turn westward. But for various reasons it is true that during the last few centuries of the Republic, "she had seen those glories fade, / Those titles vanish, and that strength decay," and no less true that this deserves "some tribute of regret."

Terraferma
As Venice's eastern empire and eastern trade came under threat, relations with the Italian mainland or *terraferma* became more evidently

important. The move westward in the fifteenth century was also a response to the dangerously increased power of such Italian neighbors as the expansionist Milan of the Visconti and, more briefly, the Padua of the ambitious Carrara family. In alliance with Milan and other local states, Venice had defeated the Scaligeri of Verona in 1339 and gained from them the city and march of Treviso, the beginning of the mainland dominion. Over-mighty neighbors mattered above all for the practical reason that Venice relied on terraferma for food and timber.

The Carrara were crushed by Milan and Venice in a war that resulted in the republic gaining control of the valuable cities of Padua, Verona and Vicenza in 1404–6. These gains were followed in 1420 by most of the Friuli region. The system of government for these territories had been piloted in Treviso. It allowed a degree of autonomy—local affairs controlled by a local assembly or council—while keeping the supreme authority clearly Venetian, in the hands of a Rector who was himself answerable to the Venetian Senate and Council of Ten. In the long term the mainland provinces brought much needed revenue to Venice. In later centuries the nobility owned large estates all over the Veneto and Friuli. The republic also gained much culturally: it acquired in Padua one of the foremost European universities, and later attracted the services of such artists as Titian, Veronese, and Palladio (from, respectively, Pieve di Cadore, Verona, and Padua via Vicenza).

There were also, however, serious dangers in this development. Gains had been made at the price of allowing Milan to become ever more powerful and, as Tommaso Mocenigo had gone on to warn in his valedictory speech, further expansion would involve ruinous expenditure. Mocenigo was specifically attacking the warlike tendencies of Francesco Foscari, the man who, as he feared, would succeed him; but with hindsight Foscari's policies seem an inevitable consequence of his predecessors' expansionism. The north Italian involvements of the next few decades added Brescia and Bergamo to Venetian territory, but weakened Venetian capacity to resist Turkish imperialism in the east. Nevertheless the republic emerged from a complex and shifting sequence of alliances made and broken with Milan, Florence, Naples, Mantua, Ferrara and others, with the terraferma conquests largely intact.

Venice won its wars now with the aid of *condottieri* (mercenary genrals), a sign to some moralists that the old days of sturdy republican virtue were over. This point of view gained some confirmation in the case of Francesco Bussone. Bussone, known more often as Carmagnola, abandoned Visconti service and signed a contract to fight for the republic in 1425. He proved at first an able but then a desultory and ungovernable general; in 1432, tricked into returning to Venice, he was arrested as he was about to leave the Ducal Palace and beheaded a month later. But more loyal service was given by Carmagnola's *condottiere* successors Gattamelata and Colleoni.

New perils appeared once the larger European power-blocs became involved in the affairs of Italy after the expedition across the Alps and as far as Naples by Charles VIII of France in 1494–5. At the same time the papacy, especially the pugnacious Pope Julius II (1503–13), was determined to get its share of any redistribution of land resulting from foreign interventions. Julius was also hostile to the independent ways of Venice and was provoked, besides, by the high-handed way in which it had seized papal territory, including the cities of Rimini and Faenza, on the death of Pope Alexander VI in 1503. Eventually in 1509 Julius succeeded, in the League of Cambrai, in arraying against Venice a huge and seemingly invincible alliance of France, Spain, the Empire, Hungary, Mantua, and Ferrara. Each of these states hoped to gain or regain Venetian territory. Having defeated Venice and divided its possessions among them they would all, the pope encouraged them to agree, go off on crusade together against the Turks. For good measure Venice was excommunicated.

When a Venetian mercenary-led army was overwhelmingly defeated by the French at Agnadello, most of the mainland cities took the opportunity to throw off the Venetian yoke. Venice itself prepared for a siege, laid in stores of wheat, and fasted three times a week in an attempt to placate the divine wrath that many felt had fallen on the city for its sins. But, with or without heavenly help, the League of Cambrai soon collapsed under the strain of the rivalries of its members. Julius was appeased by Venetian submission to his authority (a sign of how unusually desperate the city had been), symbolized in February 1510 by the Venetian envoys' humiliating hour-long kneel at the doors of

St. Peter's while the conditions were read out. And there was a widespread feeling among the people (more often than the nobility) of cities like Brescia and Verona that Venetian rule was, while not necessarily perfect, preferable to the alternatives. Allied now with the papacy, now with France, the republic had recovered all its lost territory, apart from the briefly held papal lands and part of Apulia, by 1516.

This narrow escape was, however, one of many signs of coming decline. At home, there had been a crisis of confidence during the war of the League of Cambrai. There had been an unusual degree of citizen anger against the patricians, whose claims to integrity became more difficult to uphold when, even at the height of the crisis, and in spite of the impassioned pleas of Doge Leonardo Loredan, there had been resistance in the Great Council to proposals that involved parting with money. By 1516 a much clearer division than before was emerging between a rich ruling elite within the nobility and a poorer disaffected group, unlikely to plot against the state but equally unlikely to contribute to its welfare. Increasingly, besides, noblemen concentrated on terraferma estates and interests. Yet, logically enough, this was the very time at which the Myth of Venice was most articulately formulated and confidently proclaimed. Aspects of the myth, including a history composed mainly of providential victories, were also celebrated in much of the art that flourished in the sixteenth century—by Veronese and Tintoretto, for example—and helped to give the impression of confidence and stability. This skill in self-projection was at least one element in the Venetian victory in the next major struggle with the pope, the "Crisis of the Interdict" of 1606–7, although diplomacy, luck, and the skilled leadership of Fra Paolo Sarpi also had much to do with it.

The Turkish Wars

Venice, caught up in mainland affairs, prevaricated too long to come to the aid of Constantinople in 1453. The republic held back, probably, in the knowledge that there was no avoiding the inevitable end of Byzantium and in the hope—rightly—that a new commercial treaty with the Turks would be more easily agreed if Venice did not too directly take the Greek side. Nevertheless, many individual Venetians died fighting to save the city.

Renewed conflict did, however, break out in 1463, and Venice went on, with occasional help from the papacy, fighting the Turks until the treaty of 1479 in which hostilities were, on receipt of a large payment from Venice, once more to be replaced by trade. During the war Venice had lost a major commercial and naval base, Negroponte (now Khalkis) on the island of Euboia—"the show-place of the Venetian Aegean," as Jan Morris calls it in *The Venetian Empire: a Sea Voyage*. This had grave psychological as well as practical consequences; the pattern was set for the gradual destruction of the maritime empire. Aegean islands, some under direct Venetian control, more leased or ruled by lords of Venetian descent and loyalties, were picked off by the Turks as wars and occasion allowed. They also took the Peloponnesian ports: Modon and Coron in 1500, Nauplion and Monemvasia (the famous source of "malmsey" wine) in 1540. And in 1570–1 Cyprus fell, another mainstay of Venetian trade and confidence. Any Venetians present at productions of *Othello* in Jacobean London must have heard wistfully or wryly of a Cyprus whose "general enemy Ottoman" is obligingly swept away by a storm, however unfortunate the domestic consequences in the play. The humiliation of losing Cyprus was underlined by the appalling treatment of the Venetian commander at Famagusta, Marcantonio Bragadin, when he came to hand over the keys of the city to the Turkish victors. The three hundred men with him were seized and beheaded. He himself was stabbed, dragged around the city, and then flayed alive.

As the situation worsened in the eastern Mediterranean, Pope Pius V succeeded in awakening the Christian lands to the increasing risk of further Turkish expansion at their expense. He initiated the diplomatic approaches which, in 1571, resulted in an alliance between, among others, Venice, the old enemy Genoa, and the usually no less hostile Spain. News of the fate of Famagusta and Bragadin reached the combined fleet, and fired the Venetians in particular with the desire for vengeance, a few days before the engagement against an equally matched Turkish fleet off Lepanto (Naupaktos) on October 7, 1571. Under the overall command of Don John of Austria, half-brother of King Philip II of Spain, the allies won an unambiguous victory, after ferocious bombardments and hand-to-hand fighting. Of the 208 ships, 110 were from Venice, its terraferma lands, or its surviving colonies in

Crete, the Ionian Islands, and Dalmatia, although—moved by common feeling or forced into it by lack of manpower—the Venetians allowed a good number of Spanish soldiers aboard with them. It was a huge fight: the Christians lost about 9,000 men, the Turks as many as 30,000 killed and 8,000 captured. (Many of the prisoners then proved useful as galley slaves.) Whereas only twelve of the Christian galleys sunk, on the other side 113 galleys were sunk and 117 captured.

There was much relief, bell-ringing, and dancing in Venice when, ten days later, news of Lepanto arrived. Don John, in accordance with his brother's instructions, did not consolidate the victory by pressing on into the eastern Mediterranean; Spain was concerned more with what happened in North Africa. Venice formally gave up its claim to Cyprus in 1573. But Lepanto had been extraordinarily good for morale. Its heroic place in Venetian mythology remains evident in Andrea Vicentino's painting of the battle in the Sala dello Scrutinio of the Ducal Palace. The painting bristles with oars, masts, muskets, arrows, swords, and is crammed with figures—turbaned or helmeted, shooting or shot from the crow's nests, struggling bloody in the water, on the decks or among the oars—fighting with total and equal determination beneath the rippling flags of the Crescent and the Lion of St. Mark.

The next great trial of strength between the Ottoman and Venetian forces came during the battle for Crete, when the capital, Candia (Heraklion) held out against the Turks' best efforts for twenty-one years (1648–69). Crete, the destination of many Byzantine refugees in 1453, had long been the setting for a rich interchange between Greek and Venetian culture. The Turkish victory here involved the republic in both cultural and financial loss. This time help from other European powers was not forthcoming until near the end; in June 1669 forty ships of French volunteers, flying the papal ensign, at last came to the relief of the beleaguered city. Only six days later the French were routed, and their leader, the Duke of Beaufort, killed along with fifty others when an accidental powder explosion wrecked their surprise attack on the Turkish positions. The survivors sailed away in August and the Venetian commander Francesco Morosini at last bowed to the inevitable and negotiated a surrender in return for permission for the defenders and few surviving inhabitants of Candia to depart unmolested.

The siege of Candia was not, however, the end of Morosini's career or of the Venetian presence in Greek lands. In 1685 he was sent out as Captain General of the force (part now of a league that included the pope, the emperor, and Venice) that captured the Ionian island of Santa Maura (Leukas) and then, after several months' siege, Coron. With the aid of German soldiers, the Venetians went on to recover almost the whole of the Peloponnese. In 1687, with notorious effects, Morosini attacked Athens: the Turks were using the Parthenon as a powder-store, and the German bombardiers blew it up. In March 1688, a vacancy having conveniently occurred, he was elected doge and carried on campaigning. Again the parallel with Enrico Dandolo and the reminder of the good old days of dominance in the east sprang easily to Venetian minds. Morosini died on a later expedition to Greece in 1694, aged about seventy-five. By then the conquering was over, but in the Treaty of Karlowitz of 1699 Venice succeeded at least in keeping the Peloponnese while reluctantly handing Attica back to the Turks. In 1715, after a determined Turkish campaign, the Peloponnese too was lost once more. But Venetian Greece (and a major source of production of raisins, oranges, lemons, and wine) survived, to the end of the republic, in the Ionian islands and Kythera. The Ottoman empire was itself now beginning its long decline, and represented less of a threat to Venetian interests in the last years of the republic.

The End of the Republic

The Venetian republic survived until 1797, thanks mainly to luck and to a skillfully maintained policy of neutrality in foreign disputes. Helpfully, too, the major European nations spent so much time at war with each other in the eighteenth century that they were distracted from the possibility of attacking Venice. Trade opportunities for the republic were sometimes opened up by these wars, contributing to the general revival of Venetian commerce in the mid-eighteenth century. But Austrian and French troops and ships now crossed Venetian territory with impunity. Venetian domination of the Adriatic ended, and with it the taxes and custom dues that had long and profitably been levied on foreign shipping. Faced by the financial consequences of competition from the English, Dutch, and French, as well as the

Austrian free port of Trieste, Venice debased its silver currency and sold some official positions and even places in the Great Council (to those able to raise 100,000 ducats). In 1702, as if to show how much had changed, the Ascension Day festivities (see p.90), the age-old assertion of Venetian maritime glory, were called off because the French fleet was operating nearby (in the War of the Spanish Succession).

Not surprisingly, the reputation of Venice changed. The love of pleasure, always part of the image associated with courtesans, luxury, and entertainment, now took over completely from the old picture of republican virtue and wise governance. "A people famous for centuries as the most skilful seamen, the shrewdest and most courageous merchant adventurers of their time" were now, as John Julius Norwich declares, "better known for their prowess as cheapskates and intriguers, gamblers and pimps." The eighteenth century in Venice was certainly a great age for gambling and the provision of sexual services (both unabashedly celebrated in the memoirs of Giacomo Casanova), carnival excess, high fashion and what Lady Mary Wortley Montagu in 1740 called "gallantries and raree-shows" pursued "in the midst of wars that surround us." It was also a golden age in interior decoration and painting, from the sweeping Baroque frescoes of Giambattista Tiepolo (1696–1770), reviving the color of the sixteenth-century Venetian masters, to the cityscapes and lagoon idylls of Antonio Canaletto (1697–1768) and Francesco Guardi (1712–93), and the genre scenes of Pietro Longhi (1702–85). One of Longhi's best-known pictures, in the museum of the eighteenth century at Ca' Rezzonico, shows a group of fashionable people, some masked, inspecting a rhinoceros in a rather dilatory way. This was the sort of idling, critics of "soft" eighteenth-century Venice suggested, that inhabitants of this corrupt city pursued—when not delighting in more active vices. Longhi, whose subjects also included card-players, might have agreed, but in a more gently mocking—more Venetian—spirit.

Most of these painters, but especially Canaletto, are well represented outside Venice. Canaletto himself worked in England in 1746–55, and even much of what he produced at home found its way there thanks to the patronage of the merchant Joseph Smith (1682–1770), who lived in Venice for much of his life and was British Consul from 1744. He sold many of the pictures and drawings (which sometimes subtly rearranged the places they depicted to allow finer perspectives) on to King George III. Smith was, like the paintings and their subjects, a familiar sight to the continuing flow of Grand Tour nobility and gentry for whom Venice was an important destination at this time. Their numbers were swelled by their retinues and by a few other less grand tourists. Their patronage of shops, coffee-houses, gondoliers, and tailors, as well as painters and engravers, contributed helpfully to the local economy but not necessarily, some thought, to the local culture. At Carnival time in 1740 Wortley Montagu wrote to her friend the Countess of Pomfret about the "blockheads"—her young male compatriots—who treat her apartment in Palazzo Mocenigo as their refuge:

> ...the greater part of them having kept an inviolable fidelity to the languages their nurses taught them. Their whole business abroad (as far as I can perceive) being to buy new clothes, in which they shine in some obscure coffee-house, where they are sure of meeting only one another; and after the important conquest of some waiting gentlewoman of an opera queen, who perhaps they remember as long as they live, return to England excellent judges of men and manners.

In June, she claims, the place is still "infested with English, who torment me as the frogs and lice did the palace of Pharaoh."

This city of coffee-houses and brothels, tourists and painters and exquisite light, of traditional pageantry belying modern powerlessness, was no match for the energetic, invincible, intolerant General Bonaparte, who arrived in northern Italy to prosecute war with Austria in 1796. Venice might be a republic, but it was hostile to the radical French brand of republicanism and had harbored the future Louis XVIII in Verona. (Napoleon was unimpressed by the Venetian claim to neutrality, and successfully demanded Louis' expulsion.) Venice stood by as the French overran the terraferma and bloodily put down an Easter rising in Verona. The Senate gave in to Bonaparte's successive ultimatums, but he was provoked to more drastic threats when the commander of the fortress of Sant'Andrea opened fire on a French vessel on April 20. Either as a result of the bombardment or during subsequent fighting, five Frenchmen were killed. The surviving members of the crew were taken prisoner. This was the immediate spur for Bonaparte's demand for what Norwich aptly calls "the suicide of the State."

Although for many years now the republic had been governed in reality mostly by small cliques (contrary to the whole spirit of the constitution), Doge Lodovico Manin and a gathering of other senior figures decided that they must put the French demands to the Great Council. There were still 1,169 members, although the number of noble families was rapidly decreasing as a result of the widespread practice of only one son marrying so that more wealth could be handed down to the next generation. Accordingly, 619 of them assembled on May 1 in the Ducal Palace, in the same great hall in which their ancestors had so often met, and were addressed by the doge, who seemed near to collapse. They voted, in effect, to do whatever Bonaparte demanded, starting with an agreement to release all political prisoners (whose existence was, however, mostly in the conqueror's imagination). On May 9 a more detailed directive was promulgated, providing for the replacement of the Venetian oligarchy by a municipal council and for French army units to move into the city. The Great Council met again on May 12. This time only 537 members turned up. The doge addressed them again, pale and stuttering, proposing their dissolution. Soon afterwards musket-shots were heard outside the palace. Councilors who were frightened that the French had arrived or mob rule broken out (in fact, it turned out, loyal Dalmatian soldiers had fired a parting salute) forced as rapid a vote as possible on the proposal. A total of 512 voted in favor, and this was no time to worry about the legal need for a quorum of 600 members to make the vote valid. Most of the patricians fled in fear of their lives, throwing off their conspicuous robes. The last doge was one of the few who stayed behind. Calm after all the emotion and the panic, he removed his ducal *corno* and passed the cap beneath it to a servant with the words, "Take this; I shall not be needing it again." The end of the republic seems inglorious, but the oligarchs' abdication almost undoubtedly prevented much bloodshed.

Foreign Rule

The first period of French domination was short-lived, although there was time to carry off to Paris art treasures, including the bronze horses of San Marco; by the Treaty of Campo Formio in October 1797 France agreed to hand Venice over to Austria. There was a second period of French rule between 1805 and 1814, when the city was part of the kingdom ruled by Napoleon's stepson Eugène de Beauharnais, one of whose titles was the once unthinkable "Prince of Venice." During this time Venice underwent its greatest physical transformation for several centuries. Religious institutions and fraternities were dissolved, their buildings often demolished or converted to secular use. Many houses were removed to make way for the Giardini Pubblici, designed by Giovanni Antonio Selva (architect of the Fenice theater) in 1808–12. A number of churches were also pulled down, including one in the Piazza, San Geminiano, replaced in 1807 by the *Ala Napoleonica* ("Napoleonic Wing"), which links together the arcaded *Procuratie Vecchie* and *Procuratie Nuove* (built in the early and late sixteenth century to house the Procurators of San Marco—senior dignitaries of the republic). The new wing was part of the large royal palace designed in these years and finished in the late 1830s, part of which is now the Museo Correr.

While money was poured into these grandiose schemes, Venice became poorer and less populated. Under Austrian rule (reimposed in 1814) there was at first little improvement. There were poor harvests in 1814–18. Between 1797 and 1824 the number of inhabitants declined from 137,240 to 113,827. By the 1830s the economy was stronger. Commercial revival was encouraged when Austria declared Venice a free port in 1830 (although Trieste retained a wider range of privileges) and when the railway-bridge from the mainland was opened in 1846. This was hailed as a sign of progress by some, but outraged others including John Ruskin, who sputtered that it was worse than "the Greenwich railway" (a by-word, as far as he was concerned, for all that was ugly). Gas-lights had been installed in Piazza San Marco in 1843. But an oppressive atmosphere remained: Vienna imposed the Austrian legal code, censorship, and centralized, complicatedly bureaucratic rule on its dominions. Police spies and the often conservative pro-Austrian clergy reported or deterred dissidence. Resentment eventually issued, in 1848–9, into revolution.

Revolution and Siege

Daniele Manin, a liberal lawyer who shared the last doge's name but little else, emerged as the leader of this revolution. Following increasing unrest in the winter of 1847–8, and demands for reform from Manin and like-minded citizens, he and Nicolò Tommaseo were imprisoned in January 1848. A great crowd of protesters finally forced the city governor, Count Palffy, to release them on March 16. Two days later, Austrian soldiers fired on rioters, killing eight of them. On March 22 an uprising at the Arsenale, and the refusal of Italian soldiers in the Austrian army to open fire, precipitated the revolution. That afternoon Manin, standing on a café table in the Piazza, proclaimed a new republic, asserted a long-term commitment to Italian unification (there were insurrections also in Milan, Naples, and Rome), and concluded his speech with the rallying cry "*Viva la Repubblica! Viva la libertà! Viva San Marco!*" To his more conservative colleagues this sounded worryingly like an invitation to return to the French Venice of 1797—dancing around the Liberty Tree in the Piazza—or, worse, to the guillotine-happy Paris of 1793. But in the event, Manin's policies were more balanced; he both enacted liberal ideals, including Jewish emancipation (he was half-Jewish himself) and adult male suffrage, for instance, and protected property rights and, on the whole, the social status quo.

Manin was elected president by popular demand on March 23, 1848. He was out of office for a time that summer when the Venetian assembly voted for union with the Kingdom of Piedmont only to see Piedmont make peace with Austria. Otherwise, he remained in charge, succeeding for the most part in restraining political and class-based rivalries, much helped by his personal bravery, his faith in the people, and theirs in him. On April 2, 1849, by which time most of the other Italian uprisings had foundered and the Austrians were preparing to besiege the city, the assembly voted, amid emotional scenes in the very Sala del Maggior Consiglio where their predecessors had dissolved the republic in 1797, to resist "at any cost" and to confer on Manin "unlimited powers." To general surprise, Venice had apparently recovered the old fighting spirit that seemed to have died in the previous century.

A combination of factors probably explains this new vigor: Manin's inspiring leadership, the pent-up frustration of fifty years under foreign rule, and the new role of the middle and lower classes in decision-making. Through the spring and summer the city held out against Austrian bombardment, which forced, by the end, the evacuation of Cannaregio and other areas facing the mainland. Supplies of food decreased and an outbreak of cholera killed about three thousand people in the lagoon area. At the end of May, the Venetians finally abandoned their defense of the mainland fort of Marghera. Instead, they demolished five arches of the railway-bridge, restoring the island status of the city. From the other end of the causeway the bombardment continued. The Rialto bridge and the Scuola Grande di San Rocco were hit but not badly damaged. Something of a Blitz spirit developed, with the band playing daily in the Piazza, Venetians climbing towers to watch the fireworks, and at least one projectile being picked up by a boatman and shown off as a "German watermelon" (*anguria tedesca*). On July 12, the Austrians also attempted what is thought to be the first-ever aerial bombardment. Fortunately it was less effective than such attacks would one day become: few of the twenty bomb-bearing balloons reached their destination, and some were even blown back over the Austrian lines. In one of their last gestures of defiance, at the beginning of August, the Venetians raided the lagoon fort of Brondolo and made off with its supplies of grain and wine and a herd of cattle. That evening they celebrated with a performance of Rossini's opera about William Tell, the Swiss hero of an earlier struggle with the Austrians.

But supplies were fast running out now; bread was being baked with an eighty percent proportion of rye (*una bomba nello stomaco*, said Tommaseo, to add to the other sorts of bomb). A second sortie failed. Social order began to break down; the Patriarch's residence at Palazzo Querini-Stampalia was sacked, at least ostensibly because he had argued for surrender. Food riots began. And so, at last, on August 22, Manin was persuaded to negotiate a surrender. In accordance with its terms, he and forty of his colleagues sailed off into exile two days later. All imperial subjects who had taken up arms against Austria were also required to leave. A final bloodbath had been averted. Daniele Manin worked as an Italian teacher in Paris, where he died, poor and having lost his wife and daughter, in 1857. His tomb is on the north façade of San Marco and a statue near his house in Campo Manin.

The Austrian Marshal Radetzky sailed in triumph down the Grand Canal on August 30 and celebrated with a *Te Deum* in San Marco. Radetzky was a charismatic commander, respected even by his enemies. At least he was a better man to have to welcome into the city than some colorless staff-officer, a minor Habsburg royal, or the notoriously brutal Marshal von Haynau who had originally led the assault on Venice. (Haynau had been transferred to fight another of the revolutions of 1848, in Hungary.) Soon the railway-bridge was functioning once more. Adding to the financial hardships of those who had sacrificed jewels, bonds, and money to the Venetian cause, the paper currency issued by the rebel regime was burned by "an immense fire and a large cauldron," reported Effie Ruskin. The recently married Ruskins were among the first foreign visitors to return to the city. Within a few years tourism had revived; already in 1848, according to the *Guida Commerciale di Venezia* issued that year (and cited in Paul Ginsborg's authoritative study *Daniele Manin and the Venetian Revolution of 1848–9*) there had been seventy-six goldsmiths', silversmiths', or jewelers' establishments, sixty-five tailors' shops, and eighty-two cobblers. Tourism also, as Ginsborg points out, created extra work for gondoliers. The 40,000 or so people who did, nevertheless, still need poor relief were comparatively well looked after. But the Austrian army still kept its cannon ready to fire into the Piazza, and most Venetians still yearned for independence, or at least for union with an independent Italy.

Italian Incorporation

The fulfillment of this ambition came tantalizingly closer in 1859 and 1860 as most other parts of the peninsula became part of the new Kingdom of Italy. It then became possible after the defeat of Austria by Prussia, Italy's ally, at Königgratz in 1866. Subsequently a complicated diplomatic formula was worked out by which Austria would cede the Veneto to France, which would in turn give it to Italy. A plebiscite would take place to ratify incorporation in Italy, but this was essentially a formality. And so at 8:00 AM on October 19, 1866, in a room at the Hotel Europa on the Grand Canal, a French general, Louis Leboeuf de Montgermont, handed the Veneto over to the Italian government commissioners. Wild celebrations broke out; Italian tricolors appeared on all sides. On November 7, after the 674,426 to 69 vote to join Italy, King Vittorio Emanuele II entered the city. He was met at the station by Italian dignitaries and the former British prime minister Lord John Russell, boarded a boat, and was rowed down the Grand Canal by oarsmen in historic Venetian costume. Bells rang, guns saluted, gondolas followed; the following day there was a gala in his honor at the newly re-opened Teatro La Fenice.

But for many the euphoria would be short-lived. The king came not simply to see the wonders of Venice, but as representative of the larger whole in which it would now be absorbed—or, some soon came to feel, swallowed. Venice was in fact less important as an administrative center than it had been under Austrian rule. And there were more pressing problems. Riots broke out after a tax on flour was introduced in 1868. Poverty was widespread, and unemployment alleviated only gradually once work got under away on the new port of Venice, the Stazione Marittima, after 1869.

The Stazione Marittima was largely completed in the1880s, but its economic benefit began to be felt only in the 1890s. It was then, too, that Giovanni Stucky brought modern industry to the Giudecca with his giant, still-standing, Mulino Stucky, the neo-Gothic flourmill erected by Ernst Wullekopf in 1895. Stucky himself was murdered outside the railway station by a disgruntled employee in 1910. The mill was abandoned only a few years later as the industrial focus shifted to the mainland.

Fascism and War

Venice entered the twentieth century as a thriving port once more and still, of course, a great center for tourism. Thomas Cook had brought his first parties here in the late 1860s, and the middle classes continued to come with at least as much enthusiasm as their Grand Tour predecessors and in much greater numbers.

In the aftermath of the First World War, Fascism began to flourish here as in many other parts of Italy. For some years, however, in keeping with Venetian tradition, perhaps, local Fascists preserved a measure of independence from the national leadership. At first it was Gabriele D'Annunzio rather than Mussolini who seemed the dominant Fascistic

figure in Venice. Long before Fascism was thought of, he had been well known as poet, novelist, playwright, politician (right- and left-wing in rapid succession), and daring First World War pilot who led sorties against Vienna itself. D'Annunzio, who had been born Gaetano Rapagnetta but early adopted the more impressive names suggesting a bringer of revelations (the Angel Gabriel and the Annunciation), was from the Abruzzi and had lived in Rome and Tuscany. But Venice, as extravagantly "different" from other places as he himself wanted to seem from other people, had long appealed to him. During the war he lived, when not actually fighting, in a small house, the Casetta delle Rose, set back in its gardens from the Grand Canal and next to the vast Palazzo Corner "Ca' Grande." And it was from Venice, in September 1919, that he set off on his famous exploit of seizing Fiume (now Rijeka in Croatia) in frustration at its not having been ceded to Italy at the Treaty of Saint-Germain signed with Austria that month. He ruled it as dictator until December 1921. Benito Mussolini viewed D'Annunzio with a mixture of admiration and envy; in the longer term he was able to supersede him politically while bestowing public honors and titles on him.

Another leader of the Fascist era expended his energies in different directions. Giuseppe Volpi, born in Venice in 1877, was one of the most successful entrepreneurs in modern Italy. Before he was thirty he had founded the *Società Adriatica di Elettricità*, which soon had a monopoly on the supply of electricity in the Veneto and Emilia-Romagna. He was actively involved in other industries such as iron, shipping, and petro-chemicals, and was a driving force in the expansion of the industrial zone at Porto Marghera, near Mestre, during the

1920s and 1930s. At first many of the workers there commuted from Venice, but increasingly they found it cheaper and more convenient to live on the mainland. By the 1960s, as expansion continued on reclaimed land south of Marghera, the population of the industrial zones outnumbered that of the historic center and the lagoon islands.

Volpi's skills soon came to the attention of government. In 1912 he was one of the principal negotiators of the Treaty of Ouchy, which transferred Libya and Tripolitania from Turkish rule to Italian. During the First World War he was president of the national Committee for Industrial Mobilization. In 1921 he was appointed governor of Tripolitania. With characteristically good timing he joined the rising Fascist movement; his energy, money, and extraordinary self-confidence (he enjoyed semi-jocular references to himself as the new doge) made him the dominant figure in the party in Venice and guaranteed, in turn, its domination of local politics. A senator from 1922, he became Mussolini's finance minister in 1925–8 (created Count of Misurata in 1925). But later, not having seen eye-to-eye with Mussolini on the artificially high level at which the leader insisted on fixing exchange rates, and never having become one of his close circle, he concentrated again on Venice and industry. In 1930–3, with Volpi's encouragement, the road-bridge was built. He also took on a new role as president of the international Biennale exhibition.

During the Fascist years there were attempts to make Italian art a more central feature of the shows, although many other countries continued actively to exhibit in their pavilions until as late as 1940. Certainly sales figures improved for home-grown art. In 1932, Year Ten of Mussolini's regime, a good number of prizes went to pictures of marching Blackshirts, dynamic cranes and planes, idealized Italian landscapes, and women and children saluting *Il Duce*. (Volpi's own tastes were fairly unadventurous.) Some more imaginative painting did, however, find its way to the Italian section of the 1930s shows as a result of the influence of the Futurist and Fascist Filippo Tommaso Marinetti. In his usual thought-provoking, if often unintentionally comic, way he encouraged "second generation" Futurists to be *aeropittori*—painters who showed the world from the perspective of flight.

By 1942 art at the Biennale had become sufficiently orthodox, nevertheless, for Dr. Josef Goebbels to express his approval. (Hitler had been before the war and had not liked the amount of "degenerate" art on show.) In September 1943, with the rest of central and northern Italy, Venice came under German control following the armistice declared by Marshal Badoglio and King Vittorio Emanuele III. Volpi, rightly suspected of a decreasing commitment to Fascism (his business instincts told him that its day was over), was arrested immediately but managed to escape and cross into Switzerland in 1944. He died in Rome in 1947. Venice saw little of the fierce fighting of the last phases of the Second World War, but, of course, many Venetians were involved in combat elsewhere in northern Italy whether as loyal Fascists, people obeying German orders, or with the Resistance.

In the city itself a campaign of sabotage was followed by reprisals in which five men were shot in Cannaregio on July 8, 1944; some thirty partisans were executed later that month, followed on August 3 by seven hostages in Riva dell'Impero, called subsequently, in their memory, Riva dei Sette Martiri. And nearly 200 members of the Jewish community in Venice went to their deaths (see p.144). In April 1945 the most important task of the local Resistance was to take control of the port of Venice which, with Porto Marghera, had at one point been threatened with destruction by the Germans. The city was liberated on April 28, although fighting near Padua went on into May.

Modern Perils

After the war a succession of different political groups held sway in Venice. As elsewhere in Italy, much money meant for public works found its way into private pockets. In the 1980s and 1990s, as in the other northern cities, separatist politicians benefited from a sense of frustration at the way national money was, as northerners saw it, being poured into the bottomless pit of the south. The present mayor, Massimo Cacciari, has a reputation for independence and integrity, but, with other concerned individuals and groups, faces an uphill battle to save Venice from the dangers that threaten it.

Since 1945 the division between Venice and the industrial terraferma has become steadily wider. There are now fewer than 70,000 residents of Venice and the islands as opposed to 400,000 in the Mestre area. Over a thousand people move out of the city every year, to be replaced, if at all, by wealthy outsiders who can afford the upkeep of old houses. All old buildings are defined as ancient monuments; complicated bureaucracy means that obtaining permission to modernize them can be a lengthy and expensive process. The cost of living is high and the average age of the population is forty-four. Tourism both keeps the city alive and inflicts damage on its precarious structures. There are other menaces such as industrial pollution; Volpi's idea that Marghera would provide "lungs" for Venice has come to seem steadily more ironic. At the same time, heavy ship traffic and the deep twentieth-century channels have disturbed the traditional balance of the lagoon waters; this is reflected in and compounded by subsidence, inefficient sewerage, erosion by *vaporetti* and other motor-boats and floods caused partly by land reclamation, as suggested by the marked increase in their frequency since the 1930s. It was only after the most famous flood in November 1966 that the seriousness of these problems began to be generally realized outside Venice. Then the Piazza was several feet deep in water, high tide was more than six feet higher than usual, and about $40 million of damage was done. The huge protecting stone walls or *murazzi* off the island of Pellestrina, sensibly installed to protect one of the lagoon entrances in the eighteenth century but neglected since the nineteenth, were swept away and the whole of Pellestrina submerged. Somehow nobody died, unlike in Florence where there was, for different reasons, a huge flood at the same time; because of this and because many more art treasures were damaged or destroyed there, Florence initially received most of the press coverage. Nevertheless it was principally as a result of the flood that UNESCO now felt moved to declare that "Venice is a moral obligation on the international community."

More than thirty organizations including Venice in Peril and Save Venice were established abroad to raise funds and organize restoration. They and other more local groups have made good progress, particularly in the restoration and protection of individual historic buildings. Some progress has also been made in the reduction of pollution and water-pumping. Recently it was proposed that visitors should be shown, on arrival in the city, a film about its partly tourist-induced plight. But bureaucracy and local and national politics have delayed the implementation of action on a larger scale and, besides, argument continues to rage about the best method of controlling the lagoon waters without destroying their delicate natural balance. Tidal barriers, especially, have been much delayed and much disagreed about. There were fairly major floods in 1979, 1986, and 1992, and about a hundred *acque alte* ("high waters") annually over this period. Although the view, widely expressed in the 1970s, that Venice was about to sink has fortunately proved incorrect, its future remains uncertain.

CHAPTER THREE

Monumental Venice: The Piazza and the Piazzetta

Piazza San Marco is a large square in which you can, as the fancy and the finance take you, drink coffee or enjoy, free of charge, the summer music played outside the cafés. Most of the music is played skillfully, but with deliberate extravagance—theatrical flourishes by conductors, violinists, and other specialists in the fast, the throbbing, the loudly or lovingly plangent, the sentimental red-rose-delivering romantic. There is much light opera, "I did it my way," and Lloyd Webber music that serious classical enthusiasts and serious rock enthusiasts love to hate, but anyone can be caught by it—at least temporarily—on a warm night in the Piazza. And having heard enough, you can pace away to the basilica while the music, more distant now, makes you only a character in some film set in Venice.

From the basilica you may drift on to the Piazzetta, the area between San Marco and the waterfront marked with two ancient columns. St. Theodore stands on his column with the dragon he defeated, before being in effect himself defeated—or at least replaced as patron saint—by St. Mark, whose winged lion tops the other column.

(Executions once took place on a scaffold erected between the columns.) Next you can stroll along by the water, often bright with lighted boats, to the Ponte della Paglia, at last uncrowded by mid-evening, with its view of the illuminated Ponte di Sospiri (Bridge of Sighs) and on along the Riva degli Schiavoni, where a few people linger in the restaurants.

Or if you walk out of the Piazza not to the Piazzetta but past the Torre dell'Orologio (clock tower), built in the late 1490s by Mauro Coducci, you soon enter a very different world: the shopping streets—jewelers, luxury stationers, art shops, mask-shops, couturiers, *pizzerie*, confectioners, *pasticcerie*—that join the Merceria. Already in the seventeenth century John Evelyn took the Merceria

> *to be the most delicious street in the world for the sweetness of it, being all the way on both sides continually tapestried, as it were, with cloth of gold, rich damask and other silks, which the shops expose and hang before their houses from the first floor; to this add the perfumers' and apothecaries' shops, and the innumerable cages of nightingales... that entertain you with their melody from shop to shop, so as shutting your eyes, you would imagine yourself in the country, when indeed you are in the middle of the sea.*

The country now seems far enough away. At times this becomes the most cloying and claustrophobic area of the city.

The music in the Piazza, too, sometimes contributes to the feeling that Venice is a honeymoon and weekend place, "a watering-place for the benefit of visitors," as Richard Wagner felt "the exquisite ruin of this wonderful city" to have become in 1858. In Wagner's day the music had, metaphorically at least, a sharper edge. He was pleased, he remembers in his autobiography, to find a "thorough German element of good military music" in the two Austrian regiments that played on alternate evenings "amid brilliant illuminations in the middle of the Piazza San Marco, whose acoustic properties for this class of production were really excellent." And there was something else particularly to enjoy: "I was often suddenly startled toward the end of my meal by the sound of my own overtures" [the stirring pieces that introduce *Rienzi* and *Tannhäuser*.] Then

> *as I sat at the restaurant window giving myself up to impressions of the music, I did not know which dazzled me most, the incomparable piazza*

*magnificently illuminated and filled with countless numbers of moving
people, or the music that seemed to be borne away in rustling glory on
the winds.*

Gratifyingly, the crowd listened intently. But one thing was missing, for
"no two hands ever forgot themselves so far as to applaud, as the least
sign of approbation of Austrian military music would have been looked
upon as treason to the Italian Fatherland." For eight more years, until
the end of Austrian rule, the Venetians would have to keep up their
dignified silence.

Another way of making their views clear was pointedly not to
patronize one of the two great rival cafés in the Piazza, Caffè Quadri,
founded in 1775, which was a favorite haunt of the Austrians. Loyal
Italians went instead to Caffè Florian, founded in 1720 by Florian
Francesconi. Nobody could stop the garrison using Florian's as well as
Quadri's, but there were ways of making them feel less than welcome;
according to Wagner, "the Austrian officers... floated about publicly in
Venice like oil on water." Habits like keeping cannon at the ready
outside the Palazzo Ducale did not endear them to their involuntary
hosts. Now, fortunately, a preference between these cafés and others
nearby is aesthetic or gastronomic, not political. Florian's has a more
distinctive interior, preserving its 1850s decoration, and it is outside
Florian's that the narrator of Henry James' *The Aspern Papers* (1888)
self-indulgently but irresistibly sits

> *eating ices, listening to music, talking with acquaintances: the traveller
> will recall how the immense cluster of tables and little chairs stretches like
> a promontory into the smooth lake of the Piazza. The whole place, of a
> summer's evening, under the stars and with all the lamps, all the voices
> and light footsteps on marble (the only sounds of the arcades that enclose
> it), is like an open-air saloon dedicated to cooling drinks and to a still finer
> degustation—that of the exquisite impressions received during the day.*

In the Piazza you can feed the pigeons or dodge them, buy
souvenirs or umbrellas, collapse in cafés or on steps and, of course,
watch other people. Thomas Coryat, the Jacobean traveler from
Somerset, was not the first or the last to declare that here "you may
both see all manner of fashions of attire, and hear all the languages of
Christendom, besides those that are spoken by the barbarous ethnics."

(It is impolite now to regard people as "barbarous ethnics," but actually encountering one's fellow mortals often increases tolerance; it was here that Coryat first saw a multi-racial community flourishing with relatively little friction.) At busy times "a man may very properly call" the Piazza "rather Orbis than Urbis forum, that is, a market place of the world, not of the city." You can watch the "Moors" who, cast in bronze in 1497, strike the hours on the Orologio; such figures were less exotic in the Orbis forum than in *Othello, the Moor of Venice*, performed in London just a few years before Coryat's visit. More rarely the Magi or Wise Men come out, in Ascension Week and on their feast day, the Epiphany, to bow before the Virgin.

Alternatively you can take a more active approach, as William Beckford described himself as doing in *Dreams, Waking Thoughts, and Incidents* (1783). He loved to "go and pry about the great church of St. Mark, and examine the variety of marbles, and mazes of delicate sculpture, with which it is covered," but he could not bear the "vile stench, which exhales from every recess and corner of the edifice" and which even incense "cannot subdue." The stench is probably no longer apparent even to the refined nostrils of latter-day Beckfords, but his remedy still has much to recommend it: "When oppressed by this noxious atmosphere, I run up the campanile in the piazza; and, seating myself amongst the pillars of the gallery, breathe the fresh gales which blow from the Adriatic… and survey at my leisure all Venice beneath me."

The Campanile and Museo Correr
The Campanile (bell-tower) of San Marco was completed in the twelfth century and restored in the sixteenth. The elegant Loggetta at its base was built by Jacopo Sansovino between 1537 and 1546. The tower collapsed with spectacular completeness, taking the Loggetta with it but without injuring anyone, in 1902. The present replica was finished in 1912; the city council had decided to rebuild it *com'era, dov'era*—"as it was, where it was." The view is as fine as Beckford says. In earlier days the height had practical advantages. From its first construction in the ninth century the Campanile not only housed the bells that rang the hours, but acted as a beacon to sailors; the roof was gilded and, at night, illuminated by fire. In the summer of 1609 Galileo Galilei, professor of mathematics at the University of Padua (in Venetian territory) since 1592, took a number of senators up the Campanile to demonstrate his telescope. His friend Fra Paolo Sarpi had heard, in 1608, about the invention of the instrument in the Dutch Republic; Galileo experimented with concave and convex lenses, became expert in grinding them (those produced by him or his assistants were regarded as the best for about the next twenty years) and produced his own improved version, in which the eyepiece is a plano-concave lens and the objective a plano-convex. The dignitaries presumably staggered to the top in their long robes rather than running

as the youthful Beckford claims he did, but they were willing to go up out of curiosity and in the hope of being shown something that might prove militarily or commercially useful. The telescope in question had a magnification of eight or nine times. With it you could, Galileo demonstrated, see ships two hours earlier than with the naked eye. Within months he was studying the moon, having increased the magnification to fifteen and then to twenty times. He would go on to identify four of the moons of Jupiter.

This technology might have given Venice an extraordinary advantage over enemies and rivals, except that the principle of the instrument was already widely known and it was not especially difficult to make. Nevertheless, on the occasion of his presentation of one of the telescopes to the Doge, Galileo was offered a substantial increase in pay. This would not take effect, however, until the following year. Further increases were ruled out and acceptance implied permanent commitment to the job. Galileo, always looking for a position that allowed more time for research, soon managed to negotiate himself a more congenial post at the court of the Grand Duke of Tuscany. (As canny as a Venetian, he had continued to cultivate Medici patronage during his years at Padua. Himself a Tuscan, he was professor at his native Pisa until 1592.) There was anger in Venice when Galileo removed himself to Florence in September 1610. Hindsight says that he should have stayed, since Venice could more easily have protected him from the Church and the Inquisition in the 1630s than could the sympatheitc but more Rome-influenced Grand Dukes. But teaching commitments in Padua would have denied him the leisure to evolve in the first place the views that he was forced to abjure.

The continuing importance of the Campanile to Venetians' sense of identity was dramatically demonstrated by a group of people, widely assumed to be members of the Lega del Nord or some other separatist party, who wished to mark the 200 years since the end of the republic with some éclat. On May 9, 1997, eight armed men forced a ferry to disembark their lorry at the Piazzetta, smashed through the gates of the Campanile with it, marched up the stairs to the top and there hoisted the flag of St. Mark and proclaimed themselves "soldiers of the *serenissimo* Venetian government." Not recognizing the government in question, the local *carabinieri* produced long ladders and rapidly overpowered these "soldiers." The Lega del Nord disclaimed responsibility for the incident.

Such goings-on are difficult to imagine in the ordered domain of the Museo Correr, opposite San Marco. Teodoro Correr bequeathed his collection to the city in 1830. Steadily augmented, it has occupied its present site, including the former Napoleonic and royal palace, since the early 1920s. Traces of the palace remain in the first few rooms of the museum; in the Throne Room, for instance, there is neoclassical Napoleonic decoration by Giuseppe Borsato and others, and frescos (now mounted on panels) from the Napoleon-free redecoration that began in 1814, including graceful mythological dancers by Francesco Hayez. Such pictures, with some contemporary furniture and the odd well-placed mirror, are the ideal accompaniment for the work of the greatest of neoclassical sculptors, Antonio Canova (1757-1822). The Correr has a good variety of Canovas, among them tantalizing pieces in bas-relief that he failed to execute in marble. *Daedalus and Icarus* is the work that, displayed at the Ascension Day festival in 1779, made the Academy of Painting and Sculpture waive its age restrictions and elect Canova a member. Daedalus, a kindly patriarch, concentrating and sure of what he is doing, attaches wings to Icarus, who looks along his shoulder at this amazing new equipment, almost transfigured with innocent pride, astonished that his father is really going to let him fulfill his heart's desire. Perhaps it is too obvious to say that this is pride before a fall; the aspiring young sculptor, besides, wants the viewer to think of the traditional symbolism of Daedalus as that of the artist, fitting wings of aspiration and imagination to common clay that it may soar—almost—to heaven. Here too are Canova's even earlier pair, the anguished *Orpheus and Eurydice* (1775-7), the *Italian Venus*, and—no less classically pure of line—a mighty bust of Pope Clement XIII.

The vast museum contains everything from masterpieces to curiosities like the last Doge's straw hat and gold *manine* (little hands, as the name suggests) for counting votes in the complicated elections in which the republic specialized. There are fine dogal coins, portraits, captured Turkish banners, Jacopo de' Barbari's remarkable perspective map of Venice in 1500, a whole interesting sub-museum of the Risorgimento (full of documents and pictures) on the second floor, altar-frontals, pictures of processions and arrivals—the spectacular disembarkation of Dogaressa Morosina Grimani by Andrea Vicentino, for example—and an extensive gallery of other paintings that delivers the final blow to those optimists who hope to see something of the museum in one visit. Perhaps the most arresting painting (Room 38 of the gallery), nevertheless, is Carpaccio's *Two Venetian Ladies*. Long taken for languid courtesans gazing into space from their balcony while waiting for a client, they have been known since the 1970s to be models of chastity, perhaps mother and daughter. The two doves, the peahen, and the lily and myrtle in the vases on the balcony, are all symbols of conjugal chastity. The women's expressions are of well-bred restraint. Perhaps more surprisingly, they turn out to be only the lower portion of a whole painting; the upper part of the lily is to be found in distant Malibu, in the foreground of the supposedly separate *Hunters on the Lagoon* in the J. Paul Getty Museum. The loyally expected or thought-of men must be among these figures in boats, firing arrows at birds. (The two parts were brought together for the first time in an exhibition at Palazzo Grassi in Venice in 1999.) Yet even with the Malibu addition and the signs of chastity, the ladies are likely to strike modern viewers as enigmatic or perhaps simply as a statement of the tedium of being wealthy but female in late fifteenth-century Venice.

San Marco

John Ruskin, in *The Stones of Venice*, gives a visionary description of San Marco from the Piazza:

> ... *a multitude of pillars and white domes, clustered into a long low pyramid of coloured light; a treasure-heap, it seems, partly of gold, and partly of opal and mother-of-pearl, hollowed beneath into five great vaulted porches, ceiled with fair mosaic, and beset with sculpture of alabaster, clear as amber and delicate as ivory,—sculpture fantastic and involved, of palm leaves and lilies, and grapes and pomegranates, and birds clinging and fluttering among the branches, all twined together into an endless network of buds and plumes: and in the midst of it, the solemn forms of angels, sceptred, and robed to the feet, and leaning to each other across the*

gates... And round the walls of the porches are set pillars of variegated stones, jasper and porphyry, and deep-green serpentine spotted with flakes of snow.

Much of what so entranced Ruskin, including "the Greek horses... blazing in their breadth of golden strength," was already to be seen by thirteenth-century Venetians. But the original basilica, as far as is known, was a more sober, perhaps a rather austere building. It was put up at the onset—and altered and enriched at the apogee—of the power of the republic. From the beginning it was intended to promote that power; it was the ducal chapel, not the cathedral, and it was here that such important state ceremonies as the investiture of the Doge took place. And, plain though the church consecrated in 832 must have been, it contained a priceless religious and political treasure: the body of St. Mark the Evangelist.

In the ninth century the power of a city could be reckoned, to a fair extent, by the number and prestige of the relics in its churches. Constantinople was particularly rich in such remains; the Apostoleion or church of the Holy Apostles, rebuilt by the emperor Justinian in the fifth century, contained relics of saints Andrew, Luke, and Timothy as well as the mausoleum of the first Christian emperor, Constantine. The first San Marco may well have been partly modeled on the Apostoleion, probably following its Greek cross plan, as befitted a saint of real authority like Mark.

Mark was not only a premier saint, but had—or was supplied with—better local connections than the earlier patron of Venice, the Greek warrior Theodore, whose church would be incorporated as a chapel in the later basilica. Mark was supposed to have evangelized the province of Upper Adria; where Venice would one day rise an angel came to him with the words: "Peace be with you, Mark my evangelist. Your body will rest here." (These are the Latin words—*Pax tibi, Marce evangelista meus. Hic requiescet corpus tuum*—the first five of which appear on the open books clutched by the familiar lions of San Marco.) This was the excuse, developed of course partly with hindsight, for seizing the evangelist's body from Alexandria in about 829. The robbery was made more palatable not only because Egypt was in "infidel" Muslim hands, but also because Venice did not openly or directly commit it. It was left, says the chronicle of Martino da Canale, to three enterprising Venetian merchants. They were prepared to offer the guardian of the body good money to let them take the saint, but he explained that this was easier said than done because "the pagans hold him above all price" and they would cut the merchants to pieces rather than yield the body up to them. The Venetians' solution was ingenious: they put St. Mark in a basket, covered over with cabbage and pork, put his clothes on a lesser saint and sealed the tomb again. Some pagans, alerted by the sudden spreading of a sweet odor of sanctity, searched the tomb but were reassured when they saw there his clothes on what they took to be his body. More suspicious types suspected what the Venetians were doing and came to inspect their ship. St. Mark had been attached to the mast, between two quarters of pork. Seeing the pork, the infidels "began to cry *hanzir! hanzir!*—'pork! pork!'—and fled from the vessel." Off sailed the merchants. With the help of the saint the party soon reached the city. (His first pro-Venetian deed was to wake the captain and tell him he would run aground if he did not immediately lower his sails). Much the same story is told in mosaic above one of the doors of the main façade.

The ninth-century basilica, damaged but not destroyed by fire in 976, was immediately repaired or partially rebuilt. More extensive rebuilding, beginning in 1063, produced the present church, consecrated by Doge Vitale Falier in 1094. The reconstruction was properly completed when, soon after the consecration, the body of St. Mark, which had apparently been lost after its removal to a place of safety during the fire of 976, made its miraculous reappearance (as told in mosaics of about 1305 at the end of the right transept). In the new church brick vaulting replaced wooden roofs, the atrium or narthex was added to the front of the church, and the crypt was made. The saint was reburied in the crypt, remaining there until 1836, when he was transferred to a position beneath the high altar.

The Apostoleion in Constantinople was again the main model; Venice now had the resources and the technical skill to imitate it more closely than in the ninth century, but comparison is made difficult by the fact that the Apostoleion was destroyed in the fifteenth century. San Marco, however, blended western and Byzantine traditions and was affected, internally in particular, by the different emphases of the Roman and Orthodox rites. The mosaics, for instance, have a more linear, narrative focus and a wider range of subjects than is permitted in Greek tradition, and the main altar is placed not in the center but farther east. The architect was very probably Greek, but the work was supervised and carried out, it would seem, by Italian stonemasons, mosaicists, and others. There are five hemispherical domes, one at the center and four on the arms of the Greek cross. The domes themselves remain the same shape—visible inside the church—as when they were completed nine hundred years ago, but in about 1230 they were capped by higher lead-covered domes surmounted by smaller cupolas. The inspiration for these new features may have been Islamic, probably Egyptian.

Other thirteenth-century changes also reflected contact with the wider world, mainly in the form of loot sent from Constantinople in the long aftermath of the Fourth Crusade. The spoils of conquest were grouped in particular profusion on the south façade, aptly facing the Ducal Palace. Here there are reliefs, panels and columns from Constantinople. At the southwest corner is what is left of a trophy from a later war, the porphyry pillar known as the *Pietra del bando*. This was taken in 1258 from Acre, where it had symbolized Genoese rule. (It was demolished when the Campanile fell in 1902.) Further along are two pillars also long believed to be from Acre but now known, like so much else, to be from Constantinople.

Beyond the pillars is the ancient porphyry group of the Tetrarchs, the two senior and two junior emperors who, on Diocletian's initiative, divided control of the Roman empire between them in 293. To possess this group was, in effect, to lay claim to imperial power; one of the tetrarchs is Constantius, father of the Byzantine founder Constantine.

How many people realized this is, however, debatable. The tetrarchs clasp each other's royally mantled shoulders with one hand and the hilts of their swords of power with the other, but their gesture of solidarity has become "charming" in some modern guides, and in the early seventeenth century Tom Coryat was told that they were four "Noble Gentlemen of Albania that were brothers." They had arrived at some early period of Venetian history "in a ship laden with great store of riches." Two went ashore, two stayed on board, and each pair plotted to poison the other and make off with the riches. All, like the young men in a similar situation in Chaucer's *The Pardoner's Tale*, died. "Whereupon the Signiory of Venice seized upon all their goods as their own, which was the first treasure that ever Venice possessed." They also put up the statue "in memorial of that uncharitable and unbrotherly conspiracy." As one might expect in a Venetian story, the emphasis is as much on the enrichment of the state as on the moral conclusion.

But the most striking and famous Byzantine loot was the team of four bronze horses prominently displayed above the main door. They seem to move with an easy, confident grace; as the young Benjamin Disraeli wrote to his father in September 1826, "the four brazen horses amble, not prance, as some have described." Not surprisingly, people wanted to attribute them to the ancient Greek sculptor Lysippus, although they are more probably from Roman imperial times. They "amble" with the easy certainty of horses made to crown a triumphal arch; they are thought to have performed some such function at the Hippodrome in Constantinople. Clearly their new position was intended to be no less triumphal, celebrating a triumph, in the first instance, over the Byzantines, one more annexing of the symbols of their power. Nearly six hundred years later they became, in turn, Napoleon's loot, but were brought back after his fall. In the twentieth century they were moved three more times for their own protection: to Rome during the world wars and, in 1979, indoors to the Museo della Basilica. You can examine the originals before going out to see the replicas that now stand on the façade. (They are also represented in the mosaic of about 1260–70, showing the arrival of St. Mark's body at the basilica, above the leftmost door, the Porta Sant' Alipio.)

In the thirteenth century, then, the exterior of San Marco was

adorned and encrusted to produce Ruskin's "treasure-heap." To enter the atrium you must pass between double-tiered columns, beneath golden mosaics ranging in date from the thirteenth to the nineteenth century, marble slabs, the bronze horses, Gothic sculpture, and gables (added in the fifteenth century). Having entered the atrium, you are offered more instances of Venetian glory in the form of magnificent thirteenth-century mosaics; on the domes, arches and lunettes here is the Old Testament story, starting with the Creation in the center of the furthest dome on the right—Adam and Eve, amid the greenery of Paradise, figure mainly in the outer ring—and proceeding to the Israelites' crossing of the Red Sea at the other end. The lozenge near the central door commemorates the moment when, under glorious Venetian auspices, Frederick Barbarossa knelt in submission to the Pope (see pp.14-15). In niches in the front wall of the atrium are the tombs of some of the medieval doges who contributed to the glory, including Vitale Falier (to the right of the main door).

On entering the interior proper one's main impression is of gold—gold glinting in every direction, complemented by the softer sheen of mosaic paving—and then of Ruskin's "continual succession of crowded imagery, one picture passing into another, as in a dream." The atmosphere is not, except perhaps during a service, noticeably religious. But then no more is it noticeably secular; easy though it is to represent the acquisition and incorporation of spoils as naked greed and self-aggrandizement, most citizens were devoted to St. Mark and believed that the city prospered, was rich and victorious, thanks to his protection. Neither quite sacred nor merely secular, neither purely Greek nor Italian, the interior seems, even on repeated visits, unique. And as through arches glimmer other arches, inscriptions and vaults, it seems less finite than most church interiors. San Marco has often been likened to a medieval illuminated manuscript; as you turn one glowing page and then, still partly seeing the next, look back, new details seem continually to appear.

Much has rightly been made of the wall and ceiling mosaics of the basilica. But the floor is almost equally exciting. The polychrome mosaic pavement is mainly twelfth- and thirteenth-century (with later restorations). Much of it is made, again, from ancient or eastern marble and porphyry. Some of this was brought back by merchants, who were ordered by Doge Domenico Selvo in 1071, during the building of the church, to include such valuables in every cargo; much again was looted from Constantinople in 1204 and the years following. There are marbles and mosaics in lozenges, suns, roundels, arches, and in colors including white, red, reddish-brown, green, and pale yellow; larger slabs of variegated gray-white; knots, leaf-patterns, and peacocks. While the left aisle has been leveled out, elsewhere whole areas of paving are rucked up, rippled; they look satisfyingly like a geological rather than an artistic occurrence.

Clearly produced by human efforts, but cumulatively, over several hundred years, is the Pala d'Oro, the golden altarpiece. The gold and enamel are punctuated by jewels: ruby, emerald, pearl, topaz, amethyst. At first it may seem simply dazzling, but it repays close attention. During the rebuilding program that followed the fire of 976, Doge Pietro Orseolo I commissioned the original *pala* from Constantinople.

It is not clear what, if anything, survives from this period. In 1105 Doge Ordelafo Falier introduced new material including, probably, the small panels with scenes from the lives of the Evangelists on three sides of the lower register. Then in 1209 Doge Pietro Ziani had the whole piece expanded. The upper register was put together to hold panels probably taken from the church of the Pantokrator, an imperial burial-place in Constantinople. The Archangel Michael, long-winged, haloed, and much bejeweled, flanked by small roundels of saints, stands between arched panels showing the Entry into Jerusalem, the Resurrection and Harrowing of Hell, the Crucifixion, Ascension, Pentecost (with apostles visibly speaking in tongues), and the death or "Dormition" of the Virgin. In the Pantokrator these panels (except for the Archangel) were part of a larger series connected with the sequence of twelve holy days, but only six scenes fitted the new *pala*.

In the mid-1340s the goldsmith Giovanni Paolo Boninsegna carried out the final spectacular framing and arrangement of the piece as we now have it. At the center of the lower register is the Byzantine Christ Pantokrator, rubies blazing on the upper part of his throne and on the Book of Life he holds, between massed jewels and roundels of the four Evangelists. This central figure is probably twelfth-century, while scholars think that the rows of saints and angels are fourteenth-century work done in Venice, although possibly by Greek artists. The whole looks surprisingly coherent, although the producers of much of the original work would probably disagree; the aim is to glorify San Marco, not to outline a religious sequence.

Too precious for everyday exposure, the pala was protected by the *pala feriale* (*ferie*, in ecclesiastical usage, are non-festival days) painted by Paolo Veneziano and his sons at the same time that Boninsegna was working on the more precious piece, and now in the Museo della Basilica.

Another important Byzantine trophy, although the date of its arrival is unknown, is the Virgin *Nikopoia*, the twelfth-century icon carried into battle before the emperors. (This is why it is called *nikopoia*, "victory bringing," not after a place as is sometimes supposed.) It had clearly not lived up to recent emperors' expectations; this, the Venetians might have pointed out, made it all the more appropriate to transfer the icon to the powerhouse of the people who were now winning the battles. It would no longer be risked in the field. Remaining in the basilica, it came to be regarded as a sign of the protection of the city by the Mother of God.

There is material for many wanderings in the basilica. The Treasury, on the right of the church, contains a rich store of icons, chalices, jeweled bowls and the like, many again Byzantine. In the Cappella Zen there are the two powerful Romanesque red marble lions that probably once guarded the southern doors of the basilica (closed in the sixteenth century). Fourteenth-century mosaics in the Baptistery tell the story of John the Baptist, including an elegantly fashionable Salome. The steep steps up to the museum, above the atrium, give memorable views down into and across the church and then, from the loggia, out over the pigeons, flags, souvenir-stalls, and milling crowds in the Piazza. Beside the replica horses, but not very high compared with church towers and campanili, you feel not so much superior to or distanced from the people below, but in a privileged relationship with them, a moving part of the façade they admire—although again it is only one of the many things they can admire in the Piazza, one aspect of the whole ensemble you seem to have been allowed to join.

San Marco is all very splendid, and there are moments when the tired or rapt visitor might almost take seriously Théophile Gautier's fantastic imaginings of the mosaics coming to life amid golden lightning: the stiff folds of the saints' robes "seem to soften and float, fixed eyes move... sealed feet begin to walk; the cherubim revolve their eight wings like wheels; angels unfurl their long purple and azure feathers, nailed to the wall by the implacable mosaicist." The phantoms, "dazzling, dizzying, hallucinatory... pass before you shaking their haloes of long golden hair." But more personal and more peaceable experiences are also possible as the church increases in familiarity until, Henry James says, "you pass in under the pictured porticoes with a feeling of habit and friendliness and a desire for something cool and dark." What you find is

> *nothing grandly balanced or far-arching: there are no long lines nor triumphs of the perpendicular. The church arches indeed, but arches like a dusky cavern. Beauty of surface, of tone, of detail, of things near enough to touch and kneel upon and lean against—it is from this the effect proceeds. In this sort of beauty the place is incredibly rich, and you may go there every day and find afresh some lurking pictorial nook.*

And indeed there are usually, James goes on, some painters trying, "with their easels set up in uncertain equilibrium on the undulating floor," to do justice to the marble slabs, "the great panels of basalt and jasper, the crucifixes of which the lonely anguish looks deeper in the vertical light, the tabernacles whose open doors disclose a dark Byzantine image spotted with dull, crooked gems." But

> *if you cannot paint these things you can at least grow fond of them. You grow fond even of the old benches of red marble, partly worn away by the breeches of many generations and attached to the base of those wide pilasters of which the precious plating, delightful in its faded brownness, with a faint grey bloom upon it, bulges and yawns a little with honourable age.*

CHAPTER FOUR

The Doges' Venice: The Ducal Palace

The Palazzo Ducale in Venice was at once a seat of government, a place of judgment, and an administrative center. It included private apartments for the doge, committee rooms, a suitably huge hall for the Great Council, and prisons. In early times (the first palace on the site was probably founded in the ninth century) it was also a fortress, but this aspect became decreasingly important, mainly because of the existence of adequate defenses at the lagoon entrances. It was decked out not with turrets and cannon, but with the finest and richest available decoration, including paintings by Veronese, Tintoretto, and the like. The aim was to assert the glory and the wealth of Venice, and the incidental effect was to provide a treasure-chest for lovers of Venetian art and architecture.

The palace was central to the life of the Venetian republic and remains essential to the city's sense of identity. Together with the domes and Campanile of San Marco, its pink-and-white Gothic upper façade (part of the mid-fourteenth-century rebuilding) dominates the view from the sea, from Santa Maria della Salute, and from San Giorgio Maggiore. The large balcony was added, partly in order to let more light into the Sala del Maggior Consiglio, in 1404. The architectural historian Deborah Howard gives a helpful account of how the façade works:

It is difficult to view such a familiar monument as the Palazzo Ducale objectively, for the eye is adjusted to the proportions as they stand through years of acquaintance. Any change in the appearance would at once look wrong or inharmonious. It is like a great piece of music, every part contributing to the unified whole, in which familiarity can easily hinder understanding. One secret of the success of the design is the way in which the large expanse of solid wall at the top of the building is made to seem light and insubstantial by the shimmering lozenge pattern in the tiles of red and white marble, while the lower arcade, where void in fact predominates over solid, appears robust and strong with its row of stocky columns and plain Gothic arches. There is no sense of top-heaviness, and the balance of light and shade is perfectly controlled.

Elements derived from Islamic architecture also contribute to the distinctiveness. Howard notes that "the traceries are as delicately carved as Moorish screen walls, and the whimsical roofline crenellations seem more appropriate to an Egyptian mosque than to an Italian communal palace." Venetian contact with the Muslim lands of the eastern Mediterranean and Iran long pre-dated the fall of Constantinople to the Turks in 1453.

At lower levels, the Molo and Piazzetta façades are richly decorated with carvings. At the corner next to the Ponte della Paglia is a large relief of the Drunkenness of Noah by Filippo Calendario, probably the principal architect of the palace itself. The limp, reeling Noah spills his goblet, the tolerant son Shem covers his father's nakedness, and to the right a frowning Ham takes an evidently different attitude. The theme of human weakness is continued by Calendario in another relief, of Adam and Eve, at the angle between the Molo and Piazzetta fronts. Weakness must be forgiven or, as in the palace and as in public executions nearby in the Piazzetta, judged; ironically Calendario himself was hanged in 1355 for his part in Doge Marino Faliero's conspiracy to overthrow the state. When the palace was extended along the Piazzetta to the basilica in the 1420s, Bartolomeo Bon drew attention to justice in his relief (next to the Porta della Carta on which he also worked) of the Judgment of Solomon. Bon seizes on the dramatic moment when the executioner pulls the defenseless small child up by the wrist and prepares to strike; the child's true mother is stricken with horror while the false mother, behind, looks on blindly; the serenely wise Solomon, sitting on his throne, stops the killing in the nick of time but with none of the urgency, none of the lack of premeditation, of less Solomonic judges. Inside the building, it was implicitly asserted, equally sure judgment would be found.

John Ruskin was fairly unimpressed by Bon's Solomon. For him, to contrast fifteenth-century carving with that of the fourteenth was to find proof of his thesis of the decline of an early, idealized Venice. (The date of this decline varied at different points in Ruskin's career.) His attention is therefore mainly directed at the capitals of the lowest level of arcading, on the Molo front, facing the sea, and the first seven capitals round the corner on the Piazzetta front. Beyond that the work is later, and sometimes simply copies the earlier designs—to woeful effect, feels Ruskin. While on the fourth capital (he numbers them leftwards from the Drunkenness of Noah) the lively youths "have the making of rough and great men in them," the children of the fifteenth century are "dull smooth-faced dunces, without a single meaning line in the features of their stolid cheeks"; they are "capable of becoming nothing but perfumed coxcombs." On the seventh capital is "Modesty, bearing a pitcher (In the Renaissance copy, a vase like a coffee-pot)."

Most people will enjoy the later capitals more than Ruskin. But his desire to prove his point, together with his inveterate habit of detailed observation, have him describing the approved early capitals with extraordinary precision and sensitivity. Usefully for his readers, the carvings entranced Ruskin with their variety and individuality. On the eighteenth capital the moon is portrayed as "a woman in a boat upon the Sea; who raises the crescent in her right hand, and with her left draws a crab out of the waves, up the boat's side; the moon's drapery ripples down to her feet, so exactly as to suggest the trembling of the moonlight on the waves." The figures on the tenth capital include Avarice, an old woman whose "throat is all made up of sinews with skinny channels deep between them, strained as by anxiety, and wasted by famine; the features hunger-bitten, the eyes hollow, the look glaring and intense, yet without the slightest caricature." It is difficult to fit all the capitals into a single detailed iconographical scheme, but they provide a fairly comprehensive picture of life. The twenty-first gathers together representatives of the "inferior" professions—stonecutter, goldsmith, cobbler, carpenter, farmer, clerk, blacksmith. The twenty-second shows the traditional Ages of Man and "influence of planets on human life"; manhood is governed by Mars, old age (the "very graceful and serene figure, in the pendant cap, reading") by Jupiter, final decrepitude by Saturn. And on the twenty-fifth capital appear the months: April with a lamb, June carrying cherries in a basket. Ruskin breaks off to observe, hungry perhaps amid all this study but observant as ever, that "this representation of June is peculiarly Venetian. The cherries grown near Venice are of a deep red colour, and large, but not of high flavour, though refreshing. They are carved upon the pillar with great care, all their stalks undercut." February, less romantically, fries fish.

A number of the capitals have been replaced by accurate copies. (The originals are in the palace, in the ground floor Museo dell'Opera.) Doge Francesco Foscari and the winged lion before which he kneels on the Porta della Carta, the grand ceremonial entrance to the courtyard, are also replicas, as most of the original figure was destroyed by the French in 1797. But the work of Bartolomeo Bon and others survives in the rest of this late Gothic masterpiece (1438–43) with its niches, pinnacles, flourishes, assured Lion of St. Mark, the saint himself in a roundel and, crowning all, Bon's Justice with her sword and balance. The Porta della Carta gets its name, "gate of paper," probably because bureaucrats worked or their documents were stored here. A vaulted passage runs from the Porta to the courtyard by way of a more classical work by some of the same sculptors, the Arco Foscari of 1462–71, evidently inspired by Roman triumphal arches and intended to appropriate their victorious and imperial associations.

Such glory was perhaps more obviously asserted in the courtyard by the Scala dei Giganti, the giants' staircase, which was designed by Antonio Rizzo as part of the rebuilding work after a fire in 1483. Its name refers to the huge statues of Mars and Neptune added by

Jacopo Sansovino in 1567. From the 1580s onward, newly elected doges walked up to stand between these giants after being saluted by the electoral committee, proclaimed and put through various ceremonies in San Marco, and carried round the Piazza. The carrying was the most popular part of the ritual, since during it the new man or one of his family distributed largesse—gold and silver coins—from a cup. At the top of the stairs, as the grand climax of the ceremonies, a senior counselor placed the distinctive *corno* on the doge's head. Here too he would later stand to receive ambassadors. And here, in Byron's verse play *Marino Faliero*, the renegade doge is beheaded. In fact Faliero died on an earlier, differently positioned staircase in 1355, more than a century before the Scala dei Giganti was built, but the setting would have appealed to the Venetians' sense of condign punishment. At the top of this grand stair, says Byron in his preface, the renegade doge was "crowned, and discrowned, and decapitated." Even the average law-abiding doge, unlikely to share Faliero's fate, was provided with a warning against vainglory immediately after his acclamation. He was escorted from the Scala dei Giganti to the Sala del Piovego to reflect on the fact that this was where his body would one day lie in state.

The new head of state was now at last free to take possession of his apartments on the first floor. He would be able to some extent to imprint his personality on these gloriously gilded and stuccoed chambers, reached by way of the spectacular Scala d'Oro, by installing his own furniture, which his heirs would have to remove within three days of his death. But even the choice of furniture was, no doubt, intended to assert the dignity of the ducal family rather than the doge's good taste. Public and ceremonial considerations remained central to his life in these apartments as elsewhere. Maps on the walls of his Sala dello Scudo or delle Mappe extended, or attempted to extend, that ceremonial order into the world beyond the palace and the city. There are proud representations of Venetian territories and of the lands visited by Marco Polo, repainted after the fire of 1483. During a later repainting, in 1762, America and other post-Polo lands were added, including places such as Greenland and Cape Verde visited by later Venetian travelers. (Polo lived somewhere in the

vicinity of Corte Prima del Milion and Corte Seconda del Milion, named from the popular title given to his account of his travels, *Il milione*, suggesting a myriad of lies or exaggerations. Giovanni Caboto or Cabot, explorer in the service of Henry VII of England, lived in a house on the corner of Via Garibaldi and Riva dei Sette Martiri, with a suitable view out onto the lagoon.)

After the doge's apartments come many other splendid rooms. The detail, whether of the decoration or of the useful information boards explaining the function of the rooms and the functioning of the republic, can become bewildering. But one unifying feature, one thread to hold on to, is the work of the sixteenth-century painters, Veronese and Tintoretto particularly, who were responsible for much of the color and atmosphere of the palace. These artists' dominance was, initially, accidental. Two great fires attacked the palace in 1574 and 1577. The first caused most damage in the Sala del Senato and the Sala del Collegio, the meeting-place of the cabinet that conducted much of the daily business of the republic. The second fire gutted the Sala del Maggior Consiglio (Hall of the Great Council) and the Sala dello Scutinio, where votes were taken, counted and recorded. Various architects including Andrea Palladio, chief architect of the republic since 1570, were called in to advise on renovation. Although there is some dispute about whether Palladio actually proposed wholesale rebuilding in the new classical—Palladian—style, he did suggest more modernization than the conservative majority in the Senate was eventually prepared to undertake. The Gothic palace was restored, not replaced.

But the situation with the paintings that had been lost was different. These represented, naturally enough, more of a medley of periods and styles than the fabric of the building. There was work by such Gothic masters as Pisanello and the Paduan artist Guariento, a fragment of whose *Coronation of the Virgin* for the Sala del Maggior Consiglio, discovered in 1903, is displayed in the Sala del Guariento. There were also paintings by such diverse later artists as Carpaccio, Giovanni Bellini, and Titian. (Titian died, aged around ninety, in 1576. His fresco of St. Christopher carrying the infant Christ [c. 1523] survives in the ducal apartments, in the Sala dei Filosofi.) Veronese, Tintoretto and their workshops and contemporaries were commissioned, or won competitions, to provide new paintings.

Veronese and Tintoretto

Paolo Veronese, born in Verona in 1528, worked much in Venice after 1553. He painted, in the words of his seventeenth-century biographer Carlo Ridolfi, "majestic deities, *gravi personaggi*, matrons full of grace," richly costumed kings, a variety of "military spoils" (the "trophies" beloved of Renaissance patrons and artists), and decorative architectural settings. Such emphases, adds another seventeenth-century commentator, Marco Boschini, led Veronese to be called "the Treasurer of Painting," the creator of a jeweled world. His distinctive preferences for satin, silk, and velvet, for golden hair and for light colors (especially silver, light blue, lemon, orange, and pink) contribute memorably to the atmosphere of the palace. "He swims before you in a silver cloud," said Henry James in 1882:

he thrones in an eternal morning. The deep blue sky burns behind him, streaked across with milky bars; the white colonnades sustain the richest canopies, under which the first gentlemen and ladies in the world both render homage and receive it. Their glorious garments rustle in the air of the sea and their sun-lighted faces are the very complexion of Venice... Never was a painter so nobly joyous, never did an artist take a greater delight in life, seeing it all as a kind of breezy festival and feeling it through the medium of perpetual success. He revels in the gold-framed ovals of the ceilings, multiplies himself there with the fluttering movement of an embroidered banner that tosses itself into the blue.

Sir Joshua Reynolds can be imagined raising an eyebrow at this "breezy festival." In the late eighteenth century, lecturing at the Royal Academy, he dismissed the Venetian painters as essentially "ornamental." Titian, he slightly grudgingly admitted, has "a sort of senatorial dignity about him," but more usually "bustle and tumult... fills every part of a Venetian picture, without the least attempt to interest the passions." Bright coloring will not produce "that solidity, steadiness, and simplicity of effect, which heroic subjects require, and which simple or grave colours only can give to a work."

For James, Veronese's *The Rape of Europa* (in the Sala dell' Anticollegio) is the "happiest picture in the world." Here Europa is not the victim of abduction but a bride hastily and enthusiastically attired by her followers, lips parted in pleasurable surprise or erotic anticipation, who waves as, bathed in light, she rides off into the sea on her bull. *The Rape of Europa* was not installed in this elaborately gilded room with its monumental fireplace until 1713. More often, however—as, for instance, next door in the allegorical scenes of the glory of Venice on the ceiling of the Sala del Collegio—Veronese's paintings formed an integral part of the design. Particular magnificence and harmony were needed, since here the Collegio would receive foreign ambassadors; in 1858 the Austrian regent Prince Maximilian chose this room as his audience chamber (rather inconveniently for anyone trying to act on Ruskin's belief that "the traveller who really loves painting ought to get leave to come to this room whenever he chooses").

After Veronese and his assistants had finished work on the Collegio ceiling, Jacopo Tintoretto and his team, including his son Domenico, provided some of their finest work for the walls, including *The Mystic Marriage of St. Catherine*. The coloring of this piece is lighter and fresher, perhaps more Veronese-like, than most reproductions suggest. White and gold associate Catherine and the otherwise contrasting figure of the elderly kneeling Doge Francesco Donà: the white of his beard, his ermine, her dress and the cloudy sky between the two; the gold of her crown and hair and his *corno*. Her veil, floating from the crown, transparent but faintly golden, shows through it the pale cloud so as to combine the colors and subtly further the association between the earthly and heavenly figures. That it would be presumptuous to make the connection too closely is emphasized by the doge's traditional expression of sobriety, of keeping one's counsel—a sort of proud humility. While he looks partly into the room, providing a point of access for the viewer, Catherine's eyes are all for the Christ-child. But the idea that the earthly doge and viewers can reach toward Christ and his mother is again suggested partly through color: moving left the eye picks out the various pinks of the lining of Donà's cloak, Catherine's sash, the cloth leading up the steps to the Virgin, and her robe. (These patterns are rendered noticeable by the careful grouping of the central figures and those around them, among them Eloquence, Prudence, Temperance, and Charity.)

Painting also adorned rooms with traditionally more fearful associations. Veronese's painting of St. Mark crowning the Theological Virtues once adorned the ceiling of the Sala della Bussola, where people waited to be interrogated in the neighboring Sala del Consiglio dei Dieci. (The painting was removed in 1797 and is still in the Louvre; a copy stands in its place.) The Sala della Bussola, named after a wooden screen at one side, contains a *bocca di leone* or "lion's mouth," into which denunciations were posted for the attention of the Council of Ten. For many years writers on Venice have been at pains to explain that old tales of wild denunciations leading to immediate arrests and torture and arbitrary executions are grossly exaggerated. Nevertheless, those waiting to be interviewed by the Ten, who were responsible for judging crimes against the state and had sweeping powers to deal with them, had reason to be nervous. Council members and suspects, engaged in the real business of the state, probably rarely had much time to look up at its allegorical celebration in the ceiling panels by Veronese. More leisured modern visitors have looked most at the corner representation of a young woman with an old man wearing a turban (perhaps intended for *Youth and Age*), a moving study in contrast and complementarity.

Veronese, Tintoretto, and many others were involved in the decoration of the largest hall, the Sala del Maggior Consiglio, where all 1,500 members of the Great Council assembled. Confidence-building representations of Venetian victories over the Turks, the Genoese, the Milanese and such surrounded them, and idealized portraits of the doges up to the death of Francesco Venier in 1556, produced mainly by Domenico Tintoretto, looked down on them. This ducal frieze did, however, admit one dire note of warning. A black cover was painted where the portrait of Marin Faliero should have been, together with a stark Latin inscription: *Hic est locus Marini Falethri decapitati pro criminibus.* Enemies of the state could not be permitted to share in the color and glory of everything else in the hall; their efficient removal, like the defeat of foreign foes in the wall paintings, made works like Veronese's oval *Triumph of Venice*, on the ceiling above the tribunal, the more convincing. Veronese worked on this painting, with his brother Benedetto among others, until just before his death in 1588. The prescribed program for it has survived: Venice is to be portrayed as the goddess Roma was in ancient times, enthroned above cities and towers; she is to be crowned by winged Victory, surrounded by Peace, Fame, Abundance, and the like with the correct classical attributes, and attended by rejoicing, various, and variously clad people. Most of these instructions were followed, but distinctively interpreted by the master. The intended "towers" are just visible on either side of the personified Venice, but the "cities"—implied besides by the crowd—become one lofty classical structure with pillars, pediments, and balustrade. The outdoing-Rome motif is satisfied by these classical allusions. More directly, this structure frames Victory, provides something solid before which Venice and the other personifications can float on their cloud, and allows some of the people to show off their fine clothes and hair while leaning on the balustrade, framed by an arch through which are visible characteristically Veronese blue sky and pink-tinged clouds.

Veronese, with Francesco Bassano, also won the competition to paint a vast *Paradise* for one wall of the Sala. When Veronese died in 1588, however, a new competition awarded the project to Jacopo Tintoretto, even though in practice his son Domenico carried out most of the work. The crowd of the Saved, with angels filling the remaining gaps, add their glorifying presence to that of the secular victors and rulers depicted in the hall.

Although the palace was so noticeably unlike a fortress, it did house the wherewithal to move quickly against insurrection. Richard Lassels, a mid-seventeenth-century visitor, found that in the armory "the muskets are always charged and discharged every three months; and they with the pikes and swords are so ordered, that by unbuckling a leather which holdeth them up, they fall in order into your hand without confusion: so that there a thousand or 1500 men may be armed in less than half an hour." There was also a more ingenious mechanism:

> a great round ball of iron twice as big as a man's head, pierced through like a close basket hilt: within it there is a spring which being let go with a cord, strikes fire into powder which lieth around this great ball in a train, and into which powder so many several ends of match as there are muskets here, do reach half of these matches hanging out, and the other half being within: so that (if need were) the first man that should come in and pluck the foresaid cord, would light all those matches, and every man catching one and a musket, the Senators would presently leap out soldiers.

An early version of Q might have enjoyed showing this off to James Bond. Displaying the weapons and machinery to foreigners like Lassels helped keep alive, in a time of decreasing actual power, the idea of an impregnable Venice; perhaps if grave senators could metamorphose so rapidly into gun-toting soldiers, Venice could respond just as efficiently on an international scale. But by 1688 François Misson, a Huguenot usually resident in England, was noting that the "machine... to light five hundred matches all at once" was "a little out of order."

In 1797, when Venice was finally forced to admit to powerlessness, the French dispersed some of the weaponry. What was left formed the nucleus of the present armory rooms. There is a suit of armor that belonged to Henri IV of France (sent, Lassels claims, in lieu of repayment of loans), some finely decorated sixteenth-century shields, vicious or unusable seventeenth-century two-handed swords, morions, cross-bows with their decorated leather quivers bristling with arrows, pistols, powder-flasks, arquebuses, and other guns—perhaps including some of Lassels' matchlocks—with a range of antique firing-mechanisms. From the windows of the last room, more peacefully, there are superb, distracting views of San Giorgio Maggiore, the Giudecca, the trees on the Lido, and innumerable boats.

The Prisons

Like other medieval and later palaces, the Ducal Palace also had its prisons. Placing them here was a matter mainly of convenience and security, but detaining or punishing offenders at the very heart of the state was also symbolically appropriate. Later generations, however, found it surprising and even shudderingly romantic that a palace and a prison could be so closely linked by the Bridge of Sighs (by Antonio Contin or Contino, 1600)—so-called only from the nineteenth century. The prison in question was the new block, also built by Contin and designed to alleviate overcrowding in the palace itself. But dungeons there also continued to be used; the worst were the constricted sixteenth-century cells of the *pozzi* or "wells" on the bottom two levels. They were not, as liberal propagandists claimed, continually flooded, but clearly they were damp, cold, and overcrowded; disease killed many of the inmates.

The pozzi are not open to visitors but the equally famous *piombi*—"leads," from their position just beneath the palace roof—can be seen on the *Itinerari segreti* or "secret tours" of the palace. These tours also go to the Sala del Tormento, where prisoners, as elsewhere in Europe, were tortured in an attempt to extract confessions. A rope and pulley were fastened to the ceiling, and the victim, with arms bound behind the back, was jerked up on the rope, suspended in agony until, as Coryat puts it, he "sustaineth so great torments that his joints are for the time loosed and pulled asunder," and then sent crashing down again. The piombi, probably fitted up in the late fifteenth century, were much less cramped and dispiriting than the pozzi, but subject to extremes of heat and cold. Silvio Pellico (1789–1854), a writer arrested in 1820 after falling foul of the Austrians for his liberal involvements, described a splendid summer view spoiled by the way the leaden roof of San Marco "hammered back at me with stunning force." Worse, there were mosquitoes. To banish thoughts of suicide Pellico forced himself to think his life through, meditating on "the duties of men and myself in particular." He scraped the results, in code, onto the table in his cell. Every day he scratched on until the table was full and, after further contemplation, scraped it all away to make ready for new thoughts. This he recorded in his book *Le mie prigioni* (*My Prisons*) in 1832. A death sentence had been pronounced on him and then commuted; eight years of hard labor at the notorious Spielberg fortress in Moravia followed.

Casanova's Escape

Giacomo Casanova (1725–98) was luckier than Pellico; amazingly lucky, if we credit all the details of his account of his escape from the piombi in 1756. At the time of his arrest he was engaged in a career of joyous sexual activity. In his *Memoirs*, composed in French and not published until 1821, he outlines the philosophy of a "reasoning voluptuary"; human beings, he asserts, are distinguished from animal nature by their ability not simply to enjoy pleasure but to foresee, seek, create it, and to reason about it afterwards. Gambling was another of Casanova's enthusiasms, partly because it helped to finance his love affairs. Since he could not always arrange to win, he also looked for other financial openings. When a jeweler, Giovanni Battista Manuzzi, told him that he could obtain diamonds for him on credit, he proved unusually gullible. Manuzzi called on him and noticed some manuscripts dealing with magic. Casanova showed him a section on how to make contact with spirits. The jeweler told him that he knew a collector who would pay largely for such works, borrowed them, and took them straight to the State Inquisition, for whom he worked as a spy. He filed a denunciation accusing Casanova of a spectacular list of bad habits, including libertinism, unbelief, and relieving foolish gentlemen of their money by persuading them that he was an alchemist

or had access to the world of spirits. Other enemies came forward with similar accusations. He was arrested at dawn on July 26, 1755, by the Messer Grande or police chief and a rather unnecessary, as it seemed to him, thirty or forty officers.

On his way to the piombi, Casanova noticed a horseshoe-shaped device nailed to the wall and used, the jailer obligingly explained, on prisoners condemned to death by strangling. Like Pellico, he experienced stifling heat. The rats were noisy and, Casanova says, as big as rabbits. Insects (fleas this time rather than mosquitoes) were highly active. At first the cell had no bed, but he managed to sleep on the floor for three hours. At midnight, woken by bells, he reached for his handkerchief and met "another hand as cold as ice." More frightened than he had thought possible, he stretched out his right hand again with the same result. He concluded that cruel jailers had put a corpse beside him while he slept; his imagination raced to connect it with the strangulation machine. Was this the body of some "innocent wretch," even perhaps one of his friends? Was the intention to warn him what fate lay in store for him too? He felt the hand a third time; this time it came to life and withdrew, and at last he realized that it was his own temporarily numbed left hand.

In the morning at last Casanova was able to send for a bed and some food. But he soon determined to escape. He succeeded in painstakingly sharpening a bolt and had managed to make a hole in the floor with it, planning to lower himself into the Sala della Bussola on a feast-day when it would be empty. But at this point Casanova was transferred to a more comfortable cell, a floor lower, on the other side of the palace. Unconsoled by a view across the lagoon to the Lido, he waited for the hole to be discovered. But when the furious jailer Lorenzo arrived, Casanova faced him down: if the matter was taken further, he would simply say that he was provided with tools by him and had given them back; and although the furniture was searched when it was moved from one cell to the other, the bolt—hidden in an armchair—was not discovered. Planning could begin again.

This time the way forward was books. He persuaded Lorenzo to let him exchange books with a prisoner on the floor above, the monk Marin Balbi, who found himself in the piombi not so much for fathering three daughters as for attempting to legitimate them. The two sent each other letters in the books. Casanova soon realized that the monk was foolish and unreliable, but had nobody else to turn to. Daunted only briefly by the discovery that the bolt was just too long to be concealed in a large Bible, Casanova found an ingenious solution: he sent Balbi a huge complimentary dish of macaroni, crammed with butter and parmesan cheese, and at the same time returned the Bible with the bolt in it. Lorenzo was prevailed upon to carry the dish on top of the book, concentrating hard on not spilling butter onto it. Now, as intended, Balbi worked away with the bolt at loose bricks in his cell until he could make secret trips out of it to chip at Casanova's nearby ceiling. (He needed the monk to do the work mainly because he himself was still under suspicion after digging his original hole.)

Eventually, on the night of October 31, 1756, Casanova having made a long rope by knotting together sheets and mattresses, the young adventurer and the often grumpy monk embarked on their escape. Breaking out onto the roof, they crawled up the fog-wet slope until they could straddle the ridge. Balbi lost his hat (luckily it fell inconspicuously into the water, not the courtyard) and Casanova nearly fell to his death, but at last they managed to break into the palace through a window. Father Balbi was often more of a hindrance than a help; by now Casanova was, he tells us, covered in cuts and scratches while his companion was completely unscathed. But Casanova changed into the spare clothes he had carried, put his plumed hat back on, and gave Balbi his cloak; they were able to pass more or less convincingly for people accidentally locked in the evening before. An attendant let them out and, trying not to move too quickly or too slowly, they marched down the Scala dei Giganti and through the Porta della Carta. Taking the first available gondola, they went to Mestre, on by coach to Treviso, and then, on foot, across the border into non-Venetian territory. After Treviso, however, Casanova successfully impressed on the irritating Balbi that they must now separate. When at first he refused, Casanova measured him up, began digging a grave for him with his trusty bolt, and intimated that he would bury him alive unless Balbi could do the same for him. The author was a brilliant story-teller, aiming partly to vindicate himself, but he certainly escaped and some at least of his yarn must be true. Such is the devious logic of Inquisitorial minds that he was persuaded to return to Venice in 1774 to work as a spy for the same organization to which he had been denounced. He fell foul of the authorities once more in 1782, was banished, and wrote his memoirs from the safe vantage-point of Austria.

To the Arsenal

Beyond the prisons the Danieli Hotel offers more luxurious accommodation in a Gothic palace that opened as a hotel in 1822, and its extension, added in 1948. (The extension broke a tradition of nearly eight centuries that, following the assassination of Doge Vitale Michiel in Calle delle Rasse in 1172, only low wooden buildings could be erected there.) The name "Danieli" comes from that of its first proprietor, Joseph dal Niel. He and his successors entertained a long list of literary guests including George Sand and Alfred de Musset in the closing days of their tempestuous affair, Balzac, the Ruskins, Dickens, and Proust. Doubtless the hotel, if it had been in business early enough, would have been pleased to welcome Petrarch too. In the 1360s the poet lived further along Riva degli Schiavoni in a house roughly on the site of the present numbers 4143–4, provided by the republic in consideration of a promise to leave his library to the city. It commanded, like the whole expanse of the Riva, a distractingly fine view and one which, for Petrarch, stretched far beyond the visible lagoon: he watched a ship going out amid winds sufficient to shake the walls of the house:

If you had seen it, you would have said it was no ship but a mountain swimming upon the sea, although under the weight of its immense wings a great part of it was hidden in the waves. The end of the voyage was to be the Don, beyond which nothing can navigate from our seas; but many of those who were on board, when they had reached that point, meant to prosecute their journey, never pausing until they had reached the Ganges or the Caucasus, India and the Eastern Ocean.

While able to share imaginatively in the merchants' quest, Petrarch preferred less ambitious journeys. He would soon retire to spend his last years in the quiet hilltop village of Arquà—now Arquà Petrarca—near Padua.

Before you reach the Petrarch plaque, you pass the church of Santa Maria della Visitazione or della Pietà, known simply as La Pietà. This is often marketed as "Vivaldi's church," but the present fabric was begun in 1744, three years after his death. Nevertheless, Giorgio Massari's near-oval church, designed with music in mind, is a satisfying setting for concerts, often including work by Vivaldi. "Tradition likes to record," says a plaque on the outside wall of the church in Calle della Pietà, that the perfect acoustics "are indebted to the inspired intuition and felicitous advice of Antonio Vivaldi." In favor of this slightly ingenious way of keeping the composer posthumously involved is the fact that Massari's original designs date from 1736. Music-making angels in Tiepolo's ceiling fresco of *The Triumph of the Faith* (completed in 1755) helpfully take up the theme. This church, like its predecessor, was the chapel of the *ospedale* of the Pietà, the fourteenth-century foundation next door (on the site of what is now the Hotel Metropole) where for much of his career Vivaldi taught.

Riva degli Schiavoni sweeps on. Yet another plaque, next to Calle del Dose, reminds us about some of the Schiavoni or Slavs in question. The Riva not only took its name from their merchants, but was the setting for the departure of the Slav or Dalmatian forces who, *valorosi soldati* though they were, were forced in 1797 to abandon the city they had been determined to defend (see p.40). Eventually it becomes Riva Ca' di Dio, from which, looking left up the Canale dell' Arsenale, you can see the twin towers at the water entrance to the Arsenal, for centuries the center of Venetian naval power—a memorial to the time when almost all Venetians, not just their Dalmatian cohorts, seem to have been *valorosi soldati*, or ship-builders, or sailors.

In front of the towers there used to be a drawbridge; there is still a bridge which leads to the land entrance. There is no admission, since this is still a military area. *Vaporetti*, however, are allowed through, giving views of the still extensive crenellated walls and once teeming wharves, and out to the Fondamenta Nuova and Murano.

The Arsenal and the Naval History Museum

The triumphal arch of the land entrance is the first identifiably Renaissance structure in Venice, built in 1460. (It is not certain who the architect was.) Its double columns are of Greek marble. Additions celebrate later Venetian conquests. The warlike lion of St. Mark was placed squarely above the gateway after the Venetian and Spanish defeat of the Turks at Lepanto in 1571; the topmost statue, of Saint Giustina, was put up because Lepanto was fought on her day. The railed and statued forecourt was built, and the two large ancient lions on either side of it arrived in triumph, following the Greek victories of Francesco Morosini in 1692. The sitting lion on the left, taken from Piraeus, is associated with earlier battles: on its left shoulder faint runes, unreadable to, and probably rarely noticed by, the Venetians, explain how Hakon, Ulf, Asmund, and Harald the Tall—evidently members of the Byzantine emperor's Scandinavian and English guard, the Varangians—have conquered Piraeus. Harald, against Greek opposition (perhaps to the vandalizing of their lion as well as to the humiliating inscription) insisted on publicly proclaiming the fact. After his time in the east, we know, Harald the Tall became King Harald Hardrad of

Norway and died, more famously, fighting Harold Godwinson at Stamford Bridge in 1066. The other large lion, like most such trophies, remains unmarked, anonymous. It is thought to have stood on the Sacred Way between Athens and Eleusis.

Venice, always keen to augment its collection of lions, with the convenient excuse that they were St. Mark's symbol, finally added a smaller ancient pair in 1718. Originally from Delos, they celebrate one of the last Venetian naval successes, the relief of Corfu from the Turks. Through the gateway you can see little sign now of the might the lions once represented. But once the Arsenal, founded in 1105, was a visibly very active place. At first it was used mainly for ship-repairs and storage of oars, ropes, and timber, but from the fourteenth century it was the massive, efficient, and security-conscious center for the construction of ships. Its name, suitably, derives from the Arabic *darsina'a*, a house of industry or workshop. The military associations of this original *Arsenale* later made the word synonymous with a weapons store, such as the one in London, which in turn passed its name on to the football club. In the early fourteenth century the Arsenal doubled in size. This was the period when Dante observed the workshops and quays in winter, creating a picture in which purposeful Venetians boil pitch for caulking, build new ships to replace those beyond repair, make oars and ropes, patch up sails. All this introduces the way the boiling tar bubbles ready for financially corrupt officials in Hell, but also gives the opportunity to salute a Venice comparable in its glory, in the exiled Dante's view, with perfidious Florence.

The building process continued to intensify. Productivity was aided by the good pay and conditions of the army of skilled workers, the *arsenalotti*; security by the workers' tradition of loyalty to the state—they provided the doge's bodyguard; financing by the practice, established in 1329, of auctioning one-year charters of state galleys to captains and syndicates.

In 1436 Pero Tafur, a Spanish traveler, saw the arsenalotti at work: *as you enter the gate there is a great street on either hand with the sea in the middle, and on one side are windows opening out of the house of the arsenal, and the same on the other side, and out came a galley towed by a boat, and from the windows they handed out to them, from one the cordage, from another the arms, and from another the ballistas and mortars, and so from all sides everything which was required, and when the galley had reached the end of the street all the men required were on board, together with the complement of oars, and she was equipped from end to end.*

Even more productive labor was needed as, in the late fifteenth century, more technically sophisticated ships were developed and the huge Turkish fleet grew in power. In 1473 it was decreed that the Arsenal should again double in size, dominating the eastern sector of the city. The growth of workshops, storehouses, and basins can be studied in detail from maps and models in the Naval History Museum, of which more presently. To compete with the Turks, the Senate decided, in the 1540s, that the Arsenal should maintain a reserve fleet including more than a hundred galleys and a number of lighter vessels. During the Cyprus emergency of 1570 the arsenalotti—as many as 3,000 of them—worked feverishly to produce a hundred galleys in two months.

But exhaustion from these efforts combined with timber shortages and the ravages of plague to begin the decline of the Arsenal even before the end of the sixteenth century. In 1633 the reserve was reduced to fifty ships. Repair and storage functions remained important and ships went on being constructed here, but an increasing number by the mid-seventeenth century were being imported from abroad. Goethe, who came to watch the remaining workers in 1786, said it was "like visiting some old family which, though past its prime, still shows signs of life."

Back on the waterfront and to the left is the Museo Storico Navale (Naval History Museum). Here, in the first rooms, are some of the practical aids used for planning the defense or recapture of imperial outposts in the troubled, Turk-dominated seventeenth century: models in wood, plaster, and papier-mâché, partly restored in the nineteenth century, of the strongholds of Corfu and Crete and the Greek coast. Such models were used by the real equivalents of the Duke and senators in *Othello*, assessing movements and feints and "disproportion'd" news before deciding on action against the "general enemy Ottoman." Now they look attractive in their own right, especially, perhaps, if you have been to the places. One, for instance, shows the fortifications at Nauplion, near Argos, the Venetian colonists' Napoli di Romania, with its high fortress of Palamidi, where today, beside blue sea views, the winged lions on the gateways seem more decorative than imposing. But of course the emphasis in the models is on towers, harbors, moles, walls, and contours. Prominent in most cases, at Khania in Crete for instance (the colonists' Canea), are the long hangar-like buildings of the local Arsenal. Some of these survive, in part, with other Venetian period remains in the Cretan capital Candia, now Herakleion.

The first floor of the museum also contains even more practical aids to attack and defense in the shape of culverins, cannon-balls, enormous sixteenth-century arquebuses, and some of the shiny black *pignatte da fuoco artificiale*—grenades or "fire-pots"—used against the Turks during the siege of Candia (1648–69), the last western outpost in Crete. The Naval History Museum also has swords, fine models of galleys and some surviving panels and decorations from them, such later craft as the MTM explosive speedboat (used off Crete and Malta in 1941), Italian naval uniforms and much else. But perhaps the most exciting exhibit is the magnificent 1828 model of the doges' state barge, the Bucintoro—a name that probably means simply "golden boat."

The first such vessel was built in 1277 and the last, which the model represents, in 1728. Its main function was to carry the doge from the Piazzetta to San Nicolò al Lido, off which he would ritually wed the sea, on behalf of Venice, by casting into it a golden ring. This last and grandest of the boats, nearly 150 feet long and about 25 high, was rowed by specially chosen arsenalotti, four of them to each of the forty-two oars. Above the oarsmen was a long covered *salone*, gaudy with gilt and fine fabrics, with seats for the doge's noble guests. He himself was enthroned at the front. The golden external decoration was provided by the sculptor Alessandro Vittoria: sea-gods and goddesses; scallops, medallions, sphinxes, fruits; at the stern, huge fish-tailed mermen or tritons pushing up from the water and supporting or clinging onto the galleries; large lions of St. Mark on either side of the rudder, trumpeting putti, a massive ancient warrior with tall spear. No column is complete without its satyrs, sea-gods, or ornate festoons. Around the prow there is a riot of decoration: a god reclining, smaller ones spouting golden water, putti fighting, a colossal figure of Venice in Justice (the museum has a smaller and simpler one probably from a sixteenth-century Bucintoro), the inevitable projecting lion. As Goethe observed on inspecting the ship, it would be wrong to call it "overladen with ornaments," since "the whole ship is one single ornament."

All this must have been more spectacular as the gold figures rode the waters, the sun dazzled the beholders, the great banks of oars rose and fell, and triumphant music was played. John Evelyn the diarist saw the penultimate dogal vessel in action soon after his arrival in Venice in June 1645; the doge in his robes of state ("very particular and after the eastern") and the gowned senators

> embarked in their gloriously painted, carved and gilded Bucintoro, environed and followed by innumerable galleys, gondolas, and boats filled with spectators, some dressed in masquerade; trumpets, music, and cannons, filling the whole air with din.

When the doge casts his ring into the sea, "a loud acclamation is echoed by the great guns of the Arsenal, and at the Lido." But such late surviving pageantry decreasingly reflected the realities of power. The panel above the stern gallery on the last Bucintoro showed ships at sea; it was intended as a reminder of the real power of Venice, out on the real sea beyond the lagoon. But if once, as Dr. John Moore noted after a visit in 1777, "the Doge had entire possession of, and dominion over, his spouse," now and "for a considerable time past, her favours have been shared by other lovers." As if to underline this weakness, the gorgeous but unseaworthy boat could only be taken out if weather conditions were right—this part of Ascension Day could be postponed if necessary. In 1797 the French broke up the gold decorations. The hull was used for a time as a prison ship. Only a few fragments of the ship survive, some here and some in the Museo Correr. Fortunately the model was planned before everything was lost or forgotten. The Arsenal as a whole, already in decline, suffered badly; engravings in the museum show it before and after the French: ships sunk, stockyards smashed up. Nearby, probably not without irony, the museum has placed the silver inkstand into which Napoleon dipped his pen in order to pass Venice on to the Austrians in the treaty of Campo Formio.

CHAPTER FIVE

Palatial Venice:
The Grand Canal

In 1498 the French envoy Philippe de Commynes was pleased to be greeted near Venice by twenty-five gentlemen in robes of scarlet silk, and to be seated as a mark of honor between the ambassadors of Milan and Ferrara on the ceremonial boat that would convey him into the heart of the city. Venice, like other Italian powers of the day, was anxious to keep, if at all possible, on the right side of the French monarchy. But what most impressed Commynes was something that could not be got up for the occasion; it was so extraordinary that to the modern reader his repeated "ands"—really a habit or convention among chroniclers—may take on a note of breathlessness:

> *They conducted me along the great street which they call the Grand Canal, which is very broad. Galleys often cross it, and I have seen ships of over four hundred tons near the houses; and it is the most beautiful street, I believe, and furnished with the best houses, that exists in all the world, and it goes right through the city. The houses are very large and tall, and built of fine stone. The old ones are all painted; the others, built within the last hundred years, are all faced with white marble, which comes to them from Istria, a hundred miles away, and there are also many great pieces of porphyry and serpentine on the façades... And it is the most triumphant city I have ever seen.*

People encountering the Grand Canal for the first time see some of the same places Commynes saw, and usually experience something of the same wonder. This sensation is probably enhanced if, looking in vain for the reception-committee in scarlet silk, you were, moments earlier, in one of the vast car-parks, the bus-station at Piazzale Roma, or the railway station. This chapter selects a few of the many places you may see or glimpse, and may wish to come back and see more fully, on a journey down the "most beautiful street."

Ca' d'Oro

Ca' d'Oro, the House of Gold, is one of the most immediately noticeable palaces on the Grand Canal. When the façade was completed in the 1430s it was an even more remarkable sight, glittering with gold leaf (whence the traditional name for the palace), ultramarine, Veronese marble varnished to make it more emphatically red, and details picked out in white lead against black oil paint. The palace and its decoration were the project of Marino (Venetian "Marin") Contarini, a member of one of the richest and longest established noble families. They had produced, among other notables, three doges, and for a time there seemed to be a good chance that Marino's father, Antonio, would succeed his ally Doge Tommaso Mocenigo. Instead, the long-lived Francesco Foscari was elected, but this branch of the numerous Contarini remained influential and, above all, rich. Richard J. Goy, whose detailed study of the palace and the wealth of surviving documents concerning it provides the facts and figures drawn on here, shows that their money was based on trade principally in cloth, but also in other wares including copper and, on occasion, the more surprising *grana*—small insects from Greece which were powdered into red or purple dye.

Marino Contarini (1386–1441) bought a palace in 1412 from the similarly wealthy and long established family of his wife, Soradamor Zeno (d. 1417). In 1418 work began on demolishing most of the old palace to make way for what would become Ca' d'Oro. Contarini took a keen personal interest, we know, in every aspect of the building; probably as a result of his amateur enthusiasm, the façade is "a fine collection of individual works of craftsmanship," "a complex mosaic" of different architectural elements (Goy). The palace was clearly intended to impress all Venice with its splendor, rivaled only at the time by the Ducal Palace itself—a fact from which people could, if they liked, deduce a political point. Fortunately, he had the money and discernment to have his wishes carried out (and no doubt sometimes modified) by such master stonemasons and sculptors as Matteo Raverti of Milan and the Venetian father and son Giovanni ("Zane") and Bartolomeo Bon. As well as working on the palace proper, the elder Bon was responsible for the stone-traceried screen between the *androne* or ground-floor hall and the Canal, and Bartolomeo produced the elaborate well-head in the courtyard. They and their assistants worked through the 1420s and early 1430s, much of their energy going into the marble-clad, arcaded, crenellated façade that "Zuan da Franza" (Jean Charlier) then painted according to Contarini's very precise instructions. One of the most prominent features was the family's heraldic arms in gold striped with ultramarine. Zuan used 114 ducats' worth of gold leaf—at least two years' pay for a skilled craftsman of the time. (The more prized Zuan was paid 60 ducats for the job.) Ultramarine was also costly. This was one of the final expenditures in a project that cost altogether, Goy estimates, 4,000 ducats. And even while fresh stone was brought in by boat from the Istrian quarries, the lions on the parapet were carved and gilded, the wooden cranes swung and the scaffolding was put up and taken down, Contarini was still rich enough, his accounts show, to spend 500 ducats in the four years up to 1431 on clothes and fabrics meant mainly for the *cassoni*—marriage-chests—of his teenage daughters Maria and Sammaritana. The purchases included rich *fazoleti* (kerchiefs), dresses, *camicie* (shifts), and cloaks. A *cassone*, minus this fine freight but painted suitably with scenes from the life and death of the loyal and chaste wife Lucretia, is to be seen inside the palace.

Ca' d'Oro passed out of Contarini ownership only a generation after Marino's death. It suffered accretions and decay though four centuries before passing into the hands of Prince Alexander Trubetskoy. In 1847 he gave it to his lover, the ballerina Marie Taglioni, under whose direction much vandalizing modernization took place. Work had already begun before she became owner; in September 1845 John Ruskin, exaggerating only slightly, had told his father about the "unhappy day I spent yesterday before the Casa d'Oro, vainly attempting to draw it while the workmen were hammering it down before my face." But in 1894 Baron Giorgio Franchetti acquired the palace and began more sensitive restoration and repair. Some elements, much of the arcading for instance, needed to be replaced by replicas. But Franchetti succeeded in rescuing Bartolomeo Bon's original well-head from a Paris antiques dealer. And even more notably he donated to the state the art collection that forms the nucleus of the present Galleria Franchetti within the palace. (Further restoration has continued since the 1960s.)

The first room of the museum, originally the first-floor *portego* or great hall, starts with Veneto-Byzantine stone-carvings of the eleventh and twelfth centuries: intricate interlacing of vegetal patterns, beasts in combat, peacocks, a lion. One twelfth-century piece re-uses the reverse of part of a Roman relief, perhaps for purely practical reasons but also no doubt to assert, as commonly elsewhere, Venice as the new and equally glorious Rome; the later carving, with similar confidence, shows a Venetian lion victorious over its bovine foe.

In the middle of the room is a fragmentary early fourteenth-century Massacre of the Innocents. Only one figure still has a head: a shocked, irremediably suffering mother. Next to her a chain-mailed soldier, now with no head or hands, still palpably wields his invisible weapon, a timeless figure of automatic violence. His elegant armor and finely curved shield survive beside the traces of raw suffering. It is difficult not to see other nearby images of women in the light of this chilling group. The Paduan sculptor Il Riccio's Madonna, once *con bambino*, seems now to looks down sadly, where originally she looked down with devotion. True, medieval convention often has her looking sad, focused on the suffering to come, preparing, as it were, for a Pietà, but here— unintentionally—there is a sense of emptiness. Her devotional book has survived, but there is nothing of the child she held. And a fifteenth-century French or German figure, probably representing Justice, looks young, a little vulnerable; here again, adding to this impression, the hands which must once have held a sword and balance are missing. This long-haired girl in a crown and fashionable gown could almost have ordered some Massacre of Innocents or almost have intervened to stop it. (Statues often seem to tremble on the brink of participation—

rounded figures who cannot act in the round, gesticulators who cannot communicate—tantalizingly close to the fictions of Pygmalion's vivified woman or Don Juan's stone guest.) The sense of precarious poise is also, in terms of what the sculptor intended, apt for Justice, which must impose reasonable judgment, uphold the law, or temper justice with mercy.

Less ambiguous figures are to be met elsewhere in the room. In a sixteenth-century Flemish tapestry of some unknown historical scene a grandly dressed female ruler sits enthroned with male courtiers on one side, female on the other. The physical situation of St. Catherine, bound amid torturers in a sixteenth-century alabaster altar-piece, is at least superficially less happy. But she receives some definite heavenly aid; angels dive-bomb elaborate torture machines. With large swords

(one now missing) they sabotage the machinery so that it tortures the tormentors. Above her is God, wise and all-seeing but also dynamically, specifically, interested in Catherine's case: evidently the one who sends in the angels. The theme of torture is continued more painfully and enigmatically in Mantegna's late *St. Sebastian*, still displayed in the alcove designed for it by Franchetti.

There is a view out onto the Grand Canal between pillars. Having savored this and looked at exhibits including Tuscan and Umbrian paintings, you go up stairs along which are fitted the rails and posts of a staircase of rich, reddish brown wood from another fifteenth-century palace. It is decorated with rosettes, leaf-patterns, delicate tracery, and two lions, one surmounting the bottom post with its prey and the other, minus prey, two floors up. Upstairs there is much else, including a bust of Procurator Domenico Duodo by Alessandro Vittoria (1525–1608). Duodo appears poised between individuality and the usual loyal-servant-of-Venetian-state mask. From some angles he seems self-satisfied, but not offensively so, to be saying that he knew life would be so, this was his due, he has no quarrel with his duly apportioned rank. Bald, lined, with drooping mustache, curled low-slung beard, and robe of state, he projects wisdom, experience, safety. Van Dyck's portrait of a gentleman in the same room reads character in an interestingly different but perhaps no less impenetrable way: the subject, complete with slightly bravura mustache, is evidently adopting a somewhat theatrical pose in familiar Van Dyck fashion. Yet the pose looks like a pause in dynamic life or active thought. No more than elsewhere does the artist really interiorize, but there is a hint of possible depths, possible interchanges that would be more difficult with servant-of-the-state Duodo.

Also on the second floor, among much else, are the faded and worn remains of frescoes of mythological scenes by Titian, which until as late as 1967 were part of the façade of the Fondaco dei Tedeschi, the German warehouse and trading center on the other side of the Canal, now the central post office. What was left of a fresco by Giorgione was removed from the same location in 1937 and is also displayed here. Polychrome traces are a reminder of the even greater range of colors which once—as in the case of Ca' d'Oro's own sparkling surface—

greeted voyagers on the Grand Canal. Giorgio Vasari tells the story, which may or may not be true, of how after the fire of 1504 the Fondaco was rebuilt and Giorgione commissioned by the Signoria to fresco the façade facing the Grand Canal. Such was the painter's acknowledged excellence that he was given a completely free hand. Accordingly, he followed his own fancy. Vasari found the result rather baffling: "in truth, there are no scenes to be found there with any order, or representing the deeds of any distinguished person, either ancient or modern." Vasari has never understood them, and he has never met anyone else who has. "In one place there is a woman, in another a man, in diverse attitudes, while one has the head of a lion near him, and another an angel in the guise of Cupid." But, he concedes, there was some good painting and lively coloring. At the same time Titian, Giorgione's close associate, had been commissioned to fresco "the façade towards the Merceria." His scenes, whatever they were, were easier to decipher. But unluckily, "many gentlemen" were unaware that two painters had been employed, and "meeting with Giorgione congratulated him in friendly fashion, saying that he was acquitting himself better in the façade toward the Merceria" than he had done on the main Canal front. Giorgione hid himself away for some time and from that day, Vasari assures us, "he would never allow Titian to associate with him or be his friend."

Having seen the gallery (which also has an unusually good bookshop) you can visit—or could have started by visiting—what was once Marino Contarini's *androne*, both a temporary storehouse for goods and a reception area for visitors arriving from the Canal. (A spacious quay, developed at the same time as Ca' d'Oro, made both unloading and welcoming easier.) Its present appearance and atmosphere are mainly the result of alterations by Franchetti, who enlarged it by replacing a central wall with a line of columns, supporting, with the help of a new arch, the first-floor *portego*. He also installed the mosaic floor, whose colorful and various abstract patterns are a shining reminder of medieval Venice, and paneled the walls in cool brown, pink, and gray-white marble. Open at one side and with a same-level view onto the Canal, this area is shaded and relatively quiet. Boat engines only momentarily interrupt the sound of lapping water.

Rialto and the Ponte di Rialto

The Rialto was the commercial center of Venice for much of its history, whence Solanio's famous question, in *The Merchant of Venice*: "Now what news on the Rialto?" Then, as now, there were markets not only for bonds and expensive goods, but for cheese, fruit, and fish (for which see p. 182). A real Shylock or Antonio might have heard official proclamations read out in Campo San Giacomo from the granite rostrum on steps which have, since the sixteenth century, been supported by the sculpted hunchback "Gobbo di Rialto." (*Gobbo* means hunchback. Conceivably he lent his name to Old Gobbo—and his son Launcelot—in the play.) The campo takes its name from another survivor from the great days of the Rialto and before, the small church of San Giacomo di Rialto, first established in the fifth century, rebuilt in 1071, and restored in the seventeenth century. With its Greek-cross plan, dome, and six ancient marble columns topped by eleventh-century capitals, the traders' church remains true to its Byzantine origins.

From the twelfth century the Rialto was linked to the opposite bank of the Grand Canal by a rather amateurish sounding but no doubt perfectly functional bridge of boats. Various wooden structures followed, the first in 1264. The bridge was always a good vantage-point; it was crammed with people when, during the wedding procession of the Marquess of Ferrara, it collapsed in 1444. The next and final wooden bridge was stronger and came equipped with a central drawbridge, as shown in Carpaccio's *Miracle of the Relic of the True Cross* in the Accademia, where the somewhat idealized water traffic is provided by suave, fashionably dressed gondoliers and their respectable passengers (including a curly white dog).

By the early sixteenth century it was apparent that the Rialto bridge, then (until the first Accademia bridge opened in 1854) the only one to cross the Grand Canal, was becoming increasingly rickety. In the short term, the Senate opted to save money by repairing rather than replacing it. Michelangelo planned a new bridge during a short visit to Venice in 1529, but nothing came of it. Some years later other proposals began to be sought out. In the 1550s Andrea Palladio, with the support of a number of modern-minded senators, planned a spectacular neoclassical bridge with either three or five arches and

plenty of sculpture. A rather simpler but still elegantly classical version was put forward by Vincenzo Scamozzi, and nearly accepted, in the mid-1580s. But at last the demands of practicality won the day. It was cheaper to build a single span, and the shops that had lined the bridge for centuries, which had no place at least in Palladio's more idealistic versions, could more easily be accommodated. The present bridge was finally built by Antonio da Ponte—suitably named, as everyone points out—between 1588 and 1591.

Beneath the bridge, reports Thomas Coryat, was a ferry, and the ferrymen did not waste time admiring the architecture. They were "the most vicious and licentious varlets about all the city," Coryat maintains, for:

> *if a stranger entereth into one of their gondolas, and doth not presently tell them whither he will go, they will incontinently carry him of their own accord to a religious house [i.e., a brothel] forsoth, where his plumes shall be well pulled before he cometh forth again.*

Ca' Foscari

Doge Francesco Foscari began to make his mark on the Grand Canal some years after the Ca' d'Oro of the aspiring Contarini began to sparkle on the waters. Ca' Foscari (now part of the University of Venice), Henry James' "high square Gothic Foscari... a masterpiece of symmetry and majesty," is less flamboyant, more regular, than Ca' d'Oro, but has a wonderfully emphatic position on the *volta del canal*—the bend where the Canal dramatically loops back on itself—and some interesting historical associations.

When he bought the palace, the veteran doge, after long years of successful warfare, was a generally revered figure. But the seeds of his tragedy had already been sown. Foscari had been elected doge in the teeth of much opposition. He, not the expected Pietro Loredano, had been chosen, and for this among other reasons what was effectively a vendetta between the Foscari and Loredano families developed. This may have been one factor in bringing down the doge's son Jacopo; in 1445 he was accused (rightly, it seems) of taking bribes and condemned—in his father's absence, decorum demanded—to exile at the trading station of Modon, in the Peloponnese. When he failed to report to Modon and remained nearer at hand in Treviso, his goods and land were automatically seized by the state. But the doge, although he in no way overstepped his legal rights, did feel able to make a personal appeal to the Council of Ten for clemency. This succeeded. Powerless though some doges seem in effect to have been, the famed, long-serving Foscari continued to command great respect.

The pardoned man came home in 1447 and appears to have kept out of trouble. But at the beginning of 1451 someone denounced him by means of a *bocca di leone* (a "lion's mouth" into which such information could be posted for the attention of the Ten) and he was arrested for the murder of Senator Ermolao Donà the previous autumn. Jacopo Foscari was tortured and then banished to Crete. This time he was obviously not guilty. But a few years later, still angry at the way he had been treated, he was guilty of dealing secretly with the Sultan. He was brought to Venice. Although Jacopo Loredano and a few others demanded his execution he was sent back to Crete to be imprisoned at Canea (Khania). His father, who was allowed to see him one last time, could only tell him to obey what the republic had commanded, but after the interview broke down and sobbed. In Byron's verse drama, *The Two Foscari,* Jacopo Foscari collapses and dies in his father's presence; in reality he died six months later in Crete. Either way, the old doge grieved inconsolably. He stopped coming to the meetings of the Senate, the Council of Ten, and the other committees through which Venice functioned. He drew a line under a lifetime of duty. In October 1457 Jacopo Loredano, as one of the three *capi* of the Ten, led the group who came to tell Foscari that his immediate abdication would be appreciated. At first he resisted, knowing that the law was on his side: he could not be deposed without a vote in the Maggior Consiglio. But he gave in when they told him that if he did not swiftly comply, his goods would be confiscated and no pension granted. As a last proud gesture he declined to leave the Ducal Palace by a discreet "private staircase." In *The Two Foscari* he

Will now descend the stairs by which I mounted
To sovereignty—the Giants' Stairs, on whose
Broad eminence I was invested duke.
My services have called me up those steps,
The malice of my foes will drive me down them.

(In the play the foes, led by the vengeful Loredano, are very largely to blame for the whole sequence of events.)

Byron's doge has taken only a few steps toward the Giants' Staircase when, soon after hearing the great bell of San Marco tolling for the election of his successor Pasquale Malipiero, he staggers and drops dead. The distortion is not great: the real Foscari did descend the steps but died, broken-hearted, only a week later. And he died in his grand and little-used Palazzo Foscari. The new doge and Signoria, immediately stricken with remorse, had the body brought back to the Ducal Palace to lie in state in his regalia as doge. He was buried with full honors at the church of the Frari.

A happier later occasion in the history of Ca' Foscari was the brief but much chronicled stay there of King Henri III of France in July 1574. The last Valois king was an intelligent, eccentric, often troubled figure, much relieved, after his unhappy months as elected King of Poland, to abdicate and flee the country in disguise as soon as he succeeded his brother as King of France in May. In Poland royal authority was limited by the complex rivalries of different groups of the nobility; France, to which Henri proceeded by way of Venice, was at least as deeply divided by the Wars of Religion which dominated most of his reign and eventually saw him driven out of Paris by his subjects in 1588 and murdered in 1589. His ten days in Venice were perhaps the happiest (if probably most dream-like) of his life.

The king wrote from Vienna on June 24 to announce his intention of visiting Venice. Between then and his arrival on July 18 the authorities, well organized as ever, masterminded a full and rich welcome for this diplomatically important guest. Having established himself at Palazzo Capello on Murano the day before his official reception, Henri had himself rowed across to the city, incognito, for a nocturnal gondola trip on the Grand Canal. For the reception he was conducted by Doge Alvise Mocenigo to the church of San Nicolò on the Lido, at the entrance to the lagoon, the traditional place to welcome mighty outsiders. In front of the church the Venetians had rapidly erected some impressive temporary structures: a triple triumphal arch (50 feet wide, 14 feet deep, 45 feet high) through which the royal and dogal party passed to a loggia (80 feet long, 40 feet wide, about 35 feet high) built by Andrea Palladio—expert in the art of the "insubstantial pageant" no less than in more permanent architecture—and decorated with paintings by the foremost painters Veronese and Tintoretto. The loggia was further decked out with garlands, royal coats-of-arms, an altar, a throne beneath a baldachin of purple, white and gold silks, expensive carpets and statuary. (Most of these details are to be found in M. della Croce's *L'historia della publica e famosa entrata in Vinegia del serenissimo Henrico III*, published in 1574 and further disseminating the glory of La Serenissima as much as the serenissimo Henri.)

Having admired all this, the guest boarded the state ship, the Bucintoro; as it approached San Marco a cannon salute boomed out from the galleys ranged along the island of San Giorgio and bells rang from the campanili of the entire city. A reception at the Ducal Palace followed. And then, at last, the king was taken to Palazzo Foscari. Here there was no diminution of splendor; the vestibule was tapestried for the occasion, its ceiling covered in blue cloth with golden stars, and in the bedrooms were marble tables, a fireplace with gilded caryatids (the work of Alessandro Vittoria), and hangings of cloth of gold, of silver, of crimson silk, of crimson velvet, and the royal feet could tread mosaic flooring designed by Veronese.

Henri actually spent comparatively little time at the palace, what with ceremonial meetings and feasts and incognito interludes elsewhere in the city. Now and then, however, he did snatch some sleep here. And on July 20, several rafts arrived beneath the palace windows bearing a large furnace and a team of workers from Murano. For hours they delighted the king with virtuoso displays of the glassblower's art, and he bought some of the results. Even more than most Renaissance princes, he was a lover of the ingenious, the "curious"; he was particularly taken, apparently, with the banquet where the plates, the glasses, the centerpieces, and his very napkin were made of sugar. The same taste for the unexpected (at least as far as a foreigner was concerned) was perhaps catered to by Veronica Franco, the well-known courtesan and poet, who may have bestowed the expected favors, but also presented him an enameled portrait of herself and a sonnet introducing it.

Henri also attended balls, grand religious services, one of the first ever operas and a meeting of the Maggior Consiglio convened in his honor. At the Arsenal he saw a ship's keel in the morning and came back in the evening to find the whole vessel fully equipped and ready for launching. (Prefabrication of parts, as well as the skill and experience of the *arsenalotti*, was the secret of this speed.) People with such ships and such shows were, the doge and Signoria were anxious to demonstrate, worthy allies for France in a Europe increasingly threatened by the might of Philip II of Spain—the doge called at Palazzo Foscari to make the point courteously but more explicitly. Henri was intended to remember his visit. Others did too: Ben Jonson's Venetian magnifico Volpone, as late as 1607, confidently expects Celia to succumb to the attractions of one who is still, he claims, just as "fresh, /As hot, as high" as when

> For entertainment of the great Valois,
> I acted young Antinous, and attracted
> The eyes and ears of all the ladies present,
> T'admire each graceful gesture, note, and footing.

The Palazzi Giustinian

After Ca' Foscari come the Palazzi Giustinian. Here in August 1858 Richard Wagner, seeking a peaceful, relationship-free space in which to work on the second act of *Tristan und Isolde*, rented two large rooms. These promised well, but conditions, including the décor, had to be just right before the work could begin. His Erard grand piano and his bed had to be brought from Zurich, and the walls of the larger room, whose gray wash did not match the more acceptable ceiling-fresco, had to be covered with deep red hangings, even if these were of "quite common quality." Having done this, Wagner could go out onto the balcony, gaze at the Grand Canal and tell himself contentedly that here *Tristan* would be finished. But there was still, as he waited for the piano to arrive, more decorating to be done. The Hungarian landlord had replaced the original valuable palazzo doors with ordinary modern ones and these had to be hung with "dark-red portières." Not content with this, on a "finely carved gilded table-pedestal" someone—no doubt the incorrigible landlord—had "placed a vulgar pinewood top which I had to cover with a plain red cloth." Then at last the Erard was delivered; "it was placed in the middle of the large room, and now wonderful Venice was to be attacked by music" (equally wonderful music, the not over-modest composer would not have minded adding).

Even now things were not perfect. Wagner suffered from a carbuncle and gastric problems; acquaintances had to be avoided or given restricted access with the reminder, in one case, that he was spending lavishly on his accommodation "simply because it was most essential that I be undisturbed, and have no neighbours, and hear no piano" (other than his own). And Wagner was aware that more than one German state was putting pressure on the Austrian authorities to expel him from Venice. He was in exile as a result of his support for the attempted revolution in Dresden in 1849. Nevertheless, he worked successfully in the red room until two each afternoon, when he would travel by gondola to the Piazzetta. The "bright Piazzetta" (followed by a meal in the Piazza) had cheered him from the beginning, but gondolas had at first depressed him, especially since he had arrived in suddenly grim weather: "when I had to go under the black awning, I could not help remembering the cholera scare some time earlier." But gondola rides soon took on more poetic associations as, on autumn and winter evenings, Wagner was rowed back along the "now more sombre and silent Grand Canal" until "I could see my solitary lamp shining from the night-shrouded façade of the old Palazzo Giustiniani." On the Canal, as well as in the glowing red silence of the palace, music might be inspired:

As I was returning home late one night on the gloomy canal, the moon appeared suddenly and illuminated the marvellous palaces and the tall figure of my gondolier towering above the stern of the gondola, slowly moving his huge sweep. Suddenly he uttered a deep wail, not unlike the cry of an animal; the cry gradually gained in strength, and formed itself, after a long-drawn "Oh!" into the simple musical exclamation "Venezia!" This was followed by other sounds of which I have no distinct recollection, as I was so much moved at the time. Such were the impressions that to me appeared the most characteristic of Venice during my stay there, and they remained with me until the completion of the second act of Tristan, and possibly even suggested to me the long-drawn wail of the shepherd's horn at the beginning of the third act.

The third act was finished in Lucerne; fresh demands for Wagner's expulsion were one of the main reasons why he left Venice in March 1859. Later he returned, however, with his second wife Cosima and their children. In September 1882 the family took up residence in Palazzo Vendramin-Callergi, on the other side of the Grand Canal near the station end. The family lived in eighteen rooms of the palace and were altogether in more comfortable circumstances than Wagner had been in 1858–9; since the mid-1860s he had enjoyed the enthusiastic patronage of King Ludwig II of Bavaria. It was at the Vendramin-Callergi that the composer died of heart failure on February 13, 1883. On the afternoon of February 16 his body, in an ornate Renaissance-style sarcophagus from Vienna, was solemnly transported by special boat the short distance to the station, where a train for Bayreuth was waiting.

Ca' Rezzonico

Ca' Rezzonico was begun for the Bon family in about 1667 by Baldassare Longhena, the architect of Santa Maria della Salute. The ground and first floors were finished when, in the 1680s, the money for the intended mansion ran out. The last of the Bon—the family, like many other noble houses, died out in the eighteenth century—lived on in the palace under a wooden roof; it was only under the much richer Rezzonico family that it was completed, after 1751, by Giorgio Massari. Massari's upper façade onto the Grand Canal blends almost seamlessly with the lower Longhena part to form one of the most unforgettable presences on the Canal. Hugh Honour admires

the heavily rusticated basement supporting the sculptured and be-columned structure above. It is a triumph of monumentality given a typically Venetian insubstantial-pageantry appearance by its deep recesses which dissolve the wall surface into a pattern of flickering light.

Henry James speaks, more boldly, of the great pile "throwing itself upon the water with a peculiar florid assurance, a certain upward toss of its cornice which gives the air of a rearing sea-horse." It "decorates immensely—and within, as well as without—the wide angle that it commands."

Massari's brief was to provide a suitable setting, "within, as well as without," for the glory of the Rezzonico family. Having recently bought their noble status, they wanted to be assured, and to assure everyone else, that they had "arrived." To have a palace on the Grand Canal was in itself prestigious, and to have a splendid and unusually large one, decorated by the likes of Giambattista Tiepolo, was no disadvantage. Added glory came when Carlo Rezzonico was elected pope as Clement XIII in 1758. His elder brother, Lodovico, had also gratified family pride earlier that year by marrying Faustina Savorgnan, a member of the old nobility. Such a "catch" gave the same sort of respectability as a front on the Grand Canal. It brought the prospect of an infusion of blue blood, although in this case the whole family had died out by 1810. Tiepolo's celebratory ceiling gives its name to the Sala dell' Allegoria Nuziale, the first room on the right beyond the ballroom. Here bride and groom travel in Apollo's chariot, blind Cupid goes before them, and they are surrounded by energetic personifications of their virtues; Merit brandishes a standard with the arms of Rezzonico and Savorgnan.

Ca' Rezzonico has, since 1936, functioned as the civic Museo del Settecento Veneziano. It succeeds in its avowed aim of displaying eighteenth-century art in the congenial context of a contemporaneous noble house. Massari's grand staircase leads up to the ballroom or Salone delle Feste, high-ceilinged and made to seem even larger by Giambattista Crosato's *trompe-l'oeil* frescoes. Finished by 1762, this room was the magnificent setting for such occasions as the celebration, that year, of Lodovico Rezzonico's elevation as a Procurator of San Marco and the visits of George III's brother the Duke of York in 1764 and the Habsburg Emperor Joseph II in 1769. Several hundred patricians came to honor Joseph and a hundred girls from the Venetian conservatories sang for him.

The rest of the museum is on a less extravagant scale. An impression of unforced opulence is given by the remaining rooms on the first floor in particular, with their candelabra of colored glass, walls hung with red damask, green silk, or yellow holland, elegant chairs and gilt consoles. The many paintings include pastel portraits by Rosalba Carriera, rather bland for most modern tastes but hugely popular from the 1720s to the 1750s and enhanced when seen in the context of a contemporary room—here against the delicately patterned red damask of the Sala dei Pastelli. There are two Canalettos (something of a rarity in Venice) dating from the early part of his career in the 1720s, when he began to supersede Luca Carlevarijs as the most popular painter of *vedute* or views. The *Grand Canal at Palazzo Balbi, Towards the Rialto* looks almost somber by comparison with the brilliant light later identified with Canaletto. Here are shadowy, brownish palaces, the odd gray cloud, the broad space of the predominantly green canal; contrasting sunshine does, however, light up some of the palaces and picks out the red of the canopy stretched over a swiftly moving boat on the right. There are capriccios, history paintings like G.B. Piazzetta's *The Death of Darius*, portraits of robed and bewigged worthies, Pietro Longhi's aristocrats at home—playing music, reading letters—and, from the end of the century, comic frescoes by Tiepolo's son Giandomenico, including *Il Mondo Nuovo,* where, perhaps with larger satirical intent, he paints, from behind, a group of people waiting to watch a magic lantern show called "The New World."

In the new world of the nineteenth century Ca' Rezzonico passed from owner to owner until, in September 1888, it was bought by Robert Browning's son "Pen," a painter and sculptor of average ability whose misfortune has been to be unfairly denigrated for lacking the genius of his poet parents. Pen, who was able to buy the palace after having married a wealthy American wife, Fannie Coddington, a year earlier, engaged enthusiastically in the decoration and furnishing of the somewhat neglected building. He had lived in Florence until the death of his mother, Elizabeth Barrett

Browning, when he was twelve in 1861, but did not come back to Italy until the 1880s. His father, who had eventually started visiting Italy again in 1878, avoided Florence with its happy and painful memories and developed instead a passion for Venice, where he and his indefatigable companion, his sister Sarianna, stayed several times with Katharine de Kay Bronson, an expatriate American friend who also knew Henry James.

In September 1889, after staying near Bronson's house in Asolo, Robert and Sarianna Browning came to join Pen and Fannie at Ca' Rezzonico. Any project of Pen's delighted his adoring father (this love was, Bronson later claimed, the poet's "Achilles heel"), who relished his installation in this grand Venetian palace and the opportunities it presented for the future. In fact, perhaps sensing that the end was near (although he told some people that he was good for ten years yet), Browning relished everything about Venice that autumn. It is easy to imagine his keen gaze scanning the Grand Canal from the landing-stage at the front of the Rezzonico. He took, as in earlier years, bracing walks on the Lido, from which, says Bronson,

> he would return full of color and health, talk of the light and life and fresh air with enthusiasm, combined with a sort of pity for those who had remained at home. "It is like coming into a room from the outer air," he said, "to reenter Venice after walking on the sea-shore."

He dined, and sometimes read his own and other poems aloud, at the houses of friends and acquaintances. For family members only he read, apologizing that the sentiments might seem like bragging, from the Epilogue to his last volume of poems, *Asolando*, about to be published: it was evident to the listeners that he himself was the

> One who never turned his back but marched breast forward,
> Never doubted clouds would break,
> Never dreamed, though right were worsted, wrong would triumph,
> Held we fall to rise, are baffled to fight better,
> Sleep to wake.

Browning went to *Carmen* a fortnight before he died. But after the opera he nearly fainted on the stairs of the palace. Signs of heart disease became more apparent; he was confined to bed three days later on December 1, and died on the evening of December 12, having had the satisfaction, earlier in the day, of seeing an advance copy of *Asolando* and learning that it was selling well.

Browning died in a room on the first floor, which is rarely open to the public. A plaque commemorates him near the main land entrance to the palace. His friend Alexandra Orr records that "arrangements were... made for a private service to be conducted by the British Chaplain in one of the great halls of the Rezzonico Palace"—the ballroom, presumably—the following day. The city laid on formal conveyance to the cemetery island of San Michele: "the coffin was carried by eight firemen (*pompieri*), arrayed in their distinctive uniform, to the massive, highly decorated municipal barge (*Barca delle Pompe funebri*) which waited to receive it. It was guarded during the transit by four *uscieri* in gala dress, two sergeants of the Municipal Guard, and two of the firemen bearing torches." Several days later, the famous body began its train journey for London and Westminster Abbey. Another death in Venice—like Wagner's six years before—added to the hoard of the city's associations.

The Accademia

An Academy gallery existed, in various premises, from 1750. It moved into its present accommodation, in the former church, convent and Scuola of Santa Maria della Carità, in the second decade of the nineteenth century. The buildings were extensively altered, but parts of the Gothic exterior, the fifteenth-century gilded ceiling of the chapter house of the Scuola, and Mauro Coducci's vaulted double staircase (1498) survive from pre-Accademia days.

All the most interesting Venetian artists (and, rather exhaustingly, most of the less interesting ones) are represented in the Accademia, from a polyptych by the Gothic master Paolo Veneziano to views by Canaletto and Guardi. There are Bellini Madonnas with luminous landscape backgrounds; Giorgione's mysterious, perhaps allegorical painting of a soldier and a semi-naked woman with a child, known, from the stormy background that separates the figures, as *La Tempesta*; Lorenzo Lotto's young man in his study, observed in a moment of intense reflection; the deep reds of Carpaccio's sequence on the life of the virgin martyr Saint Ursula, painted originally for her Scuola. One of the most absorbing Ursula pictures is the one in which she meets her betrothed Aetherius—a hero of romance with long light golden hair and clothes of embroidered silver, red, and emerald—in a spacious scene with elegant attendants, trumpeters, pennants, eastern carpets, towers, spires, loggias, ships and the many other ingredients of what John Steer (*A Concise History of Venetian Painting*) calls Carpaccio's

> *fantasy Venice, in which the colour is brighter, the marbling richer, the architecture more bizarre, and the population more splendidly costumed and better brought up than in the city herself. A Venice, too, in which, by the formal perfection of the composition, all activity is poised, as in a dream, in magic stillness.*

The Accademia is one of the two best places in Venice—the other is the church of the Frari (pp.128-30)—to see Titian. Although he was based in Venice for much of his long career (he was long thought to have lived to be nearly a hundred; certainly he made it to his late eighties), his work is widely scattered, mainly because he attracted foreign patrons, including two of the richest and most powerful men of the time, the Emperor Charles V and his son Philip II of Spain. But the Accademia has a good range, from the serene *Presentation of the Virgin* of 1534–8 to Titian's last painting, the more somber *Pietà*. The *Presentation* was painted for its present situation in what was once the Sala dell'Albergo of the Scuola della Carità and has remained in place ever since (except during 1828–95). Before an imposingly classical temple the small but self-possessed figure of the child Virgin, surrounded by holy light and gently stretching forward her left arm, ascends the steps to the High Priest. Attention is concentrated on her, but there is also room, especially at the left, where part of the backdrop is landscape rather than architecture, for many other distinctive individuals, several of them evidently portraits of members of the Scuola. In the foreground, in front of the steps and not far beneath the Virgin, is a poor old woman, both by way of contrast with the child and as a reminder of the charitable work of the confraternity.

The atmosphere and the light in the *Pietà* are, as befits the subject, very different. At the left of the picture, a passionately distraught Mary Magdalene rushes forward with arm outstretched. Both she and the kneeling male saint (Jerome, say modern scholars) are, felt Théophile

Gautier, doubtful that this body, which they are about to consign to the tomb, can ever come out again; "indeed, Titian never created a corpse so dead. Under the green flesh and in the bluish veins there is no longer any drop of blood, the living purple has gone for ever." In this "peinture sinistre et douloureuse"

for the first time the great Venetian has been abandoned by his ancient and unalterable serenity. The shadow of coming death seems to struggle with the light of the painter who always had sunshine in his palette, and to envelop the picture with a crepuscular chill.

Titian painted himself as Jerome, looking imploringly—rather than doubtfully—to the Saviour, who alone can forgive his sins. Soon after working on these figures Titian died, with the painting not quite finished. He had intended it for his tomb in the Frari, but it never found its way there. Instead, it reached the painter Jacopo Palma (later called Palma Giovane, to distinguish him from his great-uncle), who, as the inscription explains, "reverently finished it and dedicated the work to God."

Mary Magdalene in her grief helps to make this, as another nineteenth-century French observer Hippolyte Taine noted, like a scene from a "pagan tragedy." One can imagine her, perhaps, as one of Euripides' lamenting Trojan Women, and in fact she derives partly from an ancient representation of Venus grieving for Adonis. Classical, too, is the statue of the Sibyl. And she is there for a purpose: not just for her prophecies, but as a reminder that the classical world—in which, from a Christian point of view, there can only be despair in these circumstances—has been superseded. The presence of the other statue, of Moses, indicates that Christ also supersedes, but at the same time fulfills, the old dispensation or Testament. Another sign that all is not lost glows in the apse between the statues: the bird re-born from the flames, the Phoenix, symbol of resurrection. So Titian acknowledges the fear and pain of death—Christ's, his own, the viewer's—while, with Christian hindsight, allowing signs of hope to glimmer, like the Saviour's undying halo, through the somber light. The Magdalene's despair will be converted, like the Virgin's still, tender grief, to joy; Jerome's penitence and, the painter hopes, his own, will achieve forgiveness.

Veronese is often encountered around Venice, especially in the Ducal Palace and the church of San Sebastiano, but the Accademia has the painting with the most famous story attached to it. Veronese completed his lavish, 18-by-42-feet, representation of the Last Supper in April 1573 for the refectory of the monastery of Santi Giovanni e Paolo. Someone, between then and July, denounced him and his painting to the Holy Inquisition. Unlike the Venetian state Inquisition, this body (answerable to Rome) had limited powers—except where heresy was concerned. Veronese duly appeared before the tribunal, which included the Inquisitor, the Papal Nuncio and the Patriarch or their representatives, and three senators. The proceedings of the interrogation have survived in the Venetian state archives. The tribunal wanted to know why the Last Supper was attended by a man with a nose-bleed and two halberdiers "dressed in the fashion of Germany." The nose-bleed resulted from some accident, said Veronese; and then, more informatively, having asked permission to say a few (literally "twenty") words, he went on to say that "We painters take the same license that poets and madmen take." ("The lunatic, the lover, and the poet / Are of imagination all compact," agrees Theseus in *A Midsummer-Night's Dream* about twenty years later. What the Inquisitor thought of such madmen is unrecorded.) The imaginative painter "represented those two halberdiers... at the foot of the stairs, who are there in case they are needed to perform any service, since it seemed to me suitable that the master of the house, who, I was told, was great and rich, should have such servants."

The questioners, apparently unimpressed by this reply, still wanted to know about someone "dressed as a jester"—the dwarf on the left—and holding a parrot; "He is there as an ornament, *come si fa*—as is customary," came the reply. But Veronese had to agree with his interrogators that "jesters, drunkards, Germans, dwarfs, and similar *scurrilità*" have no place at the Last Supper. Now came the real reason for the Inquisition's interest: "Do you not know that in Germany and other places infected with heresy, they are accustomed, with various pictures full of *scurrilità* [evidently a favorite Inquisition hold-all term] and similar devices, to... vilify and make a laughing-stock of the things of the Holy Catholic Church, in order to teach bad doctrine to... the ignorant?" Veronese could not dispute this. Nevertheless, he continued to insist that he had felt justified in including such figures because they were "outside the space where our Lord is." Three great arches do indeed separate the busy foreground of the picture from the supper itself; in the central arch the quiet communion of Jesus with saints Peter and John contrasts markedly with the multifarious activity elsewhere. A suitably villainous looking Judas, sitting on our side of the table, looks, significantly, away from Jesus.

Veronese's inclusive Renaissance art had fallen foul of the new Counter-Reformation desire for the pure and unimpeachable. But in Venice the Inquisitors' attitude seems to have been uncommon. Although they required the painter to alter his painting, they were satisfied with an unexpectedly simple modification: he changed the title to *Feast at the House of Levi* and, in case of lingering doubt, painted an inscription, at the head of the balustrades at each side of the picture, which includes the appropriate reference to St. Luke's gospel, chapter five. There may not have been any Germans or parrots at Levi's feast, but there was "a large company of tax collectors and others," described explicitly as "sinners." Apparently this was good enough for the Inquisition.

Accademia pilgrims may like or need to avail themselves of the nearby Caffè Belle Arti, where reasonably priced drinks, pizza, sandwiches, *focaccia*, and the like can be consumed in a relaxed atmosphere.

The Peggy Guggenheim Collection
The distinctive low white Palazzo Venier dei Leoni houses the Peggy Guggenheim collection of modern art. One work of art directly confronts voyagers on the canal: on the terrace stands Marino Marini's *Angel of the Citadel*, an ecstatic bronze figure on horseback, with arms stretched out and phallus notably erect. In *Confessions of an Art Addict* (1960) Peggy Guggenheim (1898–1979) explained how the artist originally provided a detachable member—it could be put in a drawer when nuns came past in a boat on their way to be blessed by the Patriarch or for the benefit of "stuffy visitors." Sometimes she forgot, she claims; she enjoyed watching people's reactions to the sculpture from her sitting-room window. The first, removable phallus was stolen and she had a permanent replacement soldered on; there was now no easy escape for the embarrassed or the trying-not-to-look embarrassed.

When the Marini was installed, the palazzo was Guggenheim's private home. She was a member of the immensely rich family that also included her uncle Solomon. (Since her death the gallery has been administered by the Solomon R. Guggenheim Foundation.) She inherited her own fortune when her father went down on the *Titanic* in 1912. After involvement in various artistic projects in America and Britain, she settled in Venice after the Second World War and looked for somewhere to install herself and her growing collection. She exhibited it—in the Greek pavilion that was vacant because of the Greek Civil War—in the Biennale of 1948, contributing much to the reputation of the event. And then in 1949 she found the Venier dei Leoni, started in 1748 for the patrician Venier family but left unfinished and known as the *palazzo non compiuto*, the "unfinished palazzo." The Venier were alleged to have kept lions in the garden but the name "leoni" came more probably from the eighteen lions' heads on the front of the palace. After a degree of alteration, permission for which was easily obtainable because the palace was one of the few not regarded as a national monument, Guggenheim began, in 1951, to allow the public in on summer afternoons. As the number of paintings and sculptures increased, more of the living quarters (and the laundry) were taken over for viewing space. During opening hours the owner and friends escaped to sunbathe on the flat roof, causing some wagging of tongues in conservative Venetian circles, as did her artistic preferences. "Princess Pignatelli once said to me," she recalled, "'If you would only throw all those awful pictures into the Grand Canal, you would have the most beautiful house in Venice.'"

After Guggenheim's death the palace became more wholly an art gallery. Her tomb and those of her Lhasa terriers are in the garden. One of her favorite personal possessions remains in her former bedroom, where she (and sometimes the terriers) used the bed: the silver bed-head (1956) by Alexander Calder. It twists and wreathes arabesques; there are open-mouthed fish, abstract patterns that sometimes become fern-shapes and peacocks' tails, and a dragonfly dangling on a chain. Much of the collection is, besides, intimately linked to Guggenheim because she personally knew many of the artists; she promoted Jackson Pollock, for instance, and was married for a time to Max Ernst.

The collection, in clean white rooms, is strong in Surrealists, Cubists, Mondrian, Miró, and much else. Sculptures include Alberto Giacometti's beautiful *Walking Woman* (a slight swell of breasts and nipples, a genital crease, a longer crease dividing the legs). Egidio Constantini's twenty-three translucent blue glass sculptures after sketches by Picasso are displayed in front of, and shiftingly affected by, the Grand Canal. Picasso's own work includes his *Poet.* In the shaded Nasher Garden (named after the lenders of some of the work shown here) there are small pieces by Moore and Giacometti. Along a wall, Mario Merz's thin blue neon tubes proclaim *Se la forma scompare la sua radice è eterna*—"If form disappears, its root is eternal." This remark can be pondered with the aid of the Byzantine-style throne positioned between *scompare* and *la* and in front of that a standing woman by Giacometti; elsewhere in the garden, Jean Arp's bronze "Amphora-Fruit" moves effortlessly, meltingly, between one form and another. Altogether, splendid though old Venetian art may be, this is a good place to refresh your eyes after so much of it. (The Museo d'Arte Moderna at Ca' Pesaro also has a good collection, but has been closed for many years for restoration.)

Palazzo Dario

Beyond Palazzo Venier dei Leoni is Palazzo Dario, encrusted with marble panels and roundels by Pietro Lombardo or his workshop in 1487. The encrustation is the visible sign of the wealth of Giovanni Dario, a secretary in the Venetian treasury who, in the absence of a regular ambassador in Istanbul at the time, negotiated the important treaty of 1479 between Venice and Sultan Mehmed II and was richly rewarded by both parties. The palace was also a measure of the status attainable by a citizen like Dario who, though lacking patrician power, was able to accrue wealth, influence, and prestige. The Lombardo style, which was both fashionable and deeply imbued with the Veneto-Byzantine decorative tradition, also asserted Dario's proud loyalty to the republic, as more directly does the Latin inscription in which he prominently dedicates the house "to the spirit of the city." This was probably a necessary disclaimer of desire for personal glory by the successful citizen. At Dario's death the house passed to his patrician son-in-law Vincenzo Barbaro: another sign of his success.

In the nineteenth century Palazzo Dario belonged for a time to Rawdon Brown, one of the most assiduous students of the world of Dario and his colleagues. Brown compiled the early volumes of the monumental *Calendar of State Papers, Venetian*, editing and translating into English the many and detailed reports of Venetian ambassadors from the English court. While undertaking this and similar work he remained in Venice for fifty years until his death in 1883, becoming well known as guide and host to English visitors. Legend—reproduced in a late sonnet by Robert Browning—had it that he did not once return to England during this period. In the poem Brown sets off in his gondola, sighing, for the station:

"Yes, I'm departing, Toni!

Although my heart's Venetian. Yes, old crony—
Venice and London—London's Death the Bony
Compared with Life—that's Venice! What a sky,
A sea this morning! One last look!"

Soon, irresistibly, Brown commands Toni: "Down / With carpet-bag and off with valise-straps!" and promises not to leave: "*Bella Venezia, non ti lascio più!*" In reality, Brown did return to England more than once, but only very briefly.

Brown had bought Palazzo Dario for £480 in 1838 but had insufficient funds to halt its decay and was forced to sell after only four years. It owed its successful reconstruction to owners with more money, especially Comtesse Isabelle de Baume-Pluvinel, who lived here from 1898 with Augustine Bulteau. Both wrote books and entertained such better-known figures as the poet, novelist, and author of Venetian sketches Henri de Régnier.

Santa Maria della Salute and the Dogana

The Baroque church of Santa Maria della Salute, like San Marco, the Ducal Palace and the Rialto bridge, has become an emblem of Venice, a mnemonic for it. Generations of painters, among them Canaletto and Turner, had done the job even before the generations of photographers who followed them. Yet Henry James felt that the Salute, waiting "like some great lady on the threshold of her saloon," *is more ample and serene, more seated at her door, than all the copyists have told us, with her domes and scrolls, her scolloped buttresses and statues forming a pompous [i.e., stately] crown, and her wide steps disposed on the ground like the train of a robe.*

The Senate positioned the church as emphatically as it could. Since the Middle Ages there had been a settlement on the marshy area near the confluence of the Grand and Giudecca Canals, but as yet—mainly because it was so soggy—there were no particularly distinguished buildings. But it was already a place of practical importance: when the city was threatened, it was from here, from what would become the Punta della Dogana, that two huge chains had been fixed, one running across to the Bacino di San Marco, the other to the island of San Giorgio. When plague killed 46,490 Venetians, nearly a third of the population, in 1630–1, protection of some other sort was needed. It was found in the Virgin, who was believed to have heard the people's

prayers and eventually ended the outbreak. (*Salute* means both "health" and "salvation.") The emphasis remained Marian: the architect, Baldassare Longhena, said that the dedication of the church to the Blessed Virgin "made me think, with what little talent God has granted me, of designing it *in forma rotunda*, that is to say in the shape of a crown to be dedicated to her." There are statues of Mary above the entrance, on top of the main dome, and above the high altar.

The Salute, built after the other most famous monuments in Venice, was conceived in visual and intellectual relation to some of them: its domes complement those of San Marco; the plan echoes that of Palladio's votive plague-church the Redentore. (The Salute, like the Redentore, became an annual pilgrimage destination for a procession led across a bridge of boats by the doge.) But before such ambitious allusions could be made, several older buildings had to be demolished and up to a million wooden piles driven in to provide a firm enough foundation. Next, the architect had to fulfill the Senate's fairly precise and difficult stipulations, particularly that the high altar must be seen from the entrance while the other altars should not be visible until the viewer (and especially the doge's annual procession) reaches the center of the nave. This requirement, as well as devotion to the Virgin's crown, influenced the octagonal plan. The center of the nave is also the hub of an almost hypnotic sequence of concentric circles of polychrome marble paving. Here too, although the primary effect is of sparkling, recent-looking clarity, there is a sense of continuity with the past—with the great mosaic floors of San Marco or the basilica of Santa Maria e Donato on Murano. Apparently Longhena intended to decorate the central dome as well. Even without that finishing touch, he succeeded in realizing another of the Senate's requirements: that the church should display *bella figura*—make a grand impression. (At the same time, the senators added with true Venetian prudence, it must not cost too much.) Longhena lived to see the church in very nearly its full white-and-gray splendor. He died at 84 in 1682, five years before the eventual completion.

On the high altar a trophy of empire—but one yielded more willingly than the booty which adorns San Marco—establishes another link with the past: the icon of the Virgin and child, the Mesopanditissa, which Francesco Morosini (see p.36) was able to bring back after the fall of Candia to the Turks in 1669. According to tradition the red-and-gold icon with its penetrating eyes has miraculous power and was painted by St. Luke; really it dates from the twelfth century. The columns on either side come from a possession nearer home, Pola (now Pula in Croatia), whose Roman theater yielded them to the greater good of the republic. Above the icon is a 1670s sculptural group by the Flemish artist Juste Le Court. In the main scene Venice, personified as usual as a woman, implores relief, the Virgin grants her prayer with hand easily, mercifully outstretched, and the hag Plague flees, arms in the air, at some speed, and helped along by a flaming torch thrust at her waist by a vigorous cherub. The saints lower down, to left and right, again announce that this is a Venetian church. They are St. Mark and the popular local saint, Lorenzo Giustinian.

In the sanctuary are paintings originally from other churches and monasteries. There are some Titians, including an early enthroned St. Mark, and Tintoretto's *Marriage at Cana* (1551), once in the refectory of the monastery of the Crociferi. This large painting—27 feet long, 15 feet high—is technically notable for its handling of light and shade. But perhaps equally interesting are the details of everyday life and particularly the details of the wine supply: carafes rapidly emptied, fresh amphoras carried in, re-fills poured, a supply that is miraculously extended when Jesus turns water into wine. Although Jesus and his mother, at the head of the table, are somewhat separate from their fellow diners, somewhat iconic, there is a relaxed, genial atmosphere among the guests, suitable to the later stages of a wedding that has gone off well: a human way of stressing the traditional interpretation of Christ's presence at Cana as a sanctification of marriage.

The Salute is close to the entrance to the Grand Canal—the place where, says Henry James, it "begins in its glory." (It ends "in its abasement at the railway station.") If you walk on, beyond Santa Maria, past the Seminario Patriarcale to the end of the former Dogana di Mare or customs-house, you come to the Punta della Dogana and the distinctive golden ball—or, as James more entertainingly has it, "the gilded globe on which revolves the delightful satirical figure of a little weather-cock of a woman." She, "this Fortune, this Navigation, or whatever she is called—she surely needs no name—catches the wind in the bit of drapery of which she has divested her rotary bronze loveliness." She has a spectacular view. At the far left are the Procuratie Nuove and the trees of the Giardinetti Reali, laid out in 1814 as the gardens of the Napoleonic palace. Moving right, the eye scans the campanile and domes of San Marco, the columns in the Piazzetta, and the Ducal Palace. Straight ahead, the green mass of the Giardini Pubblici and the church and campanile of San Giorgio close the view. Further right, on the Giudecca, are Palladio's white churches of the Zitelle and the Redentore. Even with the Grand Canal behind you— here it has been assumed that you are traveling from the "abasement" of the station end—fresh experiences remain in prospect.

CHAPTER SIX

Religious Venice: Churches, Scuole, and Synagogues

Venice is full of churches, sparkling and grimed, disused and active, domed and with *campanili*. And the variety of churches is added to by the presence, nearby, of the halls and chapels of the religious confraternities or *scuole*. In 1732 there were more than 300. Only a few of the confraternities still function, but many of the buildings have survived. The first were founded in the 1260s by groups of flagellants, citizens who scourged themselves on great ceremonial occasions as a public declaration of repentance. Flagellant activity seems to have been at its strongest during plagues, which were seen as divine visitations on sinful humanity. The Scuola Grande di San Rocco, named after the pestilence-defeating Saint Roch, was founded during the plague of 1478 and was prominent again during that of 1575–7. By the 1580s the doge's formal visit to the church of San Rocco on the saint's day, August 16, had become an annual event. (Canaletto's painting in the National Gallery, London, shows one such occasion with pictures on display outside the scuola and the doge and his retinue carrying nosegays as a symbolic precaution against plague.)

By this time members of the confraternities no longer, it appears, actually scourged themselves; on ceremonial occasions flagellants were now available for hire. The organizations' emphasis had become mainly charitable, with richer members aiding poorer. Those whom the officials of the scuola deemed needy and pious enough (piety was measured mainly in terms of regular fulfillment of ceremonial duties) were helped with alms or accommodation. The daughters of those in difficulties might, if of good reputation, be provided with dowries. Such action was an expression both of religious devotion and of civic responsibility. It also gave the citizens who ran the scuole a sense of position and influence. (Noblemen could belong to the confraternity but in a more honorary capacity.) This suited the ruling class, who in return could call upon the confraternities for support, whether in terms of financing state galleys, providing a fixed number of oarsmen for them, or turning out to give emphatic ceremonial backing for government policy—to celebrate peace treaties, for instance, and, particularly, to support Venice when it fell foul of the papacy. For this reason it was important that the scuole were answerable not to the Patriarch and the Church, but directly to the Council of Ten; clergy did not hold important positions in the scuole and on the whole were employed simply to say mass. So when, for example, Venice came under papal interdict in 1606, the Scuola Grande di San Rocco were out in force, the body of San Rocco himself borne aloft, to demonstrate just how little chastened they felt.

So, for reasons of state propaganda, civic and fraternal pride, and religious sentiment, the scuole were as splendidly served and decorated as their members could make them. This was nowhere more true than on San Rocco's grand premises, dating from 1549. When Thomas Coryat came for the saint's festival in 1608 he was pleased with the building's "marvellous rich and stately frontispiece, being built with [sur]passing fair white stone," delighted by the three great chambers, and completely amazed by the quality of the music-making: "so good, so admirable, so rare, so delectable, so superexcellent, that it did even ravish and stupefy all those strangers that never heard the like." In the Sala Grande, the larger of the two upstairs chambers, before altars shining with "many singular ornaments, but especially with a great

multitude of silver candlesticks," Coryat heard various combinations of singers, sackbuts, cornetts, treble viols, theorbos, and viola da gamba in two three-hour concerts. There were also no fewer than "seven fair pair of organs." He was impressed, above all, by the sweetness of voice of a man of about forty who was not, he was somewhat surprised to discover, a eunuch; in spite of this, "it was nothing forced, strained, or affected, but came from him with the greatest facility that ever I heard." A nightingale might have sung better, he said, but not much.

Nobody knows exactly what was performed on such occasions, but in 1996 Paul McCreesh directed the Gabrieli Consort and Players in a very convincing approximation (Deutsche Grammophon Archiv 449 180–2), recorded at the Scuola Grande itself and taking advantage of what McCreesh describes as the "warm but clear acoustic" of the Sala

Grande. The format was probably a "spiritual recreation," including song, readings and prayers, and much of the music was probably by Giovanni Gabrieli.

Tintoretto and the Scuola Grande

The exuberant but controlled thirty-three part Gabrieli *Magnificat* with which the recording ends—a "huge tapestry of seven discoursing choirs"—is perhaps, as McCreesh suggests, most appropriately performed beneath the paintings of Tintoretto (Jacopo Robusti (1518–94), whose nickname refers to the fact that he came from a family of *tintori* or dyers). These are what people usually come to the scuola for: the "sundry delicate pictures" noticed but not specified by Coryat. Others have been less coy in their responses to the extraordinary series that Tintoretto carried out, largely unaided, between 1564 and 1588. The painter, fervently religious and a member of this (from 1565) and several other scuole, is said to have won the commission by what his rivals at least saw as sharp practice. While they, as stipulated, came along with their mere sketches and plans, Tintoretto installed his finished *San Rocco in Glory* in the ceiling of the smaller of the two upstairs rooms, the Sala dell'Albergo, dramatically withdrew the covering veil, and donated it to the brothers in (unrefusably) the name of their saint. He went on to decorate the rest of the room before turning to the enormous Sala Grande (Old Testament scenes on the ceiling, New on the walls) and, near the end of his life, the downstairs hall (Sala Terrena), where he illustrated the Life of the Virgin. Tintoretto specialized in dramatic light effects, diaphanous or almost diaphanous figures, rapid and impassioned composition, and less opulent coloring than such Venetian contemporaries as Veronese.

For many people Tintoretto's masterpiece is the *Crucifixion* on the end wall of the Sala dell'Albergo. In this room the woodwork is dark, the lighting subdued, and there are none of the grotesque, interesting, rather incongruous carvings by Francesco Pianta in the Sala Grande. The vast scale of the Crucifixion painting, just over 40 feet wide and over 17 high, emphasizes the vastness of the implications for humankind of the events on Calvary. Against dark skies, in the lurid light before a storm (St. Luke's "darkness over the whole land") is arrayed a crowd of figures: mourners, bystanders, the three crucified men, soldiers, horses. But, just as to Christians the crucifixion has a personal, direct application as well as a collective, there is also a more individual focus. Two soldiers crouching among the rocks dice for Christ's clothes; at the foot of the cross his mother swoons while others including St. John (a young man) and the golden-haired Magdalene gaze up at the cross, still apparently in shock. To the right (or Christ's left) the impenitent thief is still being attached to his cross before it is raised. Significantly he is looking away from Christ. On the left (Christ's right) the penitent thief, whose cross is in the process of being pulled upright, looks with faith and longing toward his Saviour. And the Saviour looks back, giving visual expression to his promise that "today you will be with me in paradise." The thieves—one still symbolically earthbound, the other being lifted up, exalted with Christ—enact the choice available to human beings. This point is further underlined, while perhaps a degree of worldly vanity is also allowed for, by the fact that some of Tintoretto's spectators are portraits of contemporary members of the confraternity.

John Ruskin (often, it must be admitted, as prone to extreme enthusiasms and revulsions as Mr. Toad) hardly rated Tintoretto until his first visit to the scuola in September 1845. His conversion was complete and characteristically vocal: "I never was so utterly crushed to the earth before any human intellect as I was today, before Tintoret," he wrote to his father. (In 1845 "Tintoret" for Tintoretto was no more unorthodox than "Raphael" for Raffaello Sanzio, but today it seems nicely to project Ruskin's sense of personal involvement with, beside awe in the presence of, the painter.) In the Life of Christ paintings generally "he lashes out like a leviathan, and heaven and earth come together. M. Angelo [Michelangelo] himself cannot hurl figures into space as he does, nor did M. Angelo ever paint space itself which would not look like a nutshell beside Tintoret's." But in *The Stones of Venice* he concluded that the Crucifixion is "beyond all analysis, and above all praise."

The Frari

Nearby is an even larger building, refreshingly light-filled after the dark Scuola Grande di San Rocco: the church of Santa Maria Gloriosa dei

Frari (begun in about 1330, completed in the 1440s). Where the scuola is dominated by one painter's artistic program, the Frari demands attention for works from the late Middle Ages to the neoclassical period. Yet the overall effect is harmonious. This is a good place simply for perambulating, for enjoying art without too much effort. Standing at the back of the nave you are aware less of individual features than of the spacious, mostly plain, internal structure, the large pillars, wooden beams, and vaulting picked out in red brick, and the long straight view—the church is 270 feet long—through Pietro Lombardo's late fifteenth-century screen to Titian's *Assumption* above the high altar. The singleness of effect reflects the Franciscan (*frari* are friars) emphasis on simplicity, on preaching more than on ritual. Arguably, however, more mysterious effects were possible when the friars sang, invisible to the congregation, from the choir-stalls.

The *Assumption* (1518) is often hailed as the beginning of the High Renaissance in Venice. Titian approaches the subject less as a traditional motif than as a serious, immediate, occasion for wonder and drama. The astonished apostles gesticulate or reach out to the cloud-borne Virgin who is very much *in the act* of ascending. The colors, too, are bold, especially the reds. And a certain Fra Germano, who had to supervise Titian's work without the benefit of hindsight, kept complaining that the figures were too big. The boldness and size, however, are appropriate to the larger architectural setting. As David Rosand (*Painting in Sixteenth-Century Venice*) points out, even the frame is an integral part of the scheme. With a dead Christ in relief at the bottom and the statue of a risen Christ at the top, it continues the theme of triumph over death. In the painting Mary rises in her own assumption into heaven, rises to God the Father and, in the frame, as if entering a new element, to God the Son. The arch in the choir-screen also frames the painting. Like the picture-frame it is a triumphal arch.

The saints in Titian's *Madonna di Ca' Pesaro* (completed 1526) belong somewhat more to this world. Here, over the altar in the north aisle of the nave granted to the Pesaro family as the equivalent of a chapel in 1518, St. Peter stops reading (marking the place with his finger) in order to present Bishop Jacopo Pesaro and his family to the Virgin, while St. Francis, patron of the Frari, courteously introduces them to the Christ-child. The bishop kneels on the left, opposite his gorgeously robed brother and beneath the substantial, rather luxuriously curling, red and gilded banner that commemorates his part in a papal naval victory over the Turks back in 1502. The bishop was still very much alive in 1526 (he died in 1547 and his monument is to the right of the painting) and could enjoy the expression both of his piety and of his position. A much more dignified impression of the family is given than in the overblown black-and-white baroque memorial, towering further to the left, of Doge Giovanni Pesaro, who died in 1659. Amidst "a huge accumulation of theatrical scenery," says Ruskin, the doge's statue "stands forward, with its arms expanded, like an actor courting applause." Two unusual features of Titian's Pesaro *Madonna* are often noted: the mother and child are placed untraditionally off-center, and Titian designed the whole piece, after much experimentation, revealed by X-ray, to be seen both obliquely as you approach up the nave and full-on as you stand before it. The steps leading up to the Madonna are one of the features that aid oblique entry, while the young Pesaro looking out at us on the right contributes more to the straight view.

Most viewers were immediately impressed by Titian's work for the Frari, where eventually he was buried in 1576. He had intended his own *Pietà*, now in the Accademia gallery (see pp.112-13), to hang over his tomb. Instead, in the end, a massive mid-nineteenth-century memorial in the south aisle was paid for by the Emperor Ferdinand I of Austria. Earlier in the nineteenth century the neoclassical sculptor Antonio Canova planned a Titian memorial here; a version of it by Canova's pupils was used in the north aisle for his own large monument (1827) with pyramid and mourning figures. Few visitors have reacted to this quite as strongly as Ruskin, for whom it is "consummate in science, intolerable in affectation, ridiculous in conception," but equally few have had much positive to say about it. The Museo Correr has Canova's original model, in wood and terracotta, for a more sober and decorous piece.

Those who were not at once captivated by Titian's Frari pieces were, one of his later defenders explained, all too accustomed to the "dead and cold" work of such painters as Giovanni Bellini (c. 1433–1516). But Bellini's triptych, in the sacristy of the Frari, of the Virgin and child with saints (1488) is, in its more meditative way, just as powerful as the bolder *Assumption* or more complex Pesaro *Madonna*. From a middle distance it is difficult to tell, for a moment, whether the Virgin's background—red patterned cloth behind, gold vault above—is painted or actually recessed. As a result mother and child inhabit a different and deeper reality than even the saints, although their depiction, too, hints at different levels of reality since they also move among pillars, some of which are painted and some more solidly part of the frame. The frame is richly gilded and decorated, but higher reality lies just beyond; the prayer above the Virgin's head is addressed to her, fittingly in this work of transitions from our world to the divine, as "safe doorway to heaven."

From the Frari, in the opposite direction to the Scuola di San Rocco, you can reach an interesting older scuola, that of San Giovanni

Evangelista (founded 1261), for which there are occasional signposts. (Finding it is easy, provided you first find the nearby Campo San Stin, which also has a convenient café.) The building is approached through two courts, the first with white marble portal (1481), again by the Renaissance classicizing architect Pietro Lombardo: pilasters and elegant vegetal and floral borders beneath a relief of the confraternity's Eagle of St. John. In a fourteenth-century relief on the wall of the scuola the saint himself appears with kneeling members of the confraternity. The long, largely undecorated lower hall has an air of clean simplicity very different from the more somber atmosphere at San Rocco. There is a small cowled praying figure on each column, and a crook of St. John. An end niche contains a small fifteenth-century statue of a saint who is certainly a Franciscan and probably San Bernardino, who preached in Venice in 1443. He carries a book and has a look of persuasive, but not coercive, spirituality.

A famous monumental double staircase by Mauro Coducci (1498, but rebuilt in modern times) leads up to the different world of Coducci's Sala Grande, remodeled by Giorgio Massari in the mid-eighteenth century, sparkling with light, the floor inlaid with different marbles, the high ceiling decorated by Giandomenico Tiepolo among others in the pinks and blues of the period. Altogether this is a less meditative, a less important place than the Scuola di San Rocco, but a happier one.

Further west, you can go to the church of San Nicolò da Tolentino with its joyous, movement-filled Baroque monument by Filippo Parodi (c. 1680) to Cardinal Francesco Morosini (not to be confused with his namesake, the doge and general). On the right of the monument is a smiling breast-feeding Charity; she and Fame, on the left, have defeated Time, who, for all his wings, is chained between them, policed by mere cherubs. Fame, amid rushing drapery, climbs easily upwards, indicating the tomb inscription with one hand and with the other, above her, the mitred deceased, who, only semi-recumbent, looks up in prayer. Fame begins the main vertical thrust of the monument, which continues through the cardinal and on by way of a great sculpted cloth, angel-borne shield and crown, to a Heaven whose clouds spill over onto the surrounding architecture.

Or you might cross the Grand Canal to see the church of the Scalzi, close to the station. For Henry James this is "all marble and malachite, all a hard, cold glitter and a costly, curly ugliness." But, especially after a long bout of sightseeing, it is enjoyable simply to sit and absorb the colors of the marble and malachite. The longer you sit, the more colors, variations, complementarities, you seem to see. Gray statues and gilded capitals are set against purple marbles, or, in the side-chapels, against reddish brown or gray-green. Red and white dominates in the chancel. The "barley-sugar" columns of the high altar shine with a deeper but white-flecked brown. And of course, the color-scheme shifts and changes with the light, so you can enjoy disagreeing with my perception of it.

The church and Campo of San Zaccaria can be reached by a short walk along Riva degli Schiavoni from the Ducal Palace, turning left along the Sottoportico San Zaccaria. In the campo, legend has it, a devil was once about to make off with a young noble bride but was scared off when her husband crawled round the well-head, roaring at him like the Lion of St. Mark. This happened at Michaelmas and thereafter on that day fiancés came to roar in the square in the assurance that it would guarantee the constancy of their future wives.

More orthodox beliefs were catered for in the church. The exterior is famous for its blend of Gothic and Renaissance elements, the interior especially for Giovanni Bellini's late altarpiece (1505) *The Virgin and Child Enthroned With a Musical Angel and SS. Peter, Catherine, Lucy and Jerome.* It is a calm, symmetrically grouped piece. The self-absorption of the saints, however, helps to spiritualize the calm; they do not look at each other or at us. Jerome as learned doctor of the Church reads on eternally, and next to him the soft-haired Lucy seems the sheer embodiment of serenity. (We may feel initially less serene on learning that the jar she lightly clasps is supposed to contain eyes, but she is the protector of sight.) A sense of divine mystery is also encouraged by the complex play between painted and real architecture; much of the effect would be lost in an art gallery. The color as well as the form of the real stonework accentuates that of its painted equivalent. And even the presence nearby of huge and more dramatic seventeenth-century paintings emphasizes the stillness and economy of gesture of Bellini's saints.

Greeks and Slavs

The Venice of Bellini and Titian was a cosmopolitan place with its traders from England and Egypt, ambassadorial retinues, sightseers, and colonial representatives. Greeks made up one of the larger ethnic minorities. When Constantinople fell to the Turks in 1453 many Greeks fled to Venice, attracted by its long, even if not always happy, relationship with the Byzantine empire and by the number of compatriots, mostly merchants, who had preceded them. By 1480 the Greek community was at least 4,000 strong. In 1468 Cardinal Bessarion, a Greek convert to Roman Catholicism who had settled in Italy in 1440, donated his great manuscript library to the Venetian state on the grounds that Greeks have such close links with Venice that when they land there "they feel they are entering another Byzantium." Aldus Manutius (Aldo Manuzio) made good use of refugee scholars in Venice on the editorial teams that produced, after 1495, many of his authoritative and crisply printed editions of ancient Greek texts. Such high-profile contacts helped to encourage the generally tolerant attitude of Venice to its racial and religious minorities, and in 1494 the Greek community was allowed to set up its own confraternity—the Scuola di San Nicolò dei Greci—and in 1539 to build a church, San Giorgio dei Greci (completed 1573).

The scuola (in its building of 1678, by Baldassare Longhena) now houses a Museum of Icons, including some by Mikhalis Damaskinos, an artist of the seventeenth-century Cretan Renaissance whose work combines Byzantine and Venetian influences. Next door, San Giorgio, a small utterly Greek-looking domed church, continues to uphold the Orthodox rite. Thomas Coryat, having just about succeeded in digesting "Papistical" doings, could now relate more unfamiliar scenes to his readers when "it was my hap to be there at their Greekish liturgy in the morning." He liked the "fair vaulted roof over the middle of the church, decked with the picture of God in it, made in mosaical work... and a great multitude of angels about him," but was rather disconcerted by the way the congregation "cross themselves six or seven times together" when they come in and later "wag their hands up and down very often," which "seemeth to me both very unseemly and ridiculous." Strange, too, were the people themselves: "most of these Grecians are very black, and all... do wear long hair... a fashion unseemly and very ruffian-like." But the average Venetian, familiar with diversity and its profits, presumably found it easy not to bat an eyelid whether at outlandish Orthodox Grecians or at Coryat, the rather wide-eyed Protestant gentleman of "Odcombe in the County of Somerset."

Another important group were the Slavs, mainly merchants or sailors in Venetian service, the majority from the coastal Venetian-ruled cities of what was then called Dalmatia: Ragusa (now Dbrovnik) and Zara (Zadar). In 1492 they, like the Greeks, were permitted their own confraternity. The Scuola di San Giorgio degli Schiavoni (St. George was a patron of the Dalmatians as well as the Greeks and the English) is a few minutes' walk from the Greek church and Icon Museum. Next to the Rio della Pietà where small boats often deliver fruit and building materials to the accompaniment of loud radios, the improbably quiet and modest scuola contains a famous sequence of paintings (1502–7) by Vittore Carpaccio in honor of the confraternity's three saints, George, Tryphon, and Jerome. The Carpaccios were originally installed upstairs, but look completely at home in the lower chamber to which they were moved in the 1550s, Ruskin's "little room about the size of the commercial parlour of an old-fashioned English inn." The paintings, on the upper walls, are glowingly but subtly illuminated by artificial light decorously dispensed from ornate wooden standards.

The eye is immediately struck by the head-on charge of St. George, in gleaming black armor but heroically unhelmeted, driving his splintering lance straight through the dragon's mouth while, on the right, the princess in a full red robe waits with hands clasped in prayer or relief. And then you may notice the skulls and bits of dismembered bodies on the ground below the knight and the monster. The princess has reason for relief. But the carnage also has a symbolic purpose: the dragon is a traditional image of lust and the young man and young woman whose torn bodies are visible have clearly, unlike the pure George and princess, given way to their passions and suffered the destructive consequences. Dragons could also traditionally stand for one's national enemies—most obviously the Turks for Carpaccio and his patrons. (Even in less symbolically minded days Venetian Slavs pitted against the French or the Austrians could perhaps see themselves as brave heirs of St. George; a side room in the scuola contains a plaque recording "at least the few names which have escaped oblivion" among "the Dalmatians who came to the defense of Venice in 1848–9.")

All the Carpaccios are worth looking at closely, for their narrative skill, their architectural details (part fantasy, part Renaissance Venice), for—to select some details—the great-bearded St. Jerome, bemused by the panic-stricken flight of his brethren as he offers hospitality to a lion with an injured paw, or St. Augustine amid his books, music and astrolabes, actively inspired in the first piece on the right. (Augustine is here because, as he writes to Jerome, he receives visionary foreknowledge of his death).

Slavs, or at least legendary Slavs, have a less good reputation at Santa Maria Formosa. In 944, the tale has it, some young women from the parish were on their way to the cathedral of San Pietro when they were seized and abducted by Slavs from the Narenta River area of Dalmatia, famous for its pirates. But the *casselleri*—makers of *cassoni* or wedding-chests, also of this parish—chased the Slavs and rescued the girls. They had, one might unchivalrously observe, a vested interest in weddings going ahead as planned. When the doge offered them the reward of their choice, they asked only that he should visit them once a year. In case of rain they bestowed on him a straw hat and in case he was hungry or thirsty they gave him bread and a bottle of wine. The custom was maintained at Candlemas up to the end of the Republic; one of the hats is preserved in the Museo Correr.

The tale of the maidens and their rescuers also had its place for a time in the much more elaborate *Festa delle Marie*, which at its height in the late thirteenth century involved three days of celebrations and processions. After ceremonies at San Marco and Santa Maria Formosa twelve "Marys," inspired partly by the nearly-kidnapped brides, were conducted in several boats to San Pietro, followed by a boatload of forty casselleri with drawn swords. Originally the Marys were real women, two from each *sestiere* of Venice, but later they were replaced by jeweled wooden effigies. William Dean Howells reports a local tradition that the change came about because the custom "had lost its simplicity and purity"; "the pretty girls were said to make eyes at handsome youths in the crowd, and scandals occurred in public."

Even after the substitution, the wooden figures were "followed by a disgusted and hooting populace, and assailed with a shower of turnips." Just possibly such conduct, "making eyes" and turnip lobbing, could be argued to be part of a fertility rite, suitable to the theme of weddings. (The drawn swords have their obvious symbolism here!) If such things did happen at all they were probably a brief relief from a long program of formal ceremonies. In 1379, however, the processions were replaced by a briefer ceremony in Santa Maria Formosa. Like the more homely straw hat and refreshments, this version endured until 1797.

Statues and Tombs

Campo Santi Giovanni e Paolo, dominated by the church of the same name, has an unusual feature for Venice: an equestrian statue. Venetian tradition refused to dignify individuals in so public and emphatic a manner, but the statue was the one condition on which the *condottiere* or mercenary general Bartolomeo Colleoni, who had long served Venice, bequeathed the state his very considerable fortune and lands in 1475. He in fact stipulated, quite unthinkably as far as the Republic was concerned, that the statue should be in Piazza San Marco. After years of deliberation (Venice, beset by wars in recent years, badly needed the money) it was decided that this detail could be interpreted creatively. Near the Scuola Grande di San Marco would have to do. The decorated late fifteenth-century façade of the scuola, rising to Hugh Honour's "attenuated windows and bobbly semi-circular gables," adjoins the church. Since 1819 it has been part of the city's main hospital; water-ambulances are to be seen moored along the Rio dei Mendicanti.

Even after a location for Colleoni's monument had been decided on, there were difficulties. Giorgio Vasari tells the story; hearing the name of the Florentine sculptor Andrea del Verrocchio much mentioned abroad, the Signoria sent for him and he completed a model in clay. But just as he was getting ready to cast it in bronze, "many gentlemen" came to the decision that although Verrocchio could cast the horse, a certain Vellano of Padua should be entrusted with the figure of Colleoni. The Florentine angrily departed, pausing only to break off the horse's legs and head, and the Senate decreed (claims Vasari) that if he ever returned to Venice *he* should have his head cut off.

His reply to this was prompt; he wrote to say that he knew how to re-do the horse's head but had never known how to re-attach any man's head, let alone one like his. This *pronta risposta* so pleased the senators that, Vasari records with the relish appropriate to the end of a folk-tale, they recalled the sculptor and paid him double. But, spoiling the conclusion a little and prolonging the Colleoni story even further, Verrocchio died, in 1488, before he could finish the work. It was finished in 1490 by a Venetian, Alessandro Leopardi, who immodestly inscribed his name on Colleoni's horse.

The group prompts comparisons, as was very likely intended, with those famous earlier equestrians, Marcus Aurelius on the Campidoglio in Rome and Donatello's *condottiere* Gattamelata in Padua. With what Henry James' narrator in *The Aspern Papers* calls his "small square-jawed face," "the terrible *condottiere* sits... sturdily astride of his huge bronze horse, on the high pedestal on which Venetian gratitude maintains him." Visitors' strength may be maintained at the Snack Bar Colleoni and its near neighbor the Snack al Cavallo. Each has a good view of the campo.

The church of Santi Giovanni e Paolo, run together, traditionally, as "San Zanipolo," was built by the Dominicans in the fourteenth and early fifteenth century. It is roughly the same—enormous—size as the Frari, the contemporary church of the other great preaching order, the Franciscans. The Dominicans' church contains the tombs of twenty-five doges, among other notables, giving it something of the feel and function of Westminster Abbey. The old patrician names occur repeatedly on the floors and walls: Mocenigo, Malipiero, Loredan, Delfin, Venier, Cornaro. But the great height of the church prevents it from seeming too cluttered with monuments (except, perhaps, the huge, outrageous, early eighteenth-century tribute to the self-esteem of the Valier family in the south aisle.) And many of the monuments are worth admiring as works of art. The fairly rapid turnover of doges, often fairly ancient when elected, helped keep the sculptors in work, here most notably Pietro Lombardo, his sons Tullio and Antonio, and other members of his workshop. (The real family name was Solari; they were originally from Lombardy.)

The central figure of Pietro's tomb (1476–81) for Doge Pietro Mocenigo, a noted naval commander, is described by John Julius Norwich: "Fully armed and decidedly bellicose, he stands upright on his sarcophagus in an attitude more appropriate to a triumphal arch than to a memorial tomb. A more godlessly typical example of Renaissance funerary sculpture could hardly be imagined." "Precisely," Fra Felix Fabri might have said, as a member of the reformed Dominican order visiting what he felt to be his distinctly unreformed brethren later in the 1480s. At the convent of Santi Giovanni e Paolo, he noted, "the friars live in some worldly pomp and splendor" and young people frequented the church in large numbers solely in order to listen to the music. The doges' tombs were rich and ostentatious and outdid even those of the popes in Rome. They were "raised above the ground and let into the walls, and the whole surface of the wall is bedecked with different marbles and carvings and gold and silver, and decorated to excess." Images of

Christ, the Virgin and the saints duly figured in important positions, "but around the edge are images of pagans, of Saturn, Janus, Jupiter, Juno, Minerva, Mars and Hercules, with emblems of their fables." On "the rich tomb of a certain Doge to the right of the entrance" [Pietro Mocenigo's] Hercules fights his lion and Hydra (in the panels at bottom left and right). It was the nakedness or semi-nakedness of such figures that particularly offended Fabri, figures "with swords and spears in their hands and shields about their necks, but without cuirass or breastplate or helmet, and these really are idols." "Simple people," he complained, "think these are images of saints, and they honor Hercules, thinking him Samson, and Venus, mistaking her for the Magdalene, and so forth."

Undaunted by such opposition, doges and their families continued to commission Lombardo tombs. Tullio Lombardo's style is, as far as it is possible to distinguish between different members of the workshop, rather more elegant than his father's: polished, more accurately classical in its details; some argue that he had studied in Rome. It is perhaps best exemplified by the monument (1492–5) to Doge Andrea Vendramin near the high altar. It might have afforded Fabri some little consolation that this tomb is at present difficult to see properly. The indefatigable John Ruskin did see it, however, and it made him just as angry as the friar might have been, if for different reasons. Armed with a ladder he climbed up, dusted down this costly tomb for a disastrous doge who "left Venice disgraced by sea and land," and discovered to his stupefaction that the statue of Vendramin has only one hand which, like the face and the ermine robe, is "a mere block on the inner side." Evidently it had been supposed "throughout the work that the effigy was only to be seen from below, and from one side." This, concluded Ruskin, is "a lying monument to a dishonoured doge" and, what is more, it features "fat-limbed boys sprawling on dolphins, dolphins incapable of swimming, and dragged along the sea by expanded pocket-handkerchiefs." Other examples of the work of the Lombardi, including Tullio's group on the west wall (1500–10) for Doge Giovanni Mocenigo, the brother and successor-but-one of Pietro, remain splendidly (unless you share certain of the views of Ruskin or Fabri) visible.

It seems mainly to have been on the strength of his tomb for Pietro Mocenigo that Pietro Lombardo was commissioned to build his masterpiece, Santa Maria dei Miracoli (1481–8). (Tullio worked with him on the sculptural details.) On a restricted site next to a canal, the tall, smooth marble church has been likened to a coffer or a treasure-chest. The interior especially, however, is anything but bejeweled. The first impression is that everything, apart from the ceiling-paintings, is pure, cool marble, free of the usual encrustations of mosaic, the jutting tombs, the side-chapels and undistinguished annunciations. The impression fades only a little with greater familiarity. The fine carving by the Lombardi in the chancel and on its balustrade, for instance, is worth closer inspection. The cool harmony is intended partly to encourage an undistracted focus on the relatively small miraculous image of the Virgin on the high altar, for which the church was built. But the image (an early fifteenth-century painting) fades into insignificance compared with its setting, which seems almost natural, a geological phenomenon. For the color and patterning of the panels is, in the first instance, a feature of the marble itself—the variation from gray to white to yellow and brown, the mottling, the near-diamond shapes. The panels themselves, of course, have been carefully selected and placed, giving a certain order to irregularities, alternating darker and lighter, introducing borders. But so subtle have the choices been that art and geology seem to be in dialogue, in partnership. Close up, the walls of the nave (this is, importantly, a single-nave building—there are no aisles) become a gallery of abstract effects, fine washes, seams.

A Church, the Ghetto, and a Palace

William Dean Howells was on his way to the Ghetto by gondola when he came "unawares" upon the Madonna dell'Orto church (begun in 1399; the campanile was built in 1503). He admired the façade, which is remarkable for its profusion of white late Gothic statues and decoration, including work by Bartolomeo Bon and his assistants. The central portal, with its ornamental flourishes and statues of St. Christopher above and Gabriel and the Virgin on either side, was paid for in 1460 by the Scuola di San Cristoforo dei Mercanti, whose building of a century later is also in the campo. Howells also liked the

Gothic windows and used them as an opportunity to explore some of the inconsistencies of our attitude to the past: "One longed to fall down" outside the church

and recant these happy, commonplace centuries of heresy, and have back again the good old believing days of bigotry, and superstition, and roasting, and racking, if only to have once more the men who dreamed those windows out of their faith and piety (if they did, which I doubt), and made them with their patient, reverent hands (if their hands were reverent, which I doubt).

Howells is having some fun here at the expense of Ruskin and the nineteenth-century exaltation of the medieval craftsman. He does not comment on the interior of the church, which was, thanks to the presence of a number of works by Tintoretto including a *Last Judgment* and a *Presentation of the Virgin*, inspired by Titian's treatment of the same subject in the Accademia, already securely established as Ruskin's territory. Ruskin had responded with particular energy to the Apocalypse with its

river of the wrath of God, roaring down into the gulf where the world has melted with its fervent heat, choked with the ruin of nations, and the limbs of its corpses tossed out of its whirling, like water-wheels. Bat-like, out of the holes and caverns and shadows of the earth, the bones gather, and the clay heaps heave, rattling and adhering into half-kneaded anatomies, that crawl, and startle, and struggle up among the putrid weeds, with the clay clinging to their clotted hair, and their heavy eyes sealed by the earth-darkness.

This was Tintoretto's parish church. He provided his huge paintings free of charge. In 1594 he was buried here and is commemorated in the chapel to the right of the chancel by a plaque and—suitably strong and pensive—a bust. His daughter Marietta (1560–90) and son Domenico (1560?–1635), each of whom worked with him, are also buried here.

The Ghetto is farther south, in the Cannaregio district. This was the original Ghetto: the name comes from the local word for a foundry (from *gettare*, meaning in this case to cast). Confusingly, the oldest synagogues are in Campo Ghetto Nuovo, since the former "new foundry" was the first area to which, in 1516, Jewish habitation was

confined. The Ghetto Vecchio was taken over in 1541 and a third area of much needed accommodation, the Ghetto Nuovissimo, was added in 1633. Once, these places, especially the Ghetto Nuovo, teemed with activity during the day when the many tailors and the pawnshops were freely patronized by Christians. It was a cramped and claustrophobic place at night, when only physicians were allowed in and out of the gates. Now the memory of that world survives, in this quiet corner of Cannaregio, in the form of a few shops selling Jewish artifacts and *kosher* food, high tenements—sometimes six or more stories since space was so limited—five synagogues and the Museo Ebraico.

The history of Jews in Venice has been, as elsewhere, checkered. They were often tolerated as useful money-lenders (since Christians were usually banned from this profession and Jews from most others) or physicians; sometimes expelled, often criticized by fastidious visitors for living in cramped and unhygienic conditions. Like Shylock in *The Merchant of Venice* they might be borrowed from, spat upon, or both. Violent persecution was rare under the Venetian Republic, but taxes were often heavy. Notwithstanding the restrictions, however, some Jews succeeded in becoming prosperous; Levantine Jews, in particular, were allowed to prosper as merchants. And Jewish culture flourished in Venice, from popular singing to drama and mystical writings. In the first half of the sixteenth century Jewish scholars and typesetters had worked on the 200 or so Hebrew books printed in Venice by Daniel Bomberg of Antwerp. Later, the poet Sara Coppio Sullam (c.1592–1641) lived in the Ghetto; her salon was a meeting point for Jewish and Christian intellectuals.

The seventeenth-century figure about whom we know most, however, is Rabbi Leon da Modena (1571–1648), author of many sermons, books and pamphlets, a pastoral play, and a candid autobiography. (Mark R. Cohen's English translation was published by Princeton University Press in 1988.) Here, Modena describes his money problems, his burning grief at the death of one son from disease and another assassinated by enemies within the community, the progress of the plague of 1630–1, and the marital discord of his old age as he and his wife move from one unsatisfactory tenement to another. In 1636–7 crisis threatened to overtake the whole community when two Jews were convicted for receiving 60–70,000 ducats' worth of stolen goods. As the scandal escalated there was some talk of expelling all Jews from Venice. This was averted partly by the persuasive intervention of Simone Luzzatto (1583–1663), Modena's pupil and later his successor as chief rabbi, whose *Discorso* on the Jews of Venice put to the rest of the city a clear case for the practical economic advantages of continued toleration. Having no separate homeland like other minority groups, Luzzatto argued, the Jews invested their money locally; they worked hard, and were in effect the "feet"—walked on but necessary—of the state.

In 1637 Modena had a more personal, but equally dangerous, problem. He was seized for a time, he confesses, by sheer panic when *Riti ebraici* was published, without his permission, in Paris. This book, unlike Luzzatto's pragmatic offering, dealt with sensitive theological matters; Modena had written about some matters of Jewish doctrine of which discussion was banned by the Catholic Church. But influential friends took the wise, preemptive step of submitting the rabbi's material at once to the Inquisition, and he was not prosecuted. He was able to go on with his writing and teaching and, human as ever in this most unsanctified of autobiographies, to go on wrestling as he always had with the compulsion to gamble away any money he succeeded in earning.

When Modena died in 1648 there were about 5,000 Jews in Venice. Later in the century numbers began to fall as some individuals and families left for the freer conditions on offer in Holland and Prussia. New restrictions were still being imposed in Venice as late as 1777. At the fall of the Republic in 1797 the gates of the Ghetto were demolished. Jews were allowed to live outside the Ghetto, although many stayed on. After the union with Italy in 1866 they were allowed to participate more fully in Venetian life until official intolerance returned with the racial laws of 1938. Earlier in Mussolini's regime, by contrast, many Jews had been encouraged to belong to the Fascist party; the change to some extent resulted from Nazi pressure. Bronze reliefs in the Ghetto Nuovo (1980, by the Lithuanian artist Arbit Blatas) remember the 200 or so members of the community who were taken to Fossoli near Modena at the end of 1943 and deported to extermination camps in Germany or Poland in February 1944. Only eight returned.

The Ghetto is no longer mainly populated by Jews. The community is small and, like the whole city, mostly elderly; jobs and excitement are sought on the mainland. Several of the synagogues (only two of which are still in regular use) can be seen by taking the regular tours, in English or Italian, that start from the ground floor of the museum building in the Ghetto Nuovo. Originally different groups of Jews had their separate synagogues. Above the museum, for instance, is the "German" Synagogue, Scuola Grande Tedesca (1528), which was used by Ashkenazi Jews mostly from France and Germany. All three synagogues in the Ghetto Nuovo are deliberately inconspicuous from the outside, but rich with carved wood and gilding inside. The Scuola Canton (1531; the name perhaps means "on the corner") has an elegant eighteenth-century interior. The quieter, calmer Scuola Italiana (1575) features a light women's gallery, eighteenth-century again, above contrastingly dark wood. The synagogues in the Ghetto Vecchio are more noticeable from the outside, built by wealthier groups and at a time of somewhat greater security from violent attack. The Scuola Spagnola, where Leon da Modena supervised the music and often preached, was regarded as the premier meeting place of the whole community. Its splendid Baroque interior (1655) is by Baldassare Longhena, better known for Santa Maria della Salute—Jews were not permitted to work as artists or artisans. The nearby Scuola Levantina, full of shining dark walnut and deep red curtains, features a huge, highly decorated, canopied *bimah* or pulpit by Andrea Brustolon of Belluno (1662–1732); "either its superabundant originality attracts, or its exaggerated ornamentation repels," says Roberta Curiel in the most comprehensive guide to the Ghetto (Roberta Curiel and Dov Cooperman, *The Venetian Ghetto*).

The tour ends back at the museum, which has a good selection of silver oil-lamps, candlesticks, Hanukah lamps, highly wrought Rimmonim (Torah finials), and marriage contracts. An earlier memorial to the Jews of Venice is the Jewish Cemetery on the Lido, first established in 1386. Modena, Luzzatto, and Sullam among others were buried here. Their tombstones were rediscovered during road works in the late 1920s and set up among the other white tombs in the walled, sandy, older part of the cemetery. A single stone inscribed "1631 Hebrei" survives from the mass grave of plague victims in that year.

Back on the Cannaregio Canal (where, incidentally, there are some well provisioned grocers' and fruit shops, mainly on the Ghetto side), near its junction with the Grand Canal, is Palazzo Labia. The Labia, a rich merchant family of Spanish ancestry, bought their patrician status for 100,000 ducats in 1646. They had been based here, in Campo San Geremia, for more than a century, but now needed a palace grand enough for their newly exalted social position. Andrea Cominelli completed the building in 1696. Alessandro Tremignon was responsible for the mid-eighteenth-century updating, which includes the façade on the campo; but the most important change was the creation of the ballroom and its decoration by the perspective artist or *quadraturista* Gerolamo Mengozzi Colonna and the great fresco-painter Giambattista Tiepolo. Mengozzi Colonna provided the perspective architecture which, by turns imitating, extending, or flouting the real architecture, brings Tiepolo's Antony and Cleopatra seemingly into the room.

Tiepolo is alert also to other ways of playing with reality: Cleopatra may be modeled on the lady of the house, Maria Labia; the black boy restraining a dog at the meeting of the lovers is probably the artist's own servant, Selim. Cleopatra's banquet is keenly watched, at left, by the painters themselves—Tiepolo aquiline, lively, and wearing a blue turban and robes, Mengozzi Colonna in lighter suit and with fuller face beside him.

Cleopatra, opulently dressed, spirited, golden-haired (quite unlike some later notions of her appearance and likely degree of covering) has just descended from her barge to meet Antony. Plutarch and Shakespeare describe the arrival of the barge and how she "purs'd up his heart upon the river of Cydnus"; according to Plurarch

> she furnished herself with a world of gifts, store of gold and silver, and of riches and other sumptuous ornaments, as is credible enough she might bring from... so wealthy a realm as Egypt was. But yet she carried noth-ing with her wherein she trusted more than in herself, and in the charms and enchantment of her [sur]passing beauty and grace.

Her retinue extends behind her—followers in various colored turbans, a heavily robed Egyptian priest—and to the left, beyond one of the doors of the room, stand her women Charmian and Iras. Antony, in armor but already passion's captive, is leading her toward the steps which (seem to) descend into the room.

Cleopatra continues the pursing up in the fresco of her banquet. The story derives from the Elder Pliny, who, in his encyclopedic *Natural History*, says that Cleopatra possessed the two largest pearls ever known. Once she told Antony that she was unimpressed by the magnificent feasts he kept giving. He wanted to know how he could possibly improve them. She said that *she* could spend ten million sesterces on one banquet. Bets were taken. The next day, her followers served what seemed at first a perfectly "everyday" feast. But then she had a goblet of vinegar brought in, dropped into it one of the famous pearls, worn as an earring, waited for it to dissolve—in reality, of course, it could not, but Pliny's mistake was a useful one for artists and story-tellers—and drank it off in a gesture of superb extravagance. (Such a gesture may have appealed especially to Tiepolo's patrons. A Labia lord after a banquet once, allegedly, tossed forty gold plates out of the window into the canal and announced, with punning *sang froid*: *L'abia o non l'abia, sarò sempre Labia*, "Have it, or have it not, I shall always be Labia." But, less reckless than the Queen of Egypt, he is said to have taken the precaution of putting a net just beneath the water so that he could retrieve his goods having impressed his guests.) Pliny goes on to say that Lucius Plancus, judging the lovers' wager, prevented Cleopatra from swallowing the second pearl and conceded defeat on behalf of Antony: he was, as moralists would not tire of pronouncing and romantics of proclaiming, conquered "for the love of love, and her soft hours."

In the fresco, which takes the romantic rather than the moralistic tack, everyone, except the musicians with their bespectacled leader, busy providing *Tafelmusik* from a gallery, watches expectantly as the queen holds the pearl with one hand and takes the wine-glass of improbably strong vinegar with the other. The relationship between Antony and Cleopatra is now established. She has not only changed her white dress for a pink one, but now, more like most Cleopatras, she has her breasts largely uncovered. (The effect, however, is as much one of *bravura* as of sexuality.) Antony looks on, bright-eyed, a little bemused, enraptured still. As at an earlier banquet where eating paled into insignificance, he "pays his heart, / For what his eyes eat only."

The contents of Palazzo Labia were mostly dispersed, under various owners, in the early nineteenth century. But the ballroom and its frescoes survived until someone with the money to finance restorations, an oil-rich Mexican, Carlos de Beistegui, bought the building in 1948. In 1951 he hosted a spectacular masquerade ball which Antony and Cleopatra might have enjoyed, and guests including Lady Diana Cooper, dressed as the Cleopatra of the frescoes, did. True to Tiepolo, the boundary between reality and illusion was once more blurred. Even Beistegui, however, lacked the resources to melt pearls or throw plates in the canal. In 1963 he sold the palace to the Italian radio and television corporation RAI, which still has its regional base here. Because of this, admission to see the frescoes is at set times, currently from Wednesday to Friday afternoons between 3:00 and 4:00 PM, and must be pre-arranged by phoning (041) 524 28 12. The successful restoration of the frescoes began in 1965.

CHAPTER SEVEN

Island Venice:
Cemeteries, Monasteries,
and Resorts

The Venetian lagoon is full of low, green islands of varying size, linked by channels through the muddy shallows. Many are tiny islets. Some are extensively inhabited. The Giudecca is effectively a suburb of Venice and even on Burano—in spite of the postcard image of brightly painted houses and lace-makers—there are more than 5,000 residents. There are islands as different as the fertile Le Vignole and Sant'Erasmo, north of the Lido, covered with market gardens; Burano's greener neighbor Mazzorbo; the desolate San Giorgio in Alga—"St. George in the Seaweed"—just off the Giudecca; Sant'Ariano, in the northern lagoon, the disused repository of the bones of the city dead; and San Francesco del Deserto, south of Burano, with its quiet Franciscan monastery, church and gardens, where in the 1950s Jan Morris could hear only

> *bells, chanting male voices, sober conversation, the singing of song birds,*
> *the squawking of peacocks, the clucking of ducks and hens, and sometimes*
> *a deep dissatisfied bellow, as of a soul sated with Elysium, from the rumi-*
> *nating cattle in the cow-house.*

San Michele

San Michele, from a distance, gives an impression of wholeness and calm: beyond the brown walls only massed cypresses are visible. An island of the dead ought to be a mythical sort of place. Rather sonorous music sounds in my head as I approach it; Rachmaninov's *Island of the Dead*, in fact. Inside, particularly in the modern areas, the fact of death is more flatly present, not dignified by myth.

The Orthodox cemetery, walled and partly lined with trees, is less troublingly extensive than the Catholic sectors. Here are the simple graves with just the words "Igor Stravinsky" and "Vera Stravinsky" and a cross. Nearby is Serge Diaghilev's tomb, to which devotees still attach ballet-shoes. (The founder of the *Ballets Russes* died on a visit to Venice in 1929.) Elsewhere are nineteenth-century expatriate princesses like the proudly named "Princess C. Troubetskoy née Moussine Pouchkine." In summer the main sound is of lizards darting about. The Evangelical or Protestant cemetery is fuller—here are buried Germans, English, Americans, French, a few Italian Protestants, and others—and in a somewhat sadder state. A few tombs are broken, tilting, or largely illegible, and there is an air of isolation. Once you are within these walls the Venice of splendid waters and campanili has completely disappeared. There is a marked contrast with the verdant and carefully maintained Protestant Cemetery in Rome.

There are some tombs of the famous: Ezra Pound, who died in Venice in 1972 after a quiet, sad last period in the city he had lived in, full of ideas and aspirations, in 1908; the poet and essayist Joseph Brodsky (1940-1996); the Venetian-born composer Ermanno Wolf-Ferrari (1876–1948) and several members of his family. Stones erected to the less well known allow glimpses of the shifting expatriate and visiting population, young and old. Just to the right of the entrance is Sybil Mitford, wife of William Henry Mason, born November 24, 1860, married October 13, 1885, died November 17, 1885; farther on is the Swiss consul "Giovanni Keller, morto a solo 39 anni" in 1923. (There are, however, few very young people buried in this part of San Michele since the damp air of Venice was not recommended for consumptives.) William Drinkwater, "commander of the Cunard steam-ship *Tarifa*," died in Venice in August 1872, aged 43. Eugene Schuyler, US consul general in Egypt, died in Venice in 1890, three years after Johanna, "eldest daughter of Henry Bradshaw Fearon formerly of Frognal Hampstead London who died... in the 68th year of her age on the eve of her return to England" and was buried by the wall where a palm now grows from her grave. A more sudden death brought here Sarah McLean Drake and Janet Drake her daughter, "who perished in the steamer disaster near the Lido, Venice, 19 March 1914."

The church of San Michele in Isola, with its cool white façade of Istrian stone, survives from an earlier period; it was built by Mauro Coducci in 1469–77. Here too is one important, if plain, grave, indicated by a marble lozenge in front of the main door: that of Fra Paolo Sarpi, defender of Venice against the papal interdict of 1606 (see pp.189-90).

Murano

In the sixteenth century 50,000 people lived on Murano. Now there are 9,000. It was renowned for its seventeen churches (a handful remains), its palaces, orchards, and gardens. In the Renaissance the green places were the favored retreat of wealthy Venetians and, it was said, of intellectuals pacing out their ideas. This prosperity and popularity flowed from the decision, at the end of the thirteenth century following a spate of fires, to move the Venetian glass industry exclusively to the island. For centuries the glass-workers, custodians of increasingly valuable trade secrets, were forbidden to leave Murano. But the island was also given special status. It had its *podestà* (mayor), for instance, and, its own *libro d'oro*—the book in which, as in the mother city, the names of the nobility were inscribed in gold. Eventually, however, the industry declined, amid competition ("Venetian style" glass from elsewhere) and changes of fashion, and the prosperity ebbed away—to be revived in the late nineteenth century.

Murano still feels like a smaller, but not negligible Venice. There are canals, but not too many; there *are* too many shops selling Murano glassware of variable quality, but you can easily lose them by

a few minutes' strolling. If you walk along Fondamenta Venier away from the center, for instance, turn right up Calle del Cimitero. This leads to the Campo del Cimitero, where plane trees line a path next to a small field or *campo* of grass. Beyond this is the enclosed cemetery itself, thick with pines.

There was a period of decline in the eighteenth and nineteenth centuries when many fine buildings were lost, but this has clearly not been a desolate place. The glass industry never entirely foundered; even the very particular John Ruskin, in *The Stones of Venice* (1851–3), is prepared to tolerate "the cloud which hovers above the glass furnaces of Murano," since it is "one of the last signs left of human exertion among the ruinous villages which surround us."

The basilica of Santa Maria and San Donato has always been the most notable building on Murano. Beside its campanile once stood the medieval Palazzo del Comune, the center of the island's partly autonomous administration, demolished in 1815. At the foot of the campanile now stands the war memorial of 1927 by the Muranese sculptor Napoleone Martinuzzi. Very much of its time and not to everyone's taste, the memorial is in harmony, nevertheless, with the peace, marble and brick of the rest of the square and enhanced, in summer, by its flowering oleanders.

At first the interior of the basilica may seem simply more ordinary than that of San Marco or of Torcello cathedral. One reason for this is that the church is more evidently in frequent use for services; as Hugh Honour says, it is "a pleasant patchwork of the centuries, a monument to the persistent piety of the local population." While the Veneto-Byzantine Virgin glows beyond the altar, on each side eighteenth-century statues of Saints Lorenzo Giustinian and Theodore gesture floridly. There has been much restoration. That of 1858–73 treated the exterior so heavy-handedly that for Honour it appeared "a bastard of the twelfth and nineteenth century." A plaque on one of the columns in the nave salutes those responsible, the Cardinal Patriarch, architects and civic officials, in the expectation of their being remembered more gratefully. More sensitive restoration continued through the twentieth century, most successfully in the 1970s, when the façade was made less bastard.

But if you look long enough at the twelfth-century Virgin in the apse, any awareness of modernization begins to fall away. The figure is elongated, robed in deep blue, and, holding her hands before her in prayer, has a simpler effect than the Torcello Madonna who holds the infant Jesus. The borders of the robe are picked out in gold and she stands on a golden base with sides of alternating red and green spotted with gold. "Settled sorrow," said the Earl of Crawford and Balcarres in *Sketches of the History of Christian Art* (1847), "dwells on every feature: the very spirit of the 'Stabat Mater' breathes through this affecting portraiture—the silent searching look for sympathy is irresistible. The face not beautiful, but impressive and dignified."

Other elements make clear that this is an early church. Some of the capitals of the columns in the nave are late Roman work. The floor mosaics, laid in 1141 (as stated in Latin on a roundel near the center of the nave) or soon afterwards, are the most absorbing element, comparable to those in San Marco of the same period. From some distance the larger patterns, especially the two great swirling circles near the entrance, take the eye. Closer to, there is an extraordinary variety of local detail. Peacocks (a symbol of the resurrection, since it was believed that their flesh did not decay) drink from a vase; there are other birds whose heads flow into each other, and wave patterns which, seen from the right angle, become crested birds. There are also fish, plants, chessboard, and other geometric patterns. And the mosaic pictures are surrounded, and their colors contrasted or complemented, by *opus sectile* work (thin slabs of colored marble). Deep reds and greens, yellow-brown, gray, black-and-white, and paler green and blue predominate.

Just across the bridge from San Donato is the Osteria al Duomo, good for very reasonably priced sandwiches, salads, white wine, and ice cream. These can be consumed at stone tables in the quiet, shaded garden at the back.

Thus fortified, one should go to the Museo Vetrario. Here, as is often not the case in the glass-blowers' showrooms and the shops, can be seen some of the variety and appeal of Murano and other glass, from early, mostly functional, examples to fine twentieth-century art glass. The spacious museum is housed in an originally fifteenth-century palace, renovated by the Giustiniani family in the seventeenth century. From that time there survives, in the main *salone*, a fresco of the triumph of the family saint, Lorenzo Giustiniani. Later the palace became the town hall. The collection began, in 1861, as part of a wider historical research project. It soon acquired an additional, more practical function as a teaching aid for the students of the school of glass design set up on Murano in 1862. Ten years later, in the revivalist spirit of the time, a lace-making school was established on Burano to help revive *its* traditional industry.

Among the highlights of the collection are goblets and bowls by Angelo Barovier (1405–60), a man of wide intellectual and scientific interests and the probable inventor of Venetian *cristallo*—clear crystal glass in the production of which an important element was the use of soda ash at the melting stage; a Renaissance *cesendella* or hanging oil-lamp enameled with the escutcheon of the Barbarigo family (featuring, in white outlined in gold against a blue background, what looks like a cross between an elongated dogal *corno* and Scrooge's night-cap); and from 1842–5, dynamic, brightly striped, whorled filigree bottles by Pietro Bigaglia. Later in the nineteenth century earlier Muranese designs were often copied or remodeled and old techniques rediscovered in the process. Material of more obvious contemporary appeal was also produced, however; for instance Toso Brothers, established in 1854 and specializing mostly in more historical work, were responsible for a large piece elaborately decorated with fat blue geese. In the museum, in such good company, it is interesting, a curiosity, even charming, as it would not be elsewhere in glass-crammed central Murano.

Most of these exhibits once came out of the furnaces of Murano. These are technically interesting, and absorbing as a spectacle, but have sometimes also led on to deeper insights. James Howell, a seventeenth-century Englishman who had been steward of a glassworks in London and was now reporting on the Venetian trade, was not above observing that, in local lore, "the first handsome woman that ever was made was made of Venice glass"—fair but frail (and, he chucklingly observes, "Venice is not unprovided with some of that mould, for no place abounds more with lasses and glasses"). But, he goes on:

> when I pry'd into the materials, and observed the furnaces and the calci-
> nations, the transubstantiations and the liquefactions that are incident to
> [the glass-blowers'] art, my thoughts were raised to a higher speculation,
> that if this small furnace-fire hath virtue to convert such a small lump of
> dark dust and sand into such a precious clear body as crystal, surely that
> grand universal-fire, which shall happen at the Day of Judgement, may
> by its violent ardour vitrify and turn to one lump of crystal the whole body
> of the earth.

Torcello

Torcello is a short stretch of water away from the colorful houses of Burano and the orchards and vineyards of neighboring Mazzorbo, but utterly different in aspect and atmosphere. The once powerful early medieval center, with its dwellings, towers, churches, and markets, its 20,000 inhabitants and abundance of sheep, has long been reduced to a rural, mostly empty place with, several minutes' peaceful walk along a narrow canal from the *vaporetto* stop, a few historic buildings: the cathedral of Santa Maria Assunta, its campanile, the remains of its baptistery (demolished in 1892), the church of Santa Fosca, and the museums in the former palazzi del

Consiglio and del Archivio. As if to emphasize the decline, "Attila's throne," in the grassy piazza between these buildings, is a much eroded seat and there isn't even any reason to associate it with the mighty Hun. Between the vaporetto and the historic buildings there are also several fairly expensive eating-places, of which the best known is Locanda Cipriani. The present population is a few dozen.

In *The Stones of Venice* John Ruskin described the view from the campanile toward evening: "Far as the eye can reach, a waste of wild sea-moor, of a lurid ashen-grey; ... lifeless, the colour of sackcloth, with the corrupted sea-water soaking through its acrid weeds, and gleaming hither and thither through its snaky channels." In the far distance he saw the blue line of higher land and beyond that the "misty band of mountains"; the Adriatic and "the widening branches of the wide lagoon, alternately purple and pale green, as they reflect the evening clouds or twilight sky." Also, to the south, is the "long irregular line" of the towers and palaces of Venice: "Mother and daughter, you behold them both in their widowhood—Torcello and Venice." But once there was no Venice and—Ruskin's main motive for taking readers up the bell-tower is to tell them this—on the horizon

> *there were strange fires mixed with the light of sunset, and the lament of many human voices mixed with the fretting of the waves on their ridges of sand. The flames rose from the ruins of Altinum; the lament from the multitude of its people, seeking, like Israel of old, a refuge from the sword in the paths of the sea.*

Ruskin imagines the refugees building their cathedral in haste. Its "massy stone shutters [an eleventh-century survival on the south wall] cause the whole building to resemble rather a refuge from Alpine storm than the cathedral of a populous city." The builders constructed an unusually light-filled church because "there was fear and depression upon them enough, without a material gloom." (Ruskin at this stage of his life remained suspicious of Roman Catholic darkness, real or metaphorical.) In fact, of course, it was a gradual process. The first cathedral here was founded in 639; it was largely rebuilt in 1008. But Ruskin's powerful myth-making has a purpose. He wants to provide us with an instance of Venice in its primal vigor, an idealized place of mariners, free citizens, untainted members of the Early Church who (like good Protestants again) "sought for comfort in their religion, for tangible hopes and promises, not for threatenings and mysteries." In their simple, ship-like refuge, their ark, was to be found the true, original spirit of Venice. To "learn in what spirit it was that the dominion of Venice was begun," the visitor should not consider wealth, arsenals, "the pageantry of her palaces" or "the secrets of her councils" but should

ascend the highest tier of the stern ledges that sweep round the altar of Torcello, and then, looking as the pilot did of old along the marble ribs of the goodly temple-ship, let him repeople its veined deck with the shad-ows of its dead mariners, and strive to feel in himself the strength of heart that was kindled within them, when first, after the pillars of it had settled in the sand, and the roof of it had been closed against the angry sky that was still reddened by the fires of their homesteads,—first, within the shelter of its knitted walls, amidst the murmur of the waste of waves and the beating of the wings of the sea-birds round the rock that was strange to them,—rose that ancient hymn, in the power of their gathered voices:

The sea is His, and He made it
And His hands prepared the dry land.

Inside the cathedral, the east end is dominated by the elongated Veneto-Byzantine figure of the Virgin holding the Christ-child. She stands in her blue robe against an undecorated gold expanse—a gold sky of which her halo forms a part. She is neither the sweet Madonna of later painting, nor the sterner figure of the icons. "An ethereal figure," Honour calls her, "in whom dignity and an almost intimate gentleness are combined." For Jan Morris she is terribly sad and "gazes down the church with an expression of timeless reproach, cherishing the Child in her arms as though she has foreseen all the years that are to come, and holds each one of us responsible."

The gold and blue in the apse contrast with the mostly paler colors of the main body of the church: the whites and grays of the Byzantine stone iconostasis panels (eleventh-century reliefs of peacocks and lions), the columns of the nave and their Corinthian capitals (some ancient). The floor mosaics contribute some color, but are generally more sober, more discreet, than those in San Donato or San Marco, and punctuated by large slabs of pale Greek marble.

On the outer arch of the apse, above the Virgin, the tall figures of Gabriel and Mary enact the Annunciation. Letting the eye travel downward from them, you witness what naturally follows their encounter: most importantly, the dominant mosaic of the mother and child. Beneath them are the mosaic apostles and then the visible reminders of the church they founded: the early, rather battered brick benches for the clergy and the bishop's throne, the altar and, below, the gold-masked remains of a latter-day apostle, St. Heliodorus, bishop of Altinum. All this is logically preceded by the Annunciation, yet, visually as well as theologically, it is co-present and contemporaneous. Mary remains, through time, annunciate, Jesus a child who blesses as well as an adult who dies and rises, and the church and its apostles and saints repeat the same message and aspire to the same divine timelessness.

As far as linear time is concerned, we move forward to the large mosaic of the Last Judgment—the end of human time—at the opposite end of the church. Although the content is traditional and some figures stiffly hieratic, the main impression here is one of energy, helped by the eloquent and various use of hands which seize, acclaim, indicate, implore, brandish spears, and trumpets, clasp crosses, welcome, or pray. It is difficult for modern eyes (and necks) to follow all the details of this huge scene, but they repay attention. The iconographical scheme is worked out with unusual logicality and precision. The starting-point, up on the tympanum, is the crucifixion. Next, moving down, is the *Anastasis* (resurrection), in which the appropriately large figure of Christ triumphantly smashes the gates of Hell. Beneath his feet Satan lies amid the wrecked locks and keys. Christ has come to set free Adam (the white-bearded figure whose wrist he seizes), Eve, and others, including Kings Solomon and David (the jeweled, robed, and gesticulating pair on the left). The small inset beneath the kings contains souls of the innocent unbaptized, waiting to be freed from Limbo. There are more of them on the right, beneath the old patriarchs and next to John the Baptist, who acclaims the victory of

Christ, the fulfillment of his and the Old Testament figures' prophecies. All this takes place between the authoritative figures of the archangels Michael and Gabriel ("Archangels of an almost Aztec brilliance and fearsomeness," says Honour.)

Moving downward still, the next register shows Christ, ready to pronounce judgment, between his mother and the Baptist, the jeweled archangels, and the apostles (more heavily restored than most of the scene.) From Christ's feet a river of fire flows down to the place of the damned, two registers below. Just beneath Him, on either side of the river, are wheels of fire and angels from the vision of the prophet Ezekiel. On the next level there is also preparation for judgment. On the black-draped throne is the Book of Justice. To left and right are some of the liveliest scenes; on the left two angels rush to blow their trumpets, at which the wild beasts—lion, elephant, hyena, leopard, wolf, griffin—render up their victims. A hand is to be seen emerging from the hyena's mouth, a head from the wolf's and so on. Those of the dead not so swallowed up awaken in their tombs, just above the creatures. Meanwhile on the right, even more surprisingly to the modern viewer, an angel unrolls the starry sky at the end of the world and two other angels call with their trumpets for the sea-monsters to spew up their victims.

As a result of all these processes we are left, on the bottom levels, with the saved and the damned. (In the middle, above the Virgin, good and bad deeds are weighed; the ominously well-armed devils carry bags full of sins.) On the left is Heaven. Here the virtuous share the same gold background as Christ and his angels; the ungodly, who do not share that freedom, inhabit fire, water, or darkness. Orderly groups of bishops, martyrs, monks, and good women are presented. Beneath them, ready to receive them, are old father Abraham, the Virgin and the Baptist. They stand near the gate of Paradise—to be contrasted with the broken gate of Hell—and St. Peter with his keys. Elsewhere, on the right, immersed in fire, are the proud, among whom are visible kings, queens, and churchmen. Probably iconographic tradition rather than a desire to assert the independence of the lagoon provides the monarchs with identifiably Byzantine crowns and earrings. But perhaps it is salutary to see the flames crackling around people wearing the same sort of headgear worn so triumphantly by the Emperor and Empress Justinian and Theodora in the mosaic at San Vitale in Ravenna. Satan, in the guise of an old white-bearded blue man, sits on a two-headed dragon. The Antichrist sits on his knees. Beneath suffer the lustful, the proud and the gluttonous, the wrathful (immersed in water to quench their angry heat), the envious, the avaricious (their earrings and jewels no use in the fire), and the slothful (reduced to scattered skulls and bones).

The Judgment frames the door through which the congregation would leave the cathedral. They were clearly intended to look up, as they passed through, at the threatened torments and (less graphic) promised rewards. It is to be hoped that they found comfort in the Virgin, directly above the door with her hands raised to implore mercy for sins.

San Giorgio and the Giudecca

The church and former monastery of San Giorgio Maggiore are, Thomas Coryat observed, "situate in a very delectable island about half a mile southward from St. Mark's Place... It is a passing sumptuous place, and the fairest and richest monastery without comparison in all Venice, having at least threescore thousand crowns for a yearly revenue, which amount to eighteen thousand pound sterling." Among the visible results of the Benedictines' wealth were "a very fair cloister that environeth a pretty green quadrangle," a large garden "full of great variety of dainty fruits" and, in the Refectory, a fine picture "of an exceeding breadth and length, containing the history of Christ's sitting at the table at the marriage at Cana in Galilee." The size of the picture, and the fact that it was one of Veronese's masterpieces, commended it to the attention of the Napoleonic commissioners charged with confiscating works of art; it is still in the Louvre. The monastery itself was suppressed by the French in 1806 and became a barracks. Eventually, in 1951–6, the buildings were restored by Count Vittorio Cini and now house the Giorgio Cini Foundation, a cultural center named after the count's son, who died in an air crash in 1949. The church, built on the site of earlier buildings between 1565 and 1610, was also closed in 1806

but re-opened two years later. Designed by Andrea Palladio, it dominates views from the Piazzetta and Ducal Palace and itself provides, from the campanile (rebuilt in 1791, now equipped with a lift), one of the most exciting and comprehensive views of Venice and the lagoon. And the spectacular position of San Giorgio Maggiore easily atones for the fact that its façade, as completed by Simone Sorella, does not follow Palladio's more harmonious plan. Palladio intended that, as at San Francesco della Vigna and Il Redentore, the aisle pilasters and the portico columns should rise from the same level as each other.

Coryat toured the church, dutifully copying for his readers such long Latin inscriptions as the one in the north transept detailing the history of the bones of the Protomartyr or first martyr St. Stephen, acquired by an earlier church on the site in the twelfth century. Stephen's stoning is illustrated here in a painting that may be at least partly by Tintoretto, whose late *Last Supper* and *Shower of Manna* hang in the chancel. In 1780 William Beckford, a wealthy and consciously "refined" traveler, had a different conception of the pleasures of church visiting. Having "procured a gondola" and "laid in my provision of grapes" from the market rafts and barges on the Grand Canal, he was rowed to Santa Maria della Salute, beneath whose dome he for a time "expatiated in solitude." Next he "was wafted across the waves to the specious [beautiful] platform in front of San Giorgio Maggiore, one of the most celebrated works of

Palladio." Where more hurried or less refined people might have marched straight into the church, Beckford took time to let his "first transport" of joy subside a little and then allowed himself to absorb the exterior. Having examined "the graceful design of each particular ornament," so as to unite "the just proportion and grand effect of the whole in my mind":

> *I planted my umbrella on the margin of the sea, and viewed at my leisure the vast range of palaces, of porticos, of towers, opening on every side and extending out of sight... To behold at one glance these stately fabrics, so illustrious in the records of former ages, before which, in the flourishing times of the republic, so many valiant chiefs and princes have landed, loaded with oriental spoils, was a spectacle I had long and ardently desired.*

On the island only "aged devotees creeping to their devotions" stirred, and the "buzz of the town" was far off, "so that I ate my grapes and read Metastasio [the Italian lyric poet], undisturbed by officiousness or curiosity." Only when the sun became too strong did he finally—with graceful, unrushed tread, one imagines—enter the spacious nave. Here he admired "the masterly structure of the roof" ("vaulted and hollow like a nut shell," Coryat had noted) "and the lightness of its arches"; then "my eyes naturally directed themselves to the pavement of white and ruddy marble, polished, and reflecting like a mirror the columns that rise from it."

Palladio, who had hoped to rebuild the center of Venice, was overruled by the conservative majority of the patricians. Instead, he operated on the fringes of the city, including San Giorgio and, separated from it by a narrow channel, the large island of Giudecca. Beckford, emerging from the cloisters of San Giorgio, "full of prophecies and bodings," gained his gondola and "arrived, I know not how, at the flights of steps which lead to [Palladio's] *Redentore*." Had he been less rapt he might have noticed, on the way along the Giudecca, another church designed by Palladio. Santa Maria della Presentazione is always called *Le Zitelle* (the Virgins, after the girls trained as lace-makers in the flanking hospice, founded in 1561). This forcefully plain, rather Roman-looking domed church is now a conference center, open to the public only for Sunday mass. Palladio planned it in about 1570 but it was built, by Jacopo Bozzetto, a few years after his death in 1580. In the last few years of his life Palladio had worked on the more striking Redentore (completed 1592), one of the most convincingly classical buildings in Venice: as Beckford rather hyperbolically says, "a structure so simple and elegant, that I thought myself entering an antique temple, and looked about for the statue of the God of Delphi, or some other graceful divinity." Among the annoying signs that this was, after all, a Christian church—a huge bronze crucifix, "the shapes of rueful martyrs peeping out of the niches around," the "bushy beards of Capuchin friars wagging before the altars"—were, surprisingly, "orange and citron trees" in the nave. They were there, he learned, for "grand festivals," when "they turn the whole church into a bower, strew the pavements with leaves, and festoon the dome with flowers." Traditionally the Capuchins preferred more austere surroundings. When the church was first built they complained about its splendor.

The festival on which such festooning was most likely to occur took place on the third Sunday in July, the still popular festival of the Redeemer, instituted in thanksgiving for the end of the great plague of 1576. The doge and senior senators would process each year to the Zattere and, almost like participants in some miraculous happening, move across a bridge of boats and up the steps to the church. The church itself, built by the republic as part of the thank-offering, was positioned with this dramatic climax in mind.

Visitors come to the Giudecca mainly for the Redentore, but it has another identity as a busy residential area, affording the casual stroller glimpses of an everyday Venetian life away from the coral necklaces and postcards. It used to be thought that the island got its name (*Zudeca* or *Zuecca* in Venetian dialect) from Jews who lived here before the Ghetto was established, but more recently it has been suggested that it comes from a word meaning "judgment," after land here was legally apportioned, or "judged" to returning exiles in the ninth century. The name made its most dramatic and lengthy television appearance when Stephen Fry, playing a pretentious character who presumably knew that in standard Italian double consonants are individually pronounced, referred to his time on the "Giudec." There was a seemingly endless pause as, looking upwards, he waited for the rest of the word to land—"ca."

The Lido

The long island that protects Venice from the open sea was once a place for receiving important visitors like Frederick Barbarossa in 1177, or for keeping at arm's length potentially troublesome ones like the crusaders of 1202. The main survivor of that past is the church of San Nicolò al Lido, begun in 1044 by Doge Domenico Contarini, who is commemorated in a monument above the door. On Ascension Day, having wed the sea from the Bucintoro, the doge would attend mass here. Other traces of the island's past are the Jewish cemetery (see p.145) and the remains of various sixteenth-century fortifications intended to hold back or daunt all aggressors and primarily the Turks. These are to be found especially north of San Nicolò; opposite, on the island of Le Vignole, is the still substantial Fortezza di Sant'Andrea, begun in 1543 by the foremost military builder of the time, Michele Sanmichele of Verona, whom the republic employed extensively to shore up its defenses both in the lagoon and in such further outposts as Crete. The fortress exudes dignity and a degree of mystery as well as strength; as Deborah Howard, in her *Architectural History of Venice*, explains:

In the Renaissance, military architecture was not purely functional. It was also a vehicle for the imaginative use of conventional classical elements to express the might and status of the territory within... The design of the triple-arched entrance combines the toughness of the Doric order with the roughness of raw stone. The metopes of the Doric frieze contain symbols of Venetian naval superiority, such as galleons and winged lions. At the corners, hefty square piers reinforce the half columns, protecting the dark, cavernous entrance, lapped by the waves like the haunt of a classical giant.

Since the mid-nineteenth century Lido has developed in other directions. First came sea-bathing—the first establishment dated from 1857—and then the hotels, most famously the Grand Hotel des Bains, where Thomas Mann and his Gustave von Aschenbach stayed (see pp.201-3). Facing the other way, the hotel with Campari sign atop, prominent in views from the Public Gardens end of Venice, is the Europa. Later came shops, golf, residential developments, the international film festival, and even, to the horror or convenience of those arriving from Venice, buses and cars. But in the early nineteenth century, when the island was used neither as a bulwark against invasion nor as a seaside resort, it provided an ideal space for horseriding. Byron came here regularly for that purpose, and in August 1818 he brought Percy Shelley with him.

Shelley had come on delicate business—as the representative of Mary Shelley's stepsister Claire Clairmont, mother of a child by Byron. Byron, exercising the invincible male prerogative of the day, did not see Clairmont as a suitable mother and was keeping the child, Allegra, away from her. At Palazzo Mocenigo Shelley was reassured by his friend's promises that Allegra would soon be able to spend time with her mother; she did, but in the long term would remain cruelly separated until her death in a convent at the age of five in 1822. Shelley then soon found himself in animated conversation with Byron about poetry, religion, and everything else. The poets talked on through the afternoon and the night, both in the palace and while riding at evening on the Lido. Talk often revolved around the fundamental difference in their philosophies. Shelley's idealist faith in "the power of man over his own mind" stood in contrast to Byron's skepticism, and subsequently both the ride and the debate informed Shelley's poem *Julian and Maddalo*. In the process he described the Lido in 1818:

> *I rode one evening with Count Maddalo*
> *Upon the bank of land which breaks the flow*
> *Of Adria towards Venice: a bare strand*
> *Of hillocks, heaped from ever-shifting sand,*
> *Matted with thistles and amphibious weeds,*
> *Such as from earth's embrace the salt ooze breeds,*
> *Is this: an uninhabited sea-side,*
> *Which the lone fisher, when his nets are dried,*
> *Abandons; and no other object breaks*
> *The waste, but one dwarf tree and some few stakes*
> *Broken and unrepaired, and the tide makes*
> *A narrow space of level sand thereon,*
> *Where 'twas our wont to ride while day went down.*
> *This ride was my delight. I love all waste*
> *And solitary places; where we taste*
> *The pleasure of believing what we see*
> *Is boundless, as we wish our souls to be.*

San Lazzaro degli Armeni and San Servolo

Just off the Lido on the lagoon side are the monastery, campanile and gardens of the Armenian monastery. When the Turks captured Modon in southern Greece, Peter of Manug, called Mekhitar ("the consoler") and his fellow Armenian monks fled to Venice. In 1717 the republic granted them the island of San Lazzaro, at one time a leper colony. Byron, seeking to occupy himself in some way other than riding, swimming, sex, or writing poetry, took Armenian lessons here from Father Pasqual Aucher in 1816. He told his friend Tom Moore that "my mind wanted something craggy to break upon; and this—as the most difficult thing I could discover here for an amusement—I have chosen, to torture me into attention." In return he helped to compile, and more importantly to arrange publication of, an Armenian grammar. The monks still proudly display "Byron's room" and other Byron memorabilia in the monastery.

Between San Lazzaro and Venice is the island of San Servolo, once home to a Benedictine monastery and then, from 1725, to a lunatic asylum reserved for sufferers of good family. Shelley's Julian and Maddalo come by gondola to this "windowless, deformed and dreary pile" to see a man who has been driven mad by the disappointment of early hopes and by his lover's abandonment of him—useful fodder for their debate on human nature. Now the inmates are long gone. Eventually the island became, in the 1980s and 1990s, a conservation training center. But almost whatever the use such places are put to, it remains possible to enjoy what Maddalo first brought Julian here to see at evening: the "temples and palaces" gleaming and "Earth and Sea... / Dissolved into one lake of fire."

CHAPTER EIGHT

Theatrical Venice: Opera, Carnival, and Eating

Since the Middle Ages Venice has amazed or entertained visitors with plays, music, processions, games, festivals, and costumes. The visitors' expectations—and purses—have helped to maintain some of the shows, including in modern times the Biennale (the international art exhibition established in 1895) and the film festival, which has taken place annually on the Lido since 1932, when the eclectic choice of films included René Clair's *A Nous la liberté*, James Whale's *Frankenstein* with Boris Karloff, and Leontine Sagan's *Mädchen in Uniform*. This festival has, like those of earlier days, long been an event at which to be seen, "a thing," as Jan Morris puts it, "of minks and speedboats, to which the world's exhibitionists flock as dazzled moths to lamplight." Perhaps such occasions still work, as the old Venetian state believed their carnivals and regattas did, as a useful channel for potentially more dangerous passions.

Some have concluded that Venice itself is theater. John Evelyn, without going quite this far, felt that the "Venetian dames" in particular seemed "always in masquerade" with their crisped and

dyed hair, silk flowers and jewels, "their petticoats coming from their very armpits, so high as that their very breasts flub over the tying place" and especially their tall "choppines." "These," explains Evelyn, "are high heeled shoes particularly affected by these proud dames, or as some say, invented to keep them at home."

Display and interesting concealment in costume were, of course, especially practiced by the city's many prostitutes. Tom Coryat saw them at the theater in 1608, so masked and covered "that no part of their skin could be discerned." Travelers will be wise, he says, to shut their eyes or "turn them aside from these venereous Venetian objects." But he managed keep his own eyes open in order, he claimed, to report all he could to his readers; after all, he said, "the knowledge of evil is not evil." On his fact-finding mission he encountered high-class courtesans in glorious and glittering tapestried rooms, alluring their clients not only with damask gowns fringed with gold, carnation silk stockings, elaborately dressed hair, diamond rings, and fragrant perfume, but with skilled lute-playing and "that heart-tempting harmony of her voice."

Musicians and Mountebanks

The courtesans' lute-playing and sweet singing are only one example of the many sorts of music to be heard in Venice for much of its history. Dr. Charles Burney, who came to gather material for his history of music in 1770, put the city's musical excellence down at least partly to the lack of opportunity for "walking, riding, and all field-sports." He heard serenaders in barges and buskers in the street ("unnoticed here as small-coalmen or oyster-women in England"). He went to the Pietà, where Antonio Vivaldi had taught, and marveled that, as very rarely elsewhere, "the performers, both vocal and instrumental, are all girls; the organ, violins, flutes, violoncellos, and even french-horns, are supplied by these females." If the Pietà was, Burney felt, now rather resting on its laurels, he found the music-making more dynamic at another *ospedale* (hospital, orphanage, and conservatory), the Incurabili, where the girls were trained by Baldassare Galuppi (1706–85), who was also Maestro di Cappella at San Marco from 1762. Galuppi was at the height of his fame, much in demand whether for opera, church music, or pieces for keyboard. He had been given three years off work at San Marco in order to take charge of the opera in St. Petersburg. Burney notes that "Signor Buranello [Galuppi was from the island of Burano] has preserved all his fire and imagination from the chill blasts of Russia, whence he is lately returned." Burney went to see the composer, who ushered him "into his working-room, with only a little clavichord in it, where, he told me, he dirtied paper"; "he has the appearance of a regular family man." Recently there has been some quickening of interest in the music itself, but Galuppi is more often remembered by Robert Browning's poem *A Toccata of Galuppi's*, sitting "stately at the clavichord," "good alike at grave and gay," conjuring a Venice of beautiful transience where "Balls and masks began at midnight, burning ever to mid-day."

On Assumption Day Burney duly admired Galuppi's music in San Marco but concluded that "this church is not very happily formed for music, as it has five domes or cupolas, by which the sound is too much broken and reverberated before it reaches the ear." Possibly he would have found these effects better managed had he been in the basilica nearly two centuries earlier. It was then that the acoustics were first put to resonant effect by the use of *cori spezzati*, the choir distributed in galleries. The foremost composer of the time had been Giovanni Gabrieli, Maestro di Cappella at the basilica between 1585 and 1612.

In the Piazza Burney came across "a great number of vagrant musicians," many with guitars. In their time the Piazza and Piazzetta have hosted everything from jazz concerts and public executions to the "electrical machine" seen by the English poet Samuel Rogers in October 1820. "For a sol [a small coin]," he noted, "you are electrified for your health." In the days of the republic the doge with his trumpeters and attendants often had occasion to pass by on his dignified way to and from the palace and the basilica. On election, medieval doges and their wives, the *dogaresse*, also had patiently to wait as they were saluted in turn by the masters of each *arte* or guild and their followers. Each group came forward in pairs, their gonfalon before them and their music playing. Among those represented were the smiths, tailors, furriers, mercers, glass-workers, cobblers, cloth-workers, fishmongers, and weavers.

Until the fifteenth century there were also jousts. In 1256 Martino da Canale records much breaking of lances before fair dames. In 1458, more ambitiously, the Piazza was transformed into a battlefield with mini-fortress and redoubts. After the fifteenth century, when horses were banned from the city, the mock-sea-battle or *naumachia* became more common. More peaceful regattas have lasted longer; one of the most watchable today is the *regata storica*— historic boats, costumes, and races—on the first Sunday in September. The Piazza was also, on less exalted occasions, the headquarters of the mountebanks. Coryat studied their methods: mounted usually on "a stage... compacted of benches or forms" (whence their name), they promoted their often "very counterfeit and false" wares, including "oils, sovereign waters, amorous songs printed, apothecary drugs and... other trifles" with the aid of music, jokes and inexhaustible sales patter "wherein [the mountebank] doth hyperbolically extol the virtue of his drugs and confections."

Commedia dell'Arte and Goldoni

Another attraction, from the sixteenth century on, was *commedia dell'arte*, originally meaning, in effect, "professional comedy" as opposed to the classicizing *commedia erudita* of the learned amateurs. Commedia dell'arte could be played on makeshift portable stages not unlike the mountebanks' platforms. Sometimes it also found its way into palaces and permanent theaters. Performances were as adaptable as the staging; around basic scenarios and traditional comic routines the actors could improvise almost at will. Their careers were a series of virtuoso variations on the expected behavior of the figures they habitually played, many of them with appropriate masks: old Pantalone, the braggart Capitano, the young lovers, the *zanni* or clowns Arlecchino and Brighella. ("Zany" derives from *zanni*, which itself is a form of Gianni or "Johnny.") This form of comedy was popular throughout northern Italy but probably acquired some of its familiar features in Venice. Pantalone (Shakespeare's "lean and slippered Pantaloon") is an elderly Venetian merchant, outwitted by servants and by the lovers, one of whom is usually his daughter. Arlecchino was originally from Bergamo, synonymous in Venetian eyes with country boorishness, although in later incarnations, including the English Harlequin, he became rather brighter. Most of these figures wore characteristic masks, the source of some of those in later carnivals and in the mask-shops of modern Venice.

The best known Venetian dramatist, Carlo Goldoni (1707–93) started his career devising scenarios for improvised comedy while working, without much success, as a lawyer. Later he went on to write fully scripted plays, for actors without masks, which nevertheless used and developed many of the old comic types and situations. It was Cesare d'Arbès, a famous Pantalone, who went to Pisa in 1748 to persuade Goldoni, who was working there as a still unsuccessful lawyer, to come home and take up the post of staple dramatist at the Teatro Sant'Angelo. This building was subsequently demolished, but two theaters where Goldoni worked do survive, albeit in considerably altered form. The San Giovanni Grisostomo opera house, where he was director in

CARLO GOLDONI

1737, has been since 1834 the Teatro Malibran (named after the mezzo-soprano Maria Malibran), while the San Luca, for which he worked in 1753–62, fittingly became the Teatro Goldoni in 1875. In Campo San Bartolomeo there is a bronze statue of a very genial Goldoni (1883) and at his house, Palazzo Centani in Calle dei Nomboli, is a good small theater museum.

Goldoni wrote a great number of comedies. Those most often performed today subtly blend farce with elements of social and psychological realism. D'Arbès, an actor of wider range than his experience as Pantalone might suggest, was able to exploit his role as both of the much-confused twins in *The Venetian Twins* (1748) to unsettling as well as hilarious effect. In *La casa nova* (1760) the situation approaches farcical bursting-point: an overspending nephew falls out with his rich uncle, the nephew's new wife demands a superior lifestyle, his sister feels displaced by her "airs and graces," the servants haven't been paid for months, and the builders are on strike because they haven't been paid either. But in the event, thanks also to some dexterous plotting, passions are cooled and solutions found because enough people are prepared to swallow their pride and do what love and generosity require.

Not everyone, however, liked this "reform" of the much-loved commedia dell'arte. One of Goldoni's most interesting rivals, the Venetian aristocrat Carlo Gozzi (1720–1806), kept the masks for such popular stylized fantasies as the original *Turandot* (1762). One reason for Goldoni's departure for France in 1762—as well as the hope of more lucrative employment in Paris—was Gozzi's success. In France Goldoni had some dramatic success at the Comédie Italienne and became tutor to Louis XV's daughter. At the Revolution he lost his pension and died in poverty, although the pension was afterwards paid to his widow. But in the long term it was his plays, not Gozzi's, that flourished on the Venetian stage.

Opera

Gozzi, on the other hand, did provide several stories that were later eagerly taken up by opera composers and librettists. And opera, long before and after his day, was enthusiastically promoted in Venice;

indeed its popularity was a factor in the gradual decline of commedia dell'arte. The new art-form had its late sixteenth- and early seventeenth-century origins mainly in Rome and Florence. Following the performance of an *Andromeda* at the Teatro San Cassiano in 1637, several more opera houses opened in Venice, or were converted from playhouses, in rapid succession. Most of the theaters were owned by noble families, anxious as ever to outdo each other and give splendid evidence of their greatness. (At first the audience was exclusive and wealthy, but by the end of the century competition had led to a marked reduction of admission prices.) Spectacular scenes and machines were provided by, among others, Giacomo Torelli, known as "the great sorcerer," and up-to-date music came from the elderly but inventive Claudio Monteverdi, Maestro di Cappella at San Marco since 1613, and the younger Francesco Cavalli. Partly inspired by Cavalli, Monteverdi graced his late operas *Il Ritorno d'Ulisse* and *L'Incoronazione di Poppea* with what David Kimbell in *Italian Opera* has aptly characterized as "exquisitely fashioned melodies." For Kimbell, these works are marked by "their elegant seriousness, the languorous ease with which they float up out of the recitative and dissolve back into it."

L'Incoronazione (not entirely by Monteverdi, it has long been clear), is perhaps the most exciting opera of the period. It leaves audiences with an unresolved dilemma: how to weigh the wise words of the emperor Nero's counselor Seneca (a bass role) against the persuasive sensuality of Nero and Poppea (soprano or counter-tenor and soprano). In theory, some feel, we should shake our heads and say "Ah, but we know wicked Nero killed wicked Poppea soon afterwards." But this awareness must struggle, once Seneca has been forced to suicide and Nero's banished wife gone off lamenting, with the rapturous, seemingly unending interweaving of the final duet of the lovers; its mutual *sì*; its ending, bald enough without the music, seductive with it, on '*O mia vita, o mio tesoro.*' Perhaps the point is that adulterers and murderers can indeed be dangerously enchanting. No doubt some people at the Teatro Santi Giovanni e Paolo in 1642 extracted this ambivalent moral; many visitors, and a good few religious-minded citizens of the day, perceived Venice itself as similarly sensual and corrupting.

Much the most famous opera house of later years was La Fenice, known for its fine acoustics, gorgeously gilt décor, and intimate atmosphere, and gutted by fire on the night of January 29–30, 1996. The interior was reduced to rubble. The façade, badly damaged, stayed precariously standing. The theater's archives and scores were destroyed, and there was a sense of loss not only locally—the Fenice had become one of the symbols of Venice—but more widely in Italy and abroad. At first an electrical fault was blamed, together with firefighters' inability to pump water from two canals that had been emptied for repair work. The theater itself was also closed for repairs when the disaster struck; smoke alarms and other anti-fire devices were to be installed. But soon people began to wonder whether the canals were drained only by coincidence and what caused the electrical fault. Evidence of arson began to accumulate, there were mutterings about the *mafia*, and eventually two electricians were charged. The theater is being rebuilt, like the Campanile, *com'era, dov'era*—"as it was, where it was." It is supposed to rise from the flames, living up to its name (Phoenix) as it did after the conflagration of 1836. But, delayed partly by legal wrangles, it is rising much more slowly than the two years optimistically announced soon after the fire. Dario Fo, the Italian actor, improviser, satirist and playwright, was in Venice to perform in a carnival masquerade at the Teatro Goldoni about ten days after the fire; he described this entertainment as "a comic opera funeral" for La Fenice. Characteristically, Fo had a sharper point to make: the comic opera funeral was "a symbol of Italy today." This, amid the delays in rebuilding the theater, the immense difficulty of actually getting flood barriers put in place at the entrances to the lagoon, and similar problems in other regions, still has a prophetic ring.

The original Fenice opened in 1792. Opera was always its main activity, and in what now seems thoroughly operatic fashion many patrons would arrive and leave by gondola; this was one of the easiest ways to reach the theater, located amid narrow calli and canals in the middle of Venice. From time to time, notably after Rossini's *Semiramide* in 1823, the production almost seemed to take over the canals; on that occasion the after-show aquatic festivities included a boatload of musicians playing tunes from the opera as they—and hundreds of other water-borne fans—escorted the composer's gondola back to his lodgings. Five Verdi operas were premiered here, mostly to great acclaim. The success of *Ernani* in March 1844 firmly established Verdi's reputation and also provided a good opportunity for nationalists, as they threw their red, white, and green bouquets onto the stage, to underline their point with cries of *Viva VERDI*—a thinly disguised way of saluting "Vittorio Emanuele Re d'Italia" (Victor Emmanuel King of Italy). *La traviata*, with its intensely personal focus on the doomed love of Alfredo and Violetta, failed in 1853 partly because it was less suited than most of the composer's work to that sort of emphatic political response. Nevertheless it succeeded in 1854, with some revisions, at another theater in Venice, the San Benedetto.

Almost a century later, in 1951, Igor Stravinsky, looking for an intimate theater and happy, too, about the incentive (the equivalent of $20,000) offered him by the Italian government, chose La Fenice to launch *The Rake's Progress*. This was inspired by Hogarth's prints and had a libretto by W.H. Auden who, after one terrible rehearsal, added to the musical traditions of the canals by taking a drunken gondola ride while singing extracts from *Die Walküre* (according to his fellow voyager, Stravinsky's close friend Robert Craft). In the event *The Rake's Progress* delighted most of its audience. Like many a production over the preceding 160 and succeeding 45 years it was, besides, a great social as well as musical occasion; the audience, Craft reported, was "the *ne plus ultra* of elegance."

Feats and Games

More earthy spectacles have always been available too. At one time there was bullfighting (sometimes in fact, more safely, cow-fighting) in some of the larger squares. A seventeenth-century painting by Josef or Giuseppe Heinz the Younger in the Museo Correr shows the resulting scenes of lively confusion, with spectators at all the windows and balconies of Campo San Polo (and on scaffolds in it), dogs dashing about, people knocked over, and great-feather-hatted hunters pulling on ropes attached to the bulls' horns. More organized feats, also illustrated in the games and pastimes section of the Correr, included the *forze d'Ercole* ("labors of Hercules"), human pyramids that on occasion figured not simply pyramids, but "the Three Bridges" or "the Colossus of Rhodes." Pictures suggest that the pyramids were sometimes as many as eight levels high. Boards helped at some of the lower levels, but the top man was often supported only by the hands of the man beneath him and—when he performed, briefly one hopes, a triumphant headstand—his head.

Teams from eastern and western sectors of the city, the Castellani and the Nicolotti, competed in the forze. The Castellani took their name from the Castello district, the Nicolotti from the church of San Nicolò dei Mendicoli. Their most famous competition was the *Guerra dei pugni* ("war of the fists") in which representatives of the two groups clashed, with a passion poised dangerously between sporting enthusiasm and bloodlust, most famously on the Ponte dei Pugni at Campo San Barnabà. Contemporary images show hapless participants tumbling headlong into the canal. In the end the custom was banned when, in September 1705, fisticuffs gave way, not for the first time, to stabbing.

Somewhat quieter games were *Biribissi* (a version of roulette), *Gioco Reale* (a lottery game), and *Sbaraglino* (backgammon). Early gaming boards, counters, and cards are preserved at the Correr. Gambling was so popular and so ruinous that in 1774 the Maggior Consiglio closed down the Ridotto (originally so named as the *ridotto* or annex of Palazzo Dandolo, in what is now Calle del Ridotto, west of the Piazza). Here patricians could gamble; so could anyone else, curiously, provided they wore a mask. The Council's decision, in response to a widespread view that Venice was becoming steadily more decadent, was symbolically rather than actually important. Gaming, of course, simply continued elsewhere.

Carnival

Gambling, jousts, theater, and *forze d'Ercole* either took place only at Carnival or reached their climax during it. The first reference to Venetian revelry preceding the penitential season of Lent survives from 1268, when masked merrymakers were prohibited from throwing eggs out of windows. There were repeated attempts to regulate such carnival customs over the centuries, but as long as serious violence and sacrilege were avoided, the authorities were, again, happy to tolerate and even to encourage this outlet for subversive instincts. Noisy young men who gate-crashed private parties were censured in the 1630s but could not easily be prevented or tracked down.

Carnival ran traditionally from December 26 to Shrove Tuesday, but by the eighteenth century it began effectively in October, pausing during December 15–26 before starting up again. As well as the activities already mentioned, there was much tumbling and juggling. There were dancing dogs and monkeys and puppet-shows. There was the *volo del Turco* ("flight of the Turk"), in which an acrobat ascended by rope to the top of the campanile of San Marco, came down another rope to present the Doge with flowers and a flattering poem, went up again and finally alighted on a nearby ship. (At least one person died in the attempt.) There were also fortune-tellers; according to the seventeenth-century traveler François Misson, "these pronouncers of oracles have a long tin pipe, through which they speak in the ear of the curious, who stand below the scaffold." To Misson's amusement, priests and monks of all orders were especially "busy about that pipe." Made equally credulous by the carnival atmosphere must have been those enthusiasts for the two Turkish horses who performed four times daily in January 1775. They could, said their promoters, contort themselves into two hundred different shapes, understand Italian, French, and German, do simple arithmetic, distinguish colors, tell the time—hours, quarters, and minutes—from a pocket-watch and even, more expectedly, jump.

Make-believe was, after all, everything at Carnival; Misson says that if you wanted to join in properly with the masquerading in Piazza San Marco "you must be able to maintain the character of the person whose dress you have taken. Thus, for example, when the Harlequins meet, they jeer at one another, and act a thousand fooleries. The doctors [i.e., lawyers] dispute; the bullies vapour and swagger." Even those, more timid perhaps, "who are not willing to be actors in this great theatre," dress as noblemen, Poles "or the like, which obliges them to nothing."

Byron can still begin his carnivalesque poem *Beppo* (1818):

Tis known, at least it should be, that throughout
All countries of the Catholic persuasion,
Some weeks before Shrove Tuesday comes about,
The people take their fill of recreation,
And buy repentance, ere they grow devout,
However high their rank, or low their station,
With fiddling, feasting, dancing, drinking, masking,
And other things which may be had for asking.

Soon afterwards, however, the fun seems to have stopped. Many Venetians felt that Carnival was inappropriate while the city continued under foreign rule. According to William Dean Howells, American consul in Venice from 1861,

Its shabby, wretched ghost is a party of beggars, hideously dressed out with masks and horns and women's habits, who go from shop to shop droning forth a stupid song, and levying tribute upon the shopkeepers. The crowds through which these melancholy jesters pass, regard them with a pensive scorn.

Even after the Austrians left in 1866, Carnival long remained moribund. But since the 1970s there has been a revival. This modern Carnival is more crowded and more commercial than its ancestor, but that, too, was always popular with tourists. Now again the boats and the dry land are full of people in three-cornered hats, masks and capes, plague-doctors with their canes and beaked masks, Columbines and Pantaloons, clowns, more modern Disney disguises, cross-dressing, parading, laughing, singing, face-paints, and confetti.

Markets and Bars

Food has also been used to entertain Venetians and visitors, whether at ducal banquets or in the more private contexts beloved of Giacomo Casanova. During one of his wealthier periods he was able not only to encourage a "lovely divinity" by giving her a good dinner, but to hire rooms and a superior cook for the purpose. The night before the divinity was due, Casanova tried out the menu, sampling "game, fish, oysters, truffles," and dessert, served on the finest Dresden china and silver-gilt plate and accompanied by burgundy and champagne.

The master professed himself satisfied, although eggs, anchovies, and vinaigrette had been unaccountably omitted.

Casanova's cook was, it must be admitted, French. Visitors sampling Italian fare in the same period often complained of rock-hard bread or were mystified by macaroni and lasagne. But there was, for those lucky enough to come across it, fine cooking to be had in Venice. Bread, of course, was the staple fare, but medieval and Renaissance Venetian control of the Adriatic and carefully organized grain imports and granaries helped make famine less likely, and diet more various, than in most of Europe. Fish, naturally enough, has always been important. In the Middle Ages, at the height of the eastern trade, it was (like meat) often strongly spiced. The popularity of rice has also been attributed to the experiences of eastern traders, although risotto—using fish, quails, snails, and a range of vegetables from pumpkins to spinach to artichoke hearts—became a common dish only in the early nineteenth century. Maize was arriving in large quantities in Venice from America by the seventeenth century and, cooked as polenta, soon became widespread throughout northern Italy.

The best-known food from Venice and the Veneto now includes *risotto alle seppie* or *risotto nero*—cuttlefish cooked in their own black (*nero*) ink—and *granseola alla veneziana* (spider-crab with oil and lemon). Other seafood dishes involve *gamberi* (prawns), *dorade* (red mullet), *cozze* (mussels), *cape sante* (scallops), *calamari* (squid), and much else. More surprisingly, *baccalà* or stockfish is imported from Scandinavia and served in Vicenza in oil, milk, garlic, and anchovies and in Venice, as *baccalà mantecato*, in oil, garlic, and parsley. (In other parts of Italy *baccalà* is salted cod and the word *stoccafisso*, more obviously, refers to stockfish.) Moving away from fish and crustaceans there is *risi e bisi* (soup-like risotto with fresh peas and bacon), *fegato alla veneziana* (calf's liver with oil, butter, onions, and parsley), *bigoli* (thick spaghetti), *saor* (sweet-and-sour sauce, dialect for *sapore*, flavor), and the heavier *soppressata* (a spicy pig's-blood and beef version of black pudding). The most popular meats are poultry, veal, and salami.

The raw material for such dishes is available at the Rialto markets, celebrated by Elizabeth David in 1954 for the benefit of a British public mostly convinced that Italians lived solely on pasta and tomatoes. In the early morning, in early summer, the light

> *is so limpid and still that it makes every separate vegetable and fruit and fish luminous with a life of its own, with unnaturally heightened colours and clear stencilled outlines. Here the cabbages are cobalt blue, the beet-roots deep rose, the lettuces clear pure green, sharp as glass. Bunches of gaudy gold marrow-flowers show off the elegance of pink and white marbled bean pods, primrose potatoes, green plums, green peas. The colours of the peaches, cherries, and apricots, packed in boxes lined with sugar-bag blue paper matching the blue canvas trousers worn by the men unloading the gondolas, are in the rose-red mullet and the orange vongole and cannestrelle [clams and the like] which have been prised out of their shells and heaped into baskets... In Venice even ordinary sole and ugly great skate are striped with delicate lilac lights, the sardines shine like newly-minted silver coins, pink scampi are fat and fresh, infinitely enticing in the early dawn.*

Venetian biscuits, pastries, and sweets are partly a legacy from the eastern sugar trade: shops have a wide range of *baicoli*, *zaleti*, and *forti* (biscuits made with butter, cornmeal, cocoa, and molasses), *rosada veneta* (lemon cream pudding), *fritelle di zucca* (pumpkin fritters with sugar and sultanas), *crostoli* (fritters flavored with *grappa*, the powerful local *marc* or "firewater"; not to be confused with *crostini*—fried bread with anchovies and cheese), and the now rather over-familiar *tiramisù* ("pick me up"), originally from Treviso. Perhaps equally familiar to foreign visitors are the main local wines, Valpolicella, Bardolino, and Soave, from vineyards north to north-west of Verona, by Lake Garda, and in the hills east of Verona. Less known is Prosecco, still or sparkling white wine produced between Conegliano and Valdobbiadene, north of Treviso, used also, with peach juice, in the cocktail *Bellini*.

Bellini was created in the 1930s by Giuseppe Cipriani of Harry's Bar, in Calle Vallaresso, near the San Marco *vaporetto* stops. The drink remained without a name until 1948, the year of a Giovanni Bellini exhibition in Venice; the name "Harry's Bar" has a longer history, re-told recently by Cipriani's son and successor Arrigo. In 1929 Cipriani was working as a barman at the Hotel Europa. Harry Pickering, a young man from Boston, a guest at the hotel and enthusiastic patron of the bar, suddenly stopped drinking and admitted, after questioning by the sympathetic Cipriani, that he was "broke." Further questioning revealed that this "rather reckless young man with a nice honest face" had been sent abroad with an aunt in an attempt to cure his drink problem. Instead she drank with him; the family, somehow discovering this, withdrew both the aunt and the money. He needed 10,000 lire (then the equivalent of $5,000) to pay his bills, drink a final dry martini, and go back to America. The barman lent him the money, with what turned out to be extraordinary foresight. In 1931 the now financially comfortable Pickering reappeared, paid back the loan, and added 40,000 lire more with which, he told him, he should open his own establishment. The only condition was that it was to be called Harry's Bar. Cipriani's wife found a small ground-floor rope warehouse—the present site—where business began on May 13, 1931. Americans (among others) continued to gather here, most famously Ernest Hemingway, Humphrey Bogart and Lauren Bacall, and Orson Welles, helping to make Cipriani enough money to buy Locanda Cipriani on Torcello in 1936 and to found the high-class Hotel Cipriani on the Giudecca in 1957.

Cipriani was also the inventor, in 1950, of *Carpaccio*, thin slices of raw beef in a sauce including, in its original version, mayonnaise and lemon-juice. There was a Carpaccio exhibition at the time, and the colors of the dish correspond roughly to the painter's favorite reds and whites. For those not sophisticated or foolhardy enough to eat raw meat—although in fact Cipriani devised his recipe for the benefit of a customer forbidden for health reasons to eat *cooked* meat—there have always been simpler delights. For Thomas Coryat it was fruit. (At this point, however, before telling us about that, Coryat would almost undoubtedly have made inventive play on his preference for nourishment only metaphorically raw: the *Crudities* which, the title-page of his book declares, were "hastily gobbled up" in his travels and have been "newly digested in the hungry air of Odcombe in the County of Somerset.") In Venice he was impressed not only by the buildings, the people, and such wonders as a hailstorm which "yielded stones as great as pigeons' eggs," and "a ball or globe of a certain tower" that was scorched coal-black by lightning, but (perhaps the pigeon eggs had him thinking of food) by the abundance of "corn and victuals" available in this unlikely watery setting:

As for their fruits I have observed wonderful plenty amongst them, as grapes, pears, apples, plums, apricots; ... figs most excellent of three or four sorts, as black, which are the daintiest, green, and yellow. Likewise they had another special commodity when I was there, which is one of the most delectable dishes for a summer fruit of all Christendom, namely musk melons. I wondered at the plenty of them; for there was such store brought into the city every morning and evening for the space of a month together, that not only St. Mark's Place but also all the market places of the city were superabundantly furnished with them: insomuch that I think there were sold so many of them every day for that space, as yielded five hundred pound sterling.

If Coryat's calculation is correct (it seems improbable), Cipriani's seventeenth-century equivalents should have been in musk melons.

Fruit, then as now, was a surprising, juicy, opulent experience for northern Europeans in the south. The melons "are of three sorts," Coryat explains, "yellow, green, and red, but the red is most toothsome of all." But alas, even this tasty and healthy sounding snack had its risks: "I advise thee (gentle reader)," he goes on in his best courteous manner:

> if thou meanest to see Venice, and shall happen to be there in the summer time when they are ripe, to abstain from the immoderate eating of them. For the sweetness of them is such as hath allured many men to eat so immoderately of them, that they have therewith hastened their untimely death: the fruit being indeed... sweet-sour. Sweet in the palate, but sour in the stomach, if it be not soberly eaten. For it doth often breed the Dysenteria, that is, the bloody flux.

Apparently there is no such risk with "another excellent fruit called Anguria" (watermelon). The Venetians "find a notable commodity of it in summer, for the cooling themselves in time of heat. For it hath," as many a parched visitor still finds, "the most refrigerating virtue of all the fruits of Italy."

CHAPTER NINE

Literary Venice: Magnificence and Decadence

The Futurist poet Filippo Tommaso Marinetti and his supporters were in no doubt about how to respond to Venice. In 1910 they climbed the clock tower in Piazza San Marco and cast down among the crowds copies of his pamphlet *Contro Venezia passatista* (Against Past-Loving Venice). Marinetti denounced this "putrefying city, magnificent sore from the past," this city of foreigners, "market for counterfeiting antiquarians, magnet for snobbery and universal imbecility... jeweled bathtub for cosmopolitan courtesans." The "little reeking canals" should be filled in "with the shards of its leprous, crumbling palaces"; "the imposing geometry of metal bridges and howitzers plumed with smoke" must "abolish the falling curves of the old architecture"; electricity must replace moonshine; and all—Marinetti was later for a time associated with Mussolini—to make an industrial, military Venice "that can dominate the Adriatic sea, that great Italian lake."

Images of Venice as a decadent and decaying place had been rife in literature long before Marinetti's radical proposals fluttered down into the Piazza. At the beginning of the seventeenth century, Iago can serve up for Othello's benefit a Venice of "wealthy curled darlings" and women who "do let God see the pranks / They dare not show their husbands." But Iago is not the most trustworthy of witnesses, and on the whole the reputation of the city in his time was very different. In the Middle Ages and the Renaissance foreigners came to marvel at the city's beauty, wealth, splendid ceremonies, accomplished courtesans, and republican constitution. Often they marveled at them all at once, which is perhaps why the rather uninformative description of Venice as the "most triumphant city" is so often quoted in books about Venice. It was difficult more precisely to sum up so many exciting aspects of the one place. (For the original context of Philippe de Commynes' phrase see p.93.)

Venetian settings in Renaissance plays functioned as convenient shorthand for wealth and at least the appearance of civilization. Large loans, far-ranging "argosies" and a lady "richly left" are only to be expected in *The Merchant of Venice* (c. 1595?); "news on the Rialto" might have directly concerned real merchants in Shakespeare's audience. The eponymous hero of Ben Jonson's *Volpone* (1607) wakes at the beginning of the play with the blatant cry "Good morning to the day and next my gold!" That he wakes in Venice makes it the more probable, to the original audience, that his wealth will be limitless, will be worth the pains his equally acquisitive would-be heirs are willing to go to in the hope of obtaining it. One disinherits his son in favor of the apparently dying Volpone; another, although violently jealous by nature, virtually prostitutes his innocent young wife to him; all turn up with regular donations of massy plate, bulging money-bags or pearls in the hope of persuading Volpone to leave everything to them.

When not being dazzled by Venetian riches, outsiders enjoyed reading about, or studying at first hand, the constitution of the republic. For only here, as Edward Muir puts it in *Civic Ritual in Renaissance Venice*, was it possible to encounter a republican ideology which was, for once, "bedfellow with a real, observable commonwealth." (Most discussions of how to do without a monarch had to make do with ancient examples from Athens and early Rome.) The extraordinary measure of independence from the papacy and other Catholic powers was another feature that greatly appealed to Protestant visitors and readers. Sir Philip Sidney's elderly mentor Hubert Languet urged him to confine his Italian journey to the Veneto. As a young man in 1587 Sir Henry Wotton (1568–1639), later English ambassador in

PAOLO SARPI

Venice, did go to Rome but was so mindful of the possible attentions of the Inquisition that he disguised himself as a German Catholic, "as light in my mind as in my apparel," with "a mighty blue feather" in his hat. For these reasons, among Venice's most popular exports to the north were the writings of Fra Paolo Sarpi (1552–1623).

When Venice was threatened with papal interdict in 1606 Sarpi, a Servite friar born in the city, became legal adviser to the senate. He was already well known as theologian, jurist and scientist; he worked with Galileo on his telescope. His job now, carried out with skill and conviction, was to defend the republic's stand against the pope on issues of church land-holding and whether Church or state courts should try clergy accused of serious crimes. The interdict was imposed, but Venice was able to count on the support of most countries other than Spain; Protestants naturally sided against the pope and many Catholics also had little desire to see secular independence limited by the Church. This, and the force of Sarpi's advocacy, persuaded Rome effectively to back down in 1607. Such keenly argued works as his *Trattato dell' Interdetto* (*Treatise on the Interdict*) had an appreciative audience abroad as well as at home.

Some years after the crisis had passed, Sarpi went on to produce, on a much larger scale, his *History of the Council of Trent*, a scathing exposé of the corruption and conspiracy he saw at the heart of the Church's great Counter-Reformation council. This time, since Venice had accepted the conclusions of Trent, Sarpi's work had to be published (in 1619) in England, where it subsequently helped to earn him from John Milton the title "the Great Unmasker." The republic continued as far as possible to protect its faithful servant, but he was lucky to survive three assassination attempts by papal agents. There might have been more attempts had more of the friar's *pensieri* (thoughts) been published. Here Sarpi's secularism is even more radical; David Wootton goes so far as to argue, on the basis of them, that he was actually an atheist (*Paolo Sarpi: Between Renaissance and Enlightenment*). A bronze statue (1892) commemorates Sarpi in Campo Santa Fosca, near the bridge where the first attempt on his life left him with a badly scarred face in 1607.

Sycophants and Courtesans

In an earlier generation the best-known Venice-based author was a more colorful figure. Pietro Aretino (1492–1556) was famous for sharp satire and plain speaking, for uproarious laughter and the unashamed amassing of riches, for erotic writing and experience, for his burly, great-bearded, expensively robed presence. He took his name from Arezzo in Tuscany, where he was born the son of a cobbler. His progress in the world was due, almost uniquely in his time, to prowess with the pen. He also trained for a time as a painter and would later, in Venice, become a close friend of Titian. As a young man he worked in Rome, where his patron Pope Leo X succeeded in protecting him from the many enemies he had lampooned. With Leo's successors his relationship was more uneven; he left Rome 1525. In 1527, the year of the sack of Rome by the German troops of the Emperor Charles V, Aretino decided to opt for the comparative safety and tolerance of Venice. He obtained the patronage of Doge Andrea Gritti and his son Luigi, flattered anyone else who mattered, and did his bit for the Venetian propaganda machine. He won Venetian hearts by his spoken and published contrasts between corrupt and turbulent Rome and just, liberal and tranquil Venice. When he dies, he declares hyperbolically in a letter to one inhabitant, may God make him into a gondola, or at least its canopy. If that is too much to ask, let him be one of the oars, a rowlock, a baler. How much better to be the door of the campanile of San Marco than to enjoy what popes are said to enjoy in Paradise—though he begs leave to doubt that any pope has really entered Paradise.

Soon Aretino was installed in Casa Aretino, a well-appointed palace on the Grand Canal next to Rio di San Giovanni Grisostomo. (Among its later names was Palazzo Bolani-Erizzo.) On October 21, 1537, he wrote in grateful celebration to his landlord, the patrician Domenico Bolani. From his windows he can see, at market-time, thousands of people and gondolas. Fruit and vegetables are everywhere; twenty-odd sailboats laden with melons make an island. Recently a special treat was watching a boatload of Germans, who had just come out of a tavern, deposited in the cold canal. (Their headquarters, the Fondaco dei Tedeschi, was nearby.) At other times less ridiculous objects meet the great ridiculer's eyes. Orange-trees "gild the base" of the Palazzo dei Camerlenghi. Regattas pass by. At night the lights are like scattered stars. The neighbors include the "honored" Maffio Lioni (who later had to leave Venice in a hurry having passed state secrets to the French) and his three worthy grandsons. Altogether, Bolani is gratifyingly assured, any genius Aretino's works possess comes from "the graces conferred" by the *felicità ariosa*, the "airy happiness," of the house. In 1551, however, he was to adopt a very different note, one of wounded dignity, in writing to Bolani when he refused to extend his lease. Aretino may have paid him, until then, in little or nothing but fine words.

The interior of the palace was decorated by such distinguished friends of the tenant as Titian and Sansovino. Tintoretto painted a ceiling. Gifts and letters from the mighty were prominently displayed; often even princes were persuaded to pay for his good word. Both Charles V and his great rival François I did so more than once. François also sent him, in 1533, the more ambiguous gift of a sizable gold chain with tongue-shaped pendants inscribed *Lingua eius loquetur mendacium*: "his tongue speaks a lie." Unabashed, Aretino replied that if this was the case, his flattery of the king must be untruthful. The English, befitting their reputation at the time, tried dealing with him not with wit, but with violence. In 1547, when Aretino complained that Ambassador Harwell was detaining money promised him by the recently dead Henry VIII, Harwell's servants cudgeled him unconscious. It is not clear whether the accusation had been justified, but the ensuing scandal produced both an apology and the cash.

Aretino went on spending lavishly, entertaining his friends, involved in love affairs and briefer sexual encounters, and writing plays, pamphlets, and his *Ragionamenti*—dialogues in praise of prostitution. On October 21, 1556, at a tavern with a large party of friends, he let out a loud laugh at some jest and fell from his chair in an apoplectic fit. He died soon afterwards. He had been living for five years in a fourteenth-century house (no. 4168) on Riva del Carbon and was buried at the church of San Luca, but there is no trace of his tomb.

Much less is known about Aretino's contemporary Gaspara Stampa (c.1523–54). The *Rime di Madonna Gaspara Stampa* appeared soon after her death: a vast, inventive, intense cycle of love-poems (mostly sonnets) exploring and renewing the Petrarchan tradition. Petrarch was one inspiration, the author's no longer requited love for Count Collaltino di Collalto another more personal source. Stampa moved to Venice with her mother and sister in 1531 following the death of her father, a jeweler in Padua. The women's house became established as a *ridotto*, meaning, in this case, a salon or center for the intimate performance of poetry and music. The sisters Gaspara and Cassandra were well known as musicians. Some argue that they must also have been courtesans, the women whose status—above common prostitutes but freer from constraint than respectable ladies—was most likely to enable artistic self-development.

Veronica Franco (1546–91), who was certainly a *cortigiana onesta*, a high-class courtesan, was keenly aware of the ambiguities of this position. True, men might appreciate her poems as well as her sexual favors; in her *Terze rime* she succeeds in undermining the Petrarchan tradition and its usually passive females by including rather conventional Petrarchist poems by male friends or lovers as well as her own more forceful and honest replies. But her personal position was always vulnerable. The cultivated patricians Domenico and Marco Venier treated her, it would appear, as more of an equal than they would most women of their own class and family. But Marco's cousin Maffio could attack her with impunity in a sonnet beginning *Veronica, ver unica puttana*, "Veronica, veritably unique whore." In the poem probably intended as her reply she can challenge him only, if spiritedly, to a duel of words with the weapon of his choice, whether vernacular—*lingua volgar Veneziana*—or in formal Tuscan, whether *seria* or *burlesca*. And, in contrast with Aretino's attitude to prostitution in the *Ragionamenti*, one of her *Lettere familari* firmly advises a woman not to allow her daughter to become a courtesan. It is a terrible thing, she writes, to force your body into slavery, to put yourself at risk of being robbed, killed, or infected with horrifying diseases; "to eat with the mouth of another, to sleep with the eyes of another, to move in accordance with another's desire." And damnation hereafter is inevitable.

For all that, Franco herself is in the profession. Her writings helped, and were intended to help, attract clients. This is obviously so for poems that, as Sara Maria Adler has said, counsel "a sane hedonism," examples of an art which is "generated not by the suffering of love denied but rather by aspirations toward love fulfilled, by the energy of her exuberant sensuality." But even a letter on the disadvantages of the profession could further the same aim by adding to her reputation for refinement; and this was at least likely to keep her among the "better sort" of clients and so somewhat less open to the dangers she describes. When, in 1580, she was summoned before the Inquisition on suspicion of witchcraft, her high connections as well as her sheer intelligent forthrightness soon led the case to be dismissed. Catherine McCormack's Franco routs the Inquisition conclusively in the climactic scene of *The Honest Courtesan*, a film by Marshall Herskovitz based on her writings and her relationship with Marco Venier, as studied in Margaret Rosenthal's book of the same name.

Great Expectations

Franco, like many contemporary poets, wrote also in celebration of renowned and resplendent Venice, its glittering palaces and glorious past. But it was visitors who, especially from the eighteenth century onwards, spent more time dwelling on its particular beauties, its picturesque or evocative scenes. By this time they came full of expectations generated by paintings and prints, histories, poems, and other visitors. The encounter with an actual Venice could be either problematic or enriching.

When William Beckford approached from Mestre he "began to distinguish Murano, St. Michele, St. Giorgio in Alga, and several other islands, detached from the grand cluster, which I hailed as old acquaintance; innumerable prints and drawings having long since made their shapes familiar." Beckford, who saw himself as a connoisseur both of arts and of rarefied experience, could compliment himself on having made such good "acquaintance" before setting off from England. But for the Irish traveler Lady Sydney Morgan, even when you see Venice, it "still appears rather a phantasm than a fact." Charles Dickens, in *Pictures from Italy* (1846), agrees: he finds a magical city and casts it as a dream in which he glides

> *Below stone balconies, erected at a giddy height, before the loftiest windows of the loftiest houses. Past plots of garden, theatres, shrines, prodigious piles of architecture—Gothic—Saracenic—fanciful with all the fancies of all times and countries. Past buildings that were high, and low, and black, and white, and straight and crooked; mean and grand, crazy and strong. Twining among a tangled lot of boats and barges, and shooting out at last into a Grand Canal! There, in the errant fancy of my dream, I saw old Shylock passing to and fro upon a bridge, all built upon with shops and humming with the tongues of men; a form I seemed to know for Desdemona's, leaned down through a latticed blind to pluck a flower. And, in the dream, I thought that Shakespeare's spirit was abroad upon the water somewhere: stealing though the city.*

But here the dream conceit becomes rather strained; there is a feeling that the writer may not really be quite as excited as he feels he ought to be, perhaps that he is being duly Dickensian about Venice rather than directly responding to it. Dickens is most at home when describing the ducal prisons and instruments of torture. Perhaps he should have dwelt longer on these or in sinister, congenially Dickensian back alleys; these have often been productive of good novels set in Venice while the Grand Canal has often flowed purple with descriptions of its perfection.

Rainer Maria Rilke had a longer and more complex relationship with the city: "each time," he wrote in 1912, "we never seem to finish with one another, and it would be good to see what it is we expect each from the other." He went on searching through many visits, whether based in rooms on the Zattere or in the palaces of aristocratic friends like Pia Valmarana (Palazzo Valmarana in San Vio), but concluded that "I've used Venice as I've used all my surroundings these last few years, asking more of them than they can give... trying to terrify things by aiming at them point-blank this pistol loaded with expectation." Inspiration came more easily in more solitary surroundings, much further up the Adriatic coast toward Trieste. Here, in the cliff-top castle of Princess von Thurn und Taxis, Rilke began work on *The Duino Elegies* in 1911.

Byron's "fairy city of the heart"

One of the great generators of expectation was Byron's account in the best-selling *Childe Harold's Pilgrimage*, canto four (1818), with its famous opening:

> I stood in Venice, on the Bridge of Sighs;
> A palace and a prison on each hand:
> I saw from out the wave her structures rise
> As from the stroke of the enchanter's wand:
> A thousand years their cloudy wings expand
> Around me, and a dying Glory smiles
> O'er the fair times, when many a subject land
> Look'd to the winged Lion's marble piles,
> Where Venice sat in state, throned on her hundred isles!

Byron himself was full of ideas about Venice years before he settled there in 1816. From boyhood he loved this "fairy city of the heart, / Rising like water-columns from the sea," which was "Of joy the sojourn, and of wealth the mart." Shakespeare and Thomas Otway (whose 1682 play *Venice Preserv'd* is based loosely on a Spanish-led conspiracy to overthrow the republic in 1618) had "stamp'd her image in me." He told his friend the Irish poet Thomas Moore that the city "has always been (next to the East) the greenest island of my imagination." What Byron found in the city itself—Austrian rule, the Bucintoro "rotting unrestored" while "The spouseless Adriatic mourns her lord," palaces crumbling away—might have been disillusioning. Instead it nourished the idea of a Venice where the past informed the present: the "thousand years" of the republic are past but not absent and the city is "Perchance even dearer in her day of woe, / Than when she was a boast, a marvel, and a show." ("*Venezia passatista!*" we hear Marinetti mutter.)

This perspective is easily possible in early nineteenth-century Venice, still sea-girt, full of signs of the glorious past, alive in literature. It is seemingly a world of its own, a place where fantasy can wander amid the "water-columns." Here Byron could conduct his personal life in public, in defiance of the England he had left; ever since his youthful Mediterranean expedition in 1810–12 "Abroad" had represented freedom. Escape became more urgent following his disastrous marriage to Annabella Milbanke and its scandalous aftermath. Much of the fashionable society that had heaped adulation on the poet of the first two *Childe Harold* cantos and exotic eastern tales now ostracized him. There was talk that he was mad. His debts, as ever, continued to rise. Soon after his separation became official he left, bruised but free, for the Continent. In Venice he availed himself to the full of the local tolerance for the foibles and predilections of a foreign *milord*.

During 1818–19 Byron leased Palazzo Mocenigo on the Grand Canal. Here he engaged in much casual sex (long his habit, but also intended to spite the conventional society that he had left or been expelled by) and two more substantial relationships. These affairs he both participated in and, at the same time, observed with detachment as a characteristically Venetian phenomenon. Marianna Segati, the wife of a "Merchant of Venice," a draper who was conveniently often away, was "altogether like an antelope," with "large, black, oriental eyes" of a sort rare in Europe. Byron enjoyed as well as endured the most un-English outbursts of his lovers: Segati raining jealous slaps on her sister-in-law before collapsing into his arms; Margarita Cogni, the *fornarina* or baker's wife, who came to Palazzo Mocenigo as housekeeper, knocking down her rivals "amid great confusion—and great demolition of head dresses and handkerchiefs" and, at the end of the affair, trying to knife him and throwing herself into the canal. Byron's letters perhaps exaggerate some of the details; as he writes, he is busy evolving the latest of his shifting self-images.

Byron also flung himself into Carnival, although at last even he began to flag, at which point he sent Thomas Moore his poem "So we'll go no more a roving / So late into the night"; since at last the sword wears out the sheath and the soul the breast,

Though the night was made for loving,
And the day returns too soon,
Yet we'll go no more a roving
By the light of the moon.

After-the-party melancholy often tinges writing in or about Venice. More vigorously, Byron once swam across from the Lido and up the length of the Grand Canal (3³/₄ miles). In doing this he was fulfilling his belief that deeds count for more than words. He was also furthering his already well-developed myth. He made more of his earlier swim across the Hellespont in imitation of the legendary Leander, but there was a special resonance in performing such a feat in Venice, itself a place, seemingly, of myth—associating yourself with its waters is one way of becoming part of the myth.

Smaller aquatic exploits are more likely, however, to make us laugh: one response, perhaps, by dwellers in drier places to the perceived incongruity of using canals as streets. Nevertheless the English eccentric Frederick Rolfe, "Baron Corvo" (1860–1913), who lived in Venice from 1908, managed to come out of an unpredicted dive into the Rio di San Vio with some, still rather comic, dignity. In "On Cascading into the Canal," an article published in *Blackwood's Magazine* in 1913, he tells the tale of how, having lost his balance while rowing a gondola, he heard the horrified shouts and prayers of the passers-by and so decided that he had better give them "something truly rare and wholesome to cough about." He "swam, submerged, about thirty yards up the Rio, passionlessly emerging (to a fanfare of yells) in a totally unexpected place, with a perfectly stony face, and the short pipe still stiff and rigid in an immovable mouth."

Byron left Venice mainly because he met there, and fell in love with, Countess Teresa Guiccioli and went, in her wake, to her native Ravenna. During his Venetian period, fortunately, he had written hard as well as living hard. The Venetian verse story *Beppo* helped prepared the way, in its deliberately digressive manner and virtuoso use of *ottava rima*, for his masterpiece *Don Juan*, begun at Palazzo Mocenigo in the summer of 1818. Later he wrote two verse plays on Venetian historical figures (as interpreted by later chroniclers and himself), *Marino Faliero* and *The Two Foscari*. But it was the *Childe Harold* canto that became an unavoidable part, for several generations, of European and American preconceptions about, and ways of responding to, Venice: dying glory, beautiful melancholy. His much publicized lifestyle contributed to the Venetian reputation for decadence, fueled also by Casanova's memoirs and older tales of courtesans.

Ruskin's Vision

Among those whose early mental furniture included *Childe Harold* was John Ruskin (1819–1900). Venice in his writing and drawings is often a more precisely real place than Byron's version. He studied the monuments in meticulous detail, striving to understand the principle of every pattern and motif, often recording for posterity elements that would soon be lost by neglect or misguided restoration. On the other hand, the use Ruskin puts his Venice to is no less visionary, in its way, than Byron's "fairy city" or the light-dissolved palaces and canals painted by J.M.W. Turner in the 1830s. (Turner's illustrations for the popular 1830 edition of Samuel Rogers' poem *Italy* were, together with the poem itself, another early influence on Ruskin.) For him the city is a dream, an argument, a contradiction of other people's architectural and more general notions. In *The Stones of Venice* (1851–3) Ruskin argues passionately that standards in architecture reflect "the moral or immoral temper of the State"; Byzantine and Gothic are not just architectural styles, but the fruit of whole states of moral being, which were once most clearly located, in Ruskin's powerful imaginings, in Venice. Gothic art in particular reflects a healthy society with craftsmen at its center. Renaissance palaces look picturesque only because they contrast with their true Gothic neighbors or with busy scenes and green waves. Since the Middle Ages, with some exceptions (Ruskin's arguments are usually riddled with fascinating inconsistencies), the enemies of art and morality have prevailed. Venice is under assault

from modernizers with their hideous gas-lamps "in grand new iron posts of the last Birmingham fashion" (he shudders at the thought of serenades by gaslight) and above all their railway-bridge which linked Venice to the mainland in 1845.

The damage is compounded by the attitude of those who, like Ruskin's younger self and his Romantic predecessors, unthinkingly relish the dilapidation of old buildings. The true Venice has been obscured by romantic dreams and three centuries of change. "Henry Dandolo or Francis Foscari... would literally recognise not one stone of the great city":

The remains of their Venice lie hidden behind the cumbrous masses which were the delight of the nation in its dotage; hidden in many a grass-grown court, and silent pathway, and lightless canal, where the slow waves have sapped their foundations for five hundred years, and must soon prevail over them for ever.

We must learn from this state of affairs:

It must be our task to glean and gather them forth, and restore out of them some faint image of the lost city; more gorgeous a thousand fold than that which now exists, yet not created in the day-dream of the prince, nor by the ostentation of the noble, but built by iron hands and patient hearts, contending against the adversity of nature and the fury of man.

Visionary proclamations like this also have their practical consequences for the future, since Ruskin exerted great influence on those who went beyond "gleaning and gathering" to the sensitive preservation and restoration of the buildings.

Ruskin, too passionate about his work to have much tolerance for the imperfections of his fellow beings, later complained that people—coming in ever increasing numbers now across the dreaded railway bridge—took *The Stones of Venice* with them and helped themselves "through the tedium of the business by due quantity of ices at Florian's, music by moonlight on the Grand Canal, paper lanterns" and English newspapers. But, apart from the practical results of his influence, particularly the contribution of *The Stones* to the Gothic revival (disliked by him) and to the movement to save Venice in the following century, readers were captivated by the fact that, as Jan Morris puts it

> he worked always, right or wrong, in the fire of conviction, just as the medieval master-masons of his imagination stood on the dizzy scaffold of their towers, or paced their echoing vaults, in the certainty that they were doing the work of God.

Proust and Memory

In May and October 1900 Marcel Proust stayed in Venice, partly in order to pursue his interest in Ruskin, two of whose books he translated. The Venice encountered by the narrator of *A la recherche du temps perdu* (1913–27), however, is not a place of Ruskinian absolutes. It is compounded of expectations and associations from Ruskin and other sources, memory, and their subtle intersections. The young Marcel in *Du côté de chez Swann* is so excited by the prospect of actually visiting Venice and Florence, until now cities of the imagination, so excited at the reality suggested when his father warns him to take warm clothes because in April it may still be cold on the Grand Canal, that he develops a fever and cannot go. Years later, in *Albertine disparue* (printed first as *La fugitive*), he and his mother at last spend a few weeks in Venice. It remains in some senses a city of the imagination; descriptions emphasize less some immutable essence of Venice of the variety sought by Ruskin than its personal effect, the way an individual perceives and so constructs it. The most important scene in Venice (whose importance becomes clear only in the last part of the novel, *Le temps retrouvé*) is when narrator and mother enter the Baptistery at San Marco:

> treading underfoot the marble and glass mosaics of the paving, in front of us the wide arcades whose curved pink surfaces have been slightly warped by time, thus giving the church, wherever the freshness of this colouring has been preserved, the appearance of having been built of a soft and malleable substance like the wax in a giant honeycomb and, where on the contrary time has shrivelled and hardened the material and artists have embellished it with gold tracery, of being the precious binding, in the finest Cordoba leather, of the colossal Gospel of Venice. Seeing that I needed [he is doing some work on Ruskin] to spend some time in front of the mosaics representing the Baptism of Christ, and feeling the icy coolness that pervaded the baptistery, my mother threw a shawl over my shoulders.

In *Le temps retrouvé* the Baptistery returns unexpectedly. Depressed, failing to create, unable to recapture past joy, Marcel happens to step on uneven paving stones in the courtyard of the Hôtel de Guermantes. Joy returns for no apparent reason. Worry about the future is removed. He thinks of blueness, coolness and dazzling light. Finally he realizes "It was Venice," where, in the Baptistery, he and his mother had stood on uneven tiles. This instance of "involuntary memory" makes death seem insignificant, establishes a continuity with the narrator's seemingly lost earlier self and experiences, and gives him the confidence to write the book which, as far as we are concerned, he has just written. He no longer needs to search in places outside himself for what is within, available to involuntary memory.

Death in Venice

Gustav von Aschenbach, in Thomas Mann's *Death in Venice*, cannot thus subsume or escape the actual Venice. Mann himself holidayed, rather less traumatically, with his wife and brother at the Hôtel des Bains, on the Lido, in the summer of 1911. He observed the Polish boy Wladyslaw Moes, the starting point for Tadzio in the novella.

(Aschenbach's external features are based on those of Gustav Mahler, who was acquainted with Mann and had died very recently; he has perhaps come to seem more Mahlerian since Luchino Visconti used the Adagietto of the Fifth symphony in his 1970 film of the book.) Aschenbach, the successful writer, has until now always obeyed the dictates of Apollo—high art—and not those of Dionysus—uninhibited pleasure. In Venice, freed from conventional duties and attitudes, he falls rapidly and completely in love with the beautiful boy. Coming out of the sea, "this living figure, virginally pure and austere, with dripping locks, beautiful as a tender young god... conjured up mythologies, it was like a primeval legend, handed down from the beginning of time, of the birth of form, of the origin of the gods." Recklessly, Aschenbach follows Tadzio and his sisters, "his footsteps guided by the daemonic power whose pastime is to trample on human reason and dignity." Venice, long past its golden time, contributes to this daemonic power: as his gondola follows Tadzio's, the air is foul; "the sun burnt down through a slate-covered haze";

> The marble steps of a church descended into the canal, and on them a beggar squatted, displaying his misery to view, showing the whites of his eyes, holding out his hat for alms. Farther on a dealer in antiquities cringed before his lair, inviting the passer-by to enter and be duped. Yes, this was Venice, the fair frailty that fawned and that betrayed, half fairy-tale, half snare; the city in whose stagnating air the art of painting once put forth so lusty a growth, and where musicians were moved to accords so weirdly lulling and lascivious.

This is the city which "sickened and hid its sickness for love of gain," which provides not only the sultry weather that helps cholera spread, but the people (hoteliers, officials, and others) who have a vested interest in denying this.

Once, Aschenbach tries to leave, getting as far as the station only to discover that his luggage has been sent to the wrong destination—an excuse, gleefully seized, to go back to the hotel. (The difficulty of leaving Venice is a recurrent theme. Rawdon Brown cannot leave in Browning's sonnet [see p.118]. Marcel in *Albertine disparue* nearly succeeds in staying on after the agreed leaving date, but at the last minute joins his mother on the train.)

Aschenbach tries to reprove himself for sinking to the level (as he dreams) of a wild follower of Dionysus, "who bit and tore and swallowed smoking gobbets of flesh—while on the trampled moss there now began the rites in honour of the god, an orgy of promiscuous embraces—and in his very soul he tasted the bestial degradation of his fall." But he cannot break free and, sitting watching Tadzio on the beach on the morning of the day when the Polish family are to leave, succumbs to the disease and dies. Love and death fuse: "it seemed to him the pale and lovely Summoner out there smiled at him and beckoned; as though with the hand he lifted from his hip, he pointed outward as he hovered on before into an immensity of richest expectation."

Mann's is perhaps the most famous sinister Venice, although his interest is more in the battle of the Apollonian and the Dionysiac, the metaphorically northern and southern. Ronald Hayman, in his biography of Mann, sees *Death in Venice* as "an expression of regret that the author had made too many sacrifices to Apollo and too few to Dionysus." At the same time, however, it acts as a safety-valve: "anarchic impressions are projected onto a character... as part of a carefully structured and highly polished narrative." There have been many other sinister Venices: the ones in minor nineteenth-century tales and novels full of dangerous *bravi*, arbitrary arrests and bodies in the canals; or the sensual, superficially fulfilling place in Jacques Offenbach's *Les Contes d'Hoffmann*. In a palace overlooking the Grand Canal Hoffmann's loyal, restraining friend (his Muse in human form) Nicklausse sings, with the much-admired courtesan Giulietta, the famous *barcarole* ("boat-song") in praise of seductive night, "Belle nuit, ô nuit d'amour... " Controlled by the Devil in the form of Captain Dapertutto ("Everywhere"), Giulietta will offer Hoffmann her love in exchange for his reflection (this is an "opéra fantastique" from a play based loosely on the fantastic tales of E.T.A. Hoffmann). He will also, having been helpfully handed a rapier by Dapertutto, kill a rival in a duel while, ironically, an off-stage chorus continues to sing of the "belle nuit... plus douce que le jour." And for his pains he gets only the sight of Giulietta floating past in a gondola with the diabolical captain. The *barcarole* tune had featured in an earlier Offenbach piece in connection with the Rhine, not the Grand Canal, and there were difficulties with the Venice scenes because the composer died before finishing work on them, but the setting of the cruelly beautiful city has become indelibly associated with *Hoffmann*.

No less dangerous is the modern and realistic setting of Michael Dibdin's crime novel *Dead Lagoon* (1994), where the detective Aurelio Zen, returning to his native Venice, encounters layers of corruption beyond even his practiced expectation. This is a place from which the life is ebbing away as only the areas interesting to tourists prosper, while elsewhere communities dwindle. A *campo*, which in Zen's childhood was "grand in stature, full of significance, peopled with a vast and curious cast of every age and character, inexhaustible and yet coherent," now looks "diminished, paltry, and deserted." The newspaper records six births and twenty-one deaths:

> *Twenty-one unique and irreplaceable repositories of local life and lore had been destroyed, while most of the six new citizens would be forced to emigrate in search of work and accommodation. In another fifty years, there would be no Venetians left at all.*

There is a danger, Venetian separatists maintain, that all links with the past will be broken and the city survive only as "Veniceland, a wholly-owned Disney subsidiary with actors dressed up as the Doge and the Council of Ten and catering by McDonald's." But, perhaps making this prospect in the end more likely, the separatist movement itself is, in the novel, riddled at the highest level with corruption. *Dead Lagoon* is remarkable for its convincing Venetian bar, street, and *vaporetto* scenes, or the chapter involving a night chase around much of the city from Cannaregio to the Lido on foot and by boat, but near the center of Dibdin's version of the city is the island with which the novel begins, the overgrown, snake-infested Sant'Ariano, final dumping ground for Venetian bones, and, beyond, "the desolate swamps and salt-flats of the *laguna morta*—the dead marshlands, unrefreshed by tidal currents." Venetian settings are also important in Donna Leon's series of books about Commissario Guido Brunetti. He encounters corruption, seedy bars, corpses in the canal, and even a conductor poisoned during a performance of *La traviata* at the Fenice.

In *The Comfort of Strangers* Ian McEwan brings a holidaying English couple to their doom through a superficially more familiar Venice. Especially when you re-read the novel, however, danger signals are all around. The disorienting effect of distance from home and of the city where visitors always get lost—which is, adding to the sense of disorientation, nearly but not quite explicitly Venice—will lead Colin and Mary into places and positions, let them fall victim to deceptions, for which their essentially normal relationship cannot prepare them. As in some other McEwan novels, the end should be read only by the strong of nerve. Dangerous Venices are seen in a wider context in Caryl Phillips' *The Nature of Blood*, which interweaves the three stories of a Holocaust victim, of Jews in the fifteenth-century Venetian-ruled community of Portobuffole who are charged with, and executed for, a murder they did not commit, and an African general, increasingly evidently to be identified with Othello, who is excluded by Venetian society except when it needs him.

Fictional constructions of Venice as merely "decadent" rather than mainly sinister or dangerous can have a more positive side. "This is the city of disguises," says Villanelle, one of the two early nineteenth-century narrators of Jeanette Winterson's *The Passion* (1987). "What you are one day will not constrain you on the next. You may explore yourself freely, and if you have wit or wealth, no one will stand in your way. This city is built on wit and wealth and we have a fondness for both, though they do not have to appear in tandem." Villanelle, web-footed descendant of boatmen, makes the most of this insight, particularly in the early part of the novel when she uses various disguises and plays various roles—male and female—at the Casino.

Henry James

One of the authors who has, with Ruskin, most affected the image of Venice is Henry James, who came first in 1869 and last in 1907. In the interim he felt keenly that the place was becoming more and more commercialized; it is by 1882 a "great bazaar" where that "exquisite edifice," San Marco, full of natives trying to persuade you to hire their services, is "the biggest booth." When he collected the earlier essays that make up *Italian Hours* (1910) James noted in his preface that "The fond appeal of the observer concerned is all to aspects and appearances—above all to the interesting face of things as it mainly *used* to be." But his evocation of those "aspects and appearances," of paintings, buildings, atmospheres, the play of light, "old Italian sketchability," has gone on informing modern responses. The essays cover, in reflective Jamesian mode, the familiar sights. ("There is notoriously nothing more to be said on the subject" of Venice; "it is not forbidden, however, to speak of familiar things, and I hold that for the true Venice-lover Venice is always in order.") But sometimes they also, perhaps more interestingly, visit such sites of personal significance as Ca' Alvisi, the home, near the mouth of the Grand Canal, of the wealthy expatriate American, Katharine de Kay Bronson.

Originally from Boston, Bronson was a friend and devoted admirer of Robert Browning, whom she entertained here and in her house at Asolo. (She also owned the Giustiniani-Recanati palace, adjoining Ca' Alvisi.) James was among her many other guests at what is now part of the Hotel Europa-Regina. Opposite Santa Maria della Salute, Bronson's home played

> *the part of a friendly private-box at the best point of the best tier, with the cushioned ledge of its front raking the whole scene and its withdrawing rooms behind for more detached conversation; for easy—when not indeed slightly difficult—polyglot talk, artful bibite, artful cigarettes too, straight from the hand of the hostess, who could do all that belonged to a hostess, place people in relation and keep them so, take up and put down the topic, cause delicate tobacco and little gilded glasses to circulate, without ever leaving her sofa-cushions or intermitting her good-nature.*

Venice seemed peculiarly suited to her: "The old bright tradition, the wonderful Venetian legend had appealed to her from the first, closing round her house and her well plashed water-steps, where the waiting gondolas were thick, quite as if, actually, the ghost of the defunct Carnival... still played some haunting part." This is a familiar Venetian image: the enchanted palace approached by water, where good things circulate as if by magic. Servants and gondoliers are not mentioned; it is something of a relief that James goes on to say that Bronson was kind to local people, "renewed their boats," helped with their troubles. And the presiding genius here is not some seductive Giulietta from *Hoffmann*, but the safely middle-aged and uncapricious Mrs. Bronson.

Another of James' haunts was Palazzo Barbaro, where he was the guest of two other long-term settlers, Daniel and Ariana Curtis, and later of Isabella Stewart Gardner. (A good view of the palace is to be had from the pizzeria opposite, near the Accademia bridge.) This was the main inspiration for Palazzo Leporelli in *The Wings of the Dove* (1902). Here, in keeping with James' complex, subtle, sometimes opaque late style, where much must be read between the lines, palace and city are often suggested rather than described. But we do glimpse the "high florid rooms" of the Leporelli, where

> *hard cool pavements took reflexions in their lifelong polish, and where the sun on the stirred sea-water, flickering up through open windows, played over the painted "subjects" in the splendid ceilings—medallions of purple and brown, of brave old melancholy colour, medallions as of old reddened gold, embossed and beribboned, all toned with time and all flourished and scolloped and gilded about, set in their great moulded and figured concavity.*

For the dying Milly Theale "the romance... would be to sit there for ever, through all her time, as in a fortress," but the machinations of her more worldly fellow beings will make her remaining time less easy.

The old lady and her niece in James' *The Aspern Papers* (1888) inhabit a different sort of Venetian palace: dilapidated, too big, on a minor canal and almost without contact with the outside world. James set this tale here rather than in Florence partly because the tradition of Venice as a world of its own makes it easier to imagine this isolation; and the tradition of Venetian brightness, color, and festivity provides a marked contrast. It was in Florence, James discovered, that Claire Clairmont, step-sister of Mary Shelley, intimate of P.B. Shelley and mother of a child by Byron, had lived on until 1879, many years after her famous connections. The story is inspired partly by a real Shelley enthusiast's attempt to gain access to papers in the possession of the old lady and her niece. The "publishing scoundrel," as the Clairmont equivalent in *The Aspern Papers* phrases it, will stop at almost nothing to achieve his goal, riding rough-shod over the right to a private life. James' least happy visit to Venice, following the suicide of his close friend, the novelist Constance Fenimore Woolson, in 1894, was focused on the need to preserve, however possible, the privacy of their relationship, which has been subtly and poignantly studied by Lyndall Gordon in *A Private Life of Henry James: Two Women and his Art*. Transferring the setting to another city, like making the famous poet an American, Jeffrey Aspern, pre-empted the possible charge that James himself is being similarly insensitive. That Aspern is an American, and the women ex-Americans who now seem to be of no particular nation, also enables James to pursue his abiding interest in the encounter between the New and Old Worlds.

Having succeeded in renting rooms in the palazzo at an exorbitant price, the main thing the narrator must do is wait—wait for any opportunity to further his designs. Sometimes he wanders about the town, describing it almost as James had in some of his earlier travel writings, but with slightly too much awareness of his own "exquisite impressions." Once he takes Miss Tina (Miss Tita in the first version) out in a gondola and shows her the wonders she has not seen for long years. Focused on the goal of obtaining the Aspern papers, he will be taken by surprise when, after Aunt Juliana's death, Tina offers them in exchange for his hand in marriage—a condition even he is not prepared to meet. Earlier, in one of the most memorable scenes, he had been taken physically by surprise when Juliana came upon him at night when he was about, in his desperation, to try the lid of her desk. It is only then that he sees the "extraordinary eyes" that once entranced the poet, now usually invisible behind a green shade: "They glared at me; they were like the sudden drench, for a caught burglar, of a flood of gaslight; they made me horribly ashamed."

The creative artist, Aspern or James, would not excite the same disapproval as the "publishing scoundrel." In his 1908 preface to *A Portrait of a Lady* (1881) James explores some aspects of creativity in a passage true both to the delicate nuances of his writing and to the spirit of Venice. While working on the later stages of the novel, he had stayed on the top floor of what is now Pensione Wildner, no. 4161 on Riva degli Schiavoni, with a broad view across to San Giorgio Maggiore.

> *The waterside life, the wondrous lagoon spread before me, and the cease-less human chatter of Venice came in at my windows, to which I seem to*

myself to have been constantly driven, in the fruitless fidget of composi-
tion, as if to see whether, out in the blue channel, the ship of some right
suggestion, of some better phrase, of the next happy twist of my subject, the
next true touch for my canvas, mightn't come into sight.

Such scenes, unfortunately, are "a questionable aid to concentration
when they themselves are not to be the object of it." But in the long
run, a "wasted effort of attention" often proves "strangely fertilizing," so
that both *The Portrait of a Lady* and "one's 'literary effort' at large" may
be the better for the fact that

There are pages of the book which, in the reading over, have seemed to
make me see again the bristling curve of the wide Riva, the large colour-
spots of the balconied houses and the repeated undulation of the hunch-
backed bridges, marked by the rise and drop again, with the wave, of
foreshortened clicking pedestrians. The Venetian footfall and the Venetian
cry—all talk there, wherever uttered, having the pitch of a call across the
water—come in once more at the window, renewing one's old impression
of the delighted senses and the divided, frustrated mind.

CHAPTER TEN

Beyond Venice: The Veneto

"Venice is a place to die in beautifully," Virginia Woolf wrote to a friend in April 1904; "but to live [in] I never felt more depressed—that is exaggerated, but still it does shut one in and make one feel like a Bird in a Cage after a time." She had seen the Tintorettos, "floated in gondolas," and eaten ices at Florian's, but didn't like the place. Nine years later in a letter to her sister Vanessa Bell she still describes it as "detestable," but concedes that "the obscurer reaches might be beautiful." Woolf made for Florence, but there are also some interesting more local escape routes.

Crossing the rail or road-bridge with a view of the smoke, containers, cranes and red-and-white towers of Marghera, you seem to be approaching a different world—a thriving industrial center or a circle of Dante's Inferno. Soon you are past all this to roads, fields, lanes full of the luxuriant Italian vegetation rarely even glimpsed in Venice. Poplars, oleanders, vines return. So too do the pleasures and perils of the car, the ancient Volkswagen beetle attempting precariously to perform a left turn with a hundred Fiats blaring their horns behind it and ahead. In the towns young women in sunglasses, helmetless, effortless, shoot round corners or cruise at speed across piazzas on scooters or motorbikes. Yet there are also many elements that link the

Veneto with the city which ruled most of it from the fifteenth to the eighteenth centuries: a common history, winged lions in public places, a common heritage of work by Veronese and Palladio, for instance. The mainland dominion gave the republic control of a distinguished university at Padua and increased access to the pink Verona marble which, with the white stone of Istria, now in Croatia, features in many Venetian churches and palaces.

Nearer home, Venice was able to smooth an awkward situation in 1488 by bestowing its walled hilltop town of Asolo, near Bassano del Grappa and Treviso, on Caterina Cornaro, Queen of Cyprus. In 1468, at the age of fourteen, she had been sent out to marry King James of Cyprus with the backing of the republic, which hoped to increase its influence in the region. This in the long term it did, but only after much suffering for the soon widowed Cornaro, who for much of the following twenty years was a pawn and sometimes a prisoner of Venice and the various rival factions on the island. Eventually she was persuaded to cede her throne to the republic in exchange for a generous pension and the fief of Asolo. Here, between 1489 and 1509, she presided over the cultivated court which inspired her kinsman Pietro Bembo to set there the humanist love-debates of *The Asolani* (1505).

Whatever daily life was really like at Caterina's court, Bembo helped to give her and Asolo a mythic dimension which survived the loss, by 1820, of most, apart from one tower, of her "fair and pleasant castle… built in the foothills of our mountains overlooking the marches of Treviso." It was both the view and the myth that appealed to Katharine de Kay Bronson, who liked light-heartedly to be identified with Queen Caterina, and her friend Robert Browning. Bronson's villa here had once formed part of the ramparts, whence its name La Mura. There Browning wrote some of the "disconnected poems" in his last collection *Asolando* (1889), giving them, he told Bronson, "a title-name popularly ascribed to the inventiveness" of Bembo: "*Asolare*—'to disport in the open air, amuse oneself at random.'" His own disporting—more strenuous, for a man in his seventies, than the civilized discourse of Bembo's courtiers—included a climb up to the ruins of the town's earlier fortress, the Rocca. Here he was amused to be recognized as "a great English poet" not by some tremulously grateful reader, but by the woman who, with her family, lived in the "wretched hut" where the keys were kept. "I see your shirt," she explained; "one of my friends ironed it last week."

Back in the evening cool on the loggia of La Mura the poet "never wearied," the adoring Bronson recalled, of gazing over the plain below and pointing out to anyone else on the loggia "sights he had kept clear in his mind" when including them, after a first visit to the area back in 1838, in his poems *Sordello* and *Pippa Passes*. He would point out the remains of the stronghold, at Romano d'Ezzelino, of the savage thirteenth-century lord of the March of Treviso, Ezzelino III "the Firebrand," whom Dante consigned with other tyrants to the seventh circle of his Hell. And "If the listener seemed interested"—we can only hope that Browning, famously talkative in his later years, read the signs aright—he would explain what happened at San Zenone, "scene of the most fearful tragedy in all history." In "a few fiery sentences" he would relate "the story of Alberico, betrayed in his last stronghold; how the Trevisani determined to extirpate the race of Ezzelini from the earth, and how, to this end, they destroyed Alberico, his wife, and five children, by tortures too terrible to describe."

As well as such "terrible medieval memories," the Veneto has Roman remains from the centuries when it was a prosperous province free of the attentions of such characters as the Ezzelini or their extirpators—or Attila, or Napoleon. Little of Altinum remains above ground at Altino, northeast of the lagoon, but its small museum contains a good range of the mosaic, funerary busts and artifacts of what was once an important city, a place whose villas, claimed the poet Martial, merited comparison with the luxurious dwellings of Baiae, on the Bay of Naples, and where a nexus of Roman highways met, providing links south to Bologna and Rimini, west to Genoa and across the Alps, and east to Aquileia.

Aquileia, further along the coast toward Trieste, was founded as a Roman colony in 181 BC. It grew to be a city of about 100,000 inhabitants, famous for its carving and trading of amber. Remains of the harbor, forum, amphitheater, baths, houses, Christian oratories, and tombs of the ancient city are still to be seen. The wealth and energy of the Aquileians—ancestors, with people from Altino, Padua, and elsewhere, of the Venetians—is also shown by the remarkable range of mosaics in the two museums and the fourth-century AD basilica of Patriarch Theodore. The mosaics in the basilica are particularly well-preserved: Jonah swallowed by a writhing Celtic-looking creature, more sea-serpent than whale; Victory, a traditionally pagan figure, winged and wreath-wielding, but here probably standing for the Christian victory to be achieved through baptism or martyrdom; baskets of fruit and mushrooms; a cock and a tortoise in combat and other animals putting in a more peaceable appearance—a ram, a gazelle, a goat, a lynx, pheasants, peacocks. There are more fine early medieval mosaics in the cathedral at Grado, south of Aquileia.

For centuries after Attila's devastation of the mainland cities, Venetian attention was focused eastwards. But once the republic had become politically and militarily involved with the Veneto, mainly in the fifteenth century, closer contact returned. (For the conquest and administration of the area see pp.31-2.) Architects and artists moved fairly freely within Venetian territory, working both on churches and palaces in the cities and on the country villas increasingly favored by the nobility. One of the most beautiful of these villas was built at Maser, near Asolo, by the Venetian patrician brothers Marcantonio and Daniele Barbaro. Daniele was variously ambassador in England, Patriarch Elect of Aquileia, and editor, in 1556, of the ancient architectural treatise of Vitruvius. Palladio, whose woodcuts illustrated the Vitruvius and who was described as "our architect" (his and his brother's) in Barbaro's will, worked on the villa in the mid-1550s. In the early 1560s Paolo Veronese complemented and completed the architecture with some of his most brilliant illusionistic effects: servants and family members apparently entering through frescoed doors or looking down from balconies, a perspective vine trellis, views through apparent windows to landscapes with ancient ruins. The landscapes at the back of the villa are probably intended to compensate for the lack of a view in that direction.

An area particularly popular with villa-builders and their customers was the Brenta Canal (the canalized River Brenta), surrounded by fertile land and conveniently placed for Venice and Padua, yet away from the heat of the cities in summer. The cool and peaceful impression may prevail on the canal-side of a villa, but Byron, who rented Villa Foscarini in Mira, now the post-office, complained that it was too near the road. Venetians, once they reach the mainland, he told John Cam Hobhouse in June 1817, "seem to think they never can have dust enough to compensate for their long immersion." Among the examples open to the public are Palladio's Villa Foscari, known as La Malcontenta. The name, according to a legend evidently invented only in order to provide an explanation, came about because a young Foscari woman, too keen on the pleasures of the wicked city, was exiled to this sadly rural retreat. The much larger Villa Pisani at Strà was begun following the election of Doge Alvise Pisani in 1735. It was large enough—there seem to be innumerable rooms and even the stables are magnificent—briefly to accommodate the retinue and the ego of Napoleon Bonaparte. The "villa" had been chosen as the official residence of his Viceroy, Eugène de Beauharnais, who naturally spent more time here. One of the most spectacular relics of this period is the gold and lacquer bed in the *Camera di Napoleone*, complete with yellow and white hangings, giant N and eagle, and a baldacchino on top of which Cupid looks up at Bevilacqua's ceiling painting of the myth of Psyche. Later the place was deemed grand enough to be the appropriate venue for the first discussions between the grandeur-seekers Hitler and Mussolini in June 1934.

Witnesses, witnesses' acquaintances, and historians disagree about how well the dictators got on. Certainly at this point Hitler, the new ruler, appears to have been more impressed with the senior man than he with him. It is unclear how far Mussolini hoped to put Hitler down when, in resplendent general's uniform, he came to the airport on the Lido to greet a guest led to expect informality and so wearing an unremarkable and rather crumpled civilian suit and hat. At Strà they talked without interpreters about issues including the future of Austria and relations with the Catholic Church, reaching little agreement. Mussolini's German was fairly good, but he had some difficulty with—and much boredom at—his guest's long monologues. Afterwards he complained that "instead of talking to me about current problems... he recited to me from memory his *Mein Kampf*," a tedious tome that he had never managed to read. According to one account, more difficult to credit, Mussolini became so fed up with the monologues that he went to the window, looked out at the assembled dignitaries and officers, and, indicating Hitler with his thumb, repeated *È matto, è matto*—"He's mad." The following day discussions resumed at the Alberoni golf club on the Lido. Mussolini, understandably at this stage, failed to take Hitler's measure; when, with *Blitzkrieg* six years ahead, the Führer told him how, with Italian help, he could invade France and capture its main cities in a matter of hours, *Il Duce* reportedly banged the table with his fist and shouted "No!" Relations would remain difficult, though Mussolini was later the one to be humiliated.

But the atmosphere in most of the rooms in Villa Pisani is lighter than such associations might suggest. There are Pompeiian rooms; frescoes of *ville con giardini* with eighteenth-century figures disposed here and there, perambulating; garden views; and a great *salone* or ballroom graced with *trompe-l'oeil* effects and the last great ceiling painting (1761–2) undertaken by Giambattista Tiepolo before he left for Madrid to work for King Carlos III of Spain. In this Apotheosis of the Pisani, as Michael Levey says in his study of the artist, "he combined allegory and personification with the living members of the family, portraying them positively up in the clouds, serene and assured, almost gods themselves, in a very heaven of optimism."

Padua

The cities of Padua, Vicenza, and Verona can each easily be visited from Venice. Padua, the closest, perhaps most keenly felt the burden (as well as the benefits) of being absorbed into the Venetian republic. But various factors have helped to maintain a distinctive Paduan identity. The university was founded in 1222, the second in Italy after Bologna, and was later famous for medicine as well as more abstract subjects. William Harvey was among the medical students in the early seventeenth century, and a funnel-like anatomical theater of 1594 survives. The Orto Botanico, established in 1545 was, as Coryat put it, "famoused over most places in Christendom for the sovereign virtue of medicinable herbs." Its remit became in time more generally botanical; palms were grown and, in the late sixteenth century, the first sunflowers and lilacs in Italy. From the 1830s the university was joined by another center of intellectual debate, the Caffè Pedrocchi. Distinctively Paduan too is the cult of Sant'Antonio, the thirteenth-century Portuguese missionary who was en route for Africa when a storm blew him off course to Italy, where he stayed to become the friend and disciple of St. Francis and a patron saint of childbirth, the poor, and lost property. His pilgrimage church, the basilica of Sant'Antonio,

known simply as *Il Santo*, was founded in 1232, the year after his death. The pilgrims continue to come to this oriental-looking place of many cupolas and many monuments, leaving ex votos, including small model arms, legs, and hearts, in the saint's chapel.

Outside the basilica in Piazza del Santo is Donatello's proudly secular equestrian figure of the *condottiere* Gattamelata (the wily "honeyed cat," really called, less noticeably, Erasmo da Narni), who died in Padua in 1443 after loyal service in the mainland wars of the Venetian republic. He appears completely determined, expression set, eyes probing the distance, baton and sword forming a clear long diagonal. His charger, with one hoof poised on a cannonball and tail tied taut, is almost as resolute as he is.

Padua's other most notable property is the Cappella Scrovegni, also known, since it was built near the remains of the ancient amphitheater, as the Arena chapel. It was built by Enrico Scrovegni in 1303, partly in expiation of family sins: his father, a money-lender, had been demoted to the seventh circle of Hell by Dante. In about 1305–6 it was decorated by Giotto di Bondone, the foremost painter of the day and the first painter to be widely talked about as a named individual. (He even appears as a canny, witty character in Boccaccio's tales.) He is still perceived as an innovator, one who made a clean break with Byzantine traditions, translating the art of painting, as a later commentator put it, "from Greek into Latin." At least to western eyes, he painted figures more naturalistically than his predecessors, more feelingly, and in more natural and evocative spatial relation; Henry Moore called his work "sculpture." He was also a pioneer of painting in fresco, a form less practicable in the saltier air of Venice; partly for this reason Giotto's strongest influence was on his fellow Florentines. The Arena frescoes tell, in a small space but with consistent dramatic clarity, the life of the Virgin and the life of Christ with, below them, grisaille Virtues and Vices. The many memorable scenes include the one in which, hemmed in by soldiers with clubs and brands, Christ and Judas look into each other's eyes as the betrayer's features are distorted by his kiss and by his crime.

Vicenza

John Evelyn, seeking educative, "curious," or impressively well ordered customs and objects on the long European tour that kept him at a safe distance from the less rational world of the English Civil Wars, approved of Vicenza. It is "a city full of gentlemen and splendid palaces, to which the famous Palladio, born here, has exceedingly contributed as having been the architect." In fact, Andrea Palladio was born in Padua, but he lived in Vicenza for much of his life. He "contributed" an extraordinary range of buildings in and around the city: churches, palaces, villas, arcades, and, "most conspicuous," as Evelyn says, "the Hall of Justice." This building is more often called by Palladio's own name for it, the Basilica, since, as he explains in *The Four Books of Architecture*, in Roman times "those places were called basilicas, in which the judges sat under cover to administer justice, and where sometimes great and imposing affairs were debated." Even the name is intended to emphasize the classical provenance of the design, as do, more physically, the colonnades with which Palladio transformed the exterior of the medieval Palazzo della Ragione.

Palladio's classicism, focused on his interpretation of Vitruvius' *De Architectura*, the only surviving ancient book on architecture, had first been fostered by his patron the Vicentine nobleman and poet Giangiorgio Trissino (1478–1550). He sent Palladio to Rome, advanced his early education and career, and even gave him the name by which he became known, suggesting skill and wisdom, from the goddess Pallas Athene. Trissino was one of a group of local patricians who participated enthusiastically in the desire for a classical revival. In 1556 they founded an Olympic Academy. They and other citizens considered Palladio's work as a matter for civic pride; its classicism was both what was regarded as modern at the time and, on the other hand, a link with the past of this ancient, once-Roman settlement. And on both counts it could be used to bolster a sense of equality with, or even superiority to, Venice, their architecturally conservative and post-Roman ruler. (Confidence was also bolstered by the city's flourishing silk trade.) Their most ambitiously classical building was the Teatro Olimpico.

It was in the Basilica, in 1562, that a production of Trissino's play *Sofonisba*, written in 1515 in Italian blank verse but inspired by ancient drama, had been staged. Partly because it was Palladio who had converted the Basilica into a temporary theater for the occasion, the Olympic Academy later commissioned him to design a permanent theater for them. The architect, with his Vitruvius and his vast experience at the ready, began work but died, in 1580, with only the outer walls completed. Vincenzo Scamozzi took over, completing and, where the stage itself was concerned, substantially modifying his predecessor's plans. The perspective streets, beyond the arches of what was intended to reproduce the Roman *frons scenae*, built by Scamozzi for the opening performance in 1585, are still in place. This somewhat limits the dramatic possibilities; a few years later, at the ducal theater in Sabbioneta, Scamozzi himself widened the arch and replaced the streets with one landscape. Changeable scenery, besides, was already being used in some other theaters. Goethe was pleased to find the theater still functioning, but speaks for many when he concludes that the Olimpico is "indescribably beautiful," yet "compared to our modern theatres, it looks like an aristocratic, rich, and well-educated child as against a clever man of the world who, though not as rich, distinguished, or educated, knows better what it is in his means to do." In short, it is an academic theater.

Nevertheless, it must have been exciting to be at the first production, *Oedipo Tiranno*, a version of Sophocles' play by Orsatto Giustiniani with music by Andrea Gabrieli. The participation of this renowned Venetian composer, uncle of Giovanni Gabrieli, was no doubt felt to contribute to the prestige of the occasion and of Vicenza. The actors' dignified robes and gestures survive in fresco on the walls of the Anteodeon, next to the auditorium. Aural, visual, and even olfactory effects were included: *Oedipo* was introduced with "a sudden fragrance."

Near the city is one of Palladio's most successful villas, built in the late 1560s for Monsignor Paolo Almerico but usually known as La Rotonda. Almerico, the architect tells us, "having traveled many years out of a desire of honor, all his relatives being dead, came to his native country, and for his recreation retired to one of his country-houses." There he built "according to the following [Palladio's] invention" the villa:

> *The site is as pleasant and delightful as can be found; it is upon a small hill, of very easy access, and is watered on one side by the Bacchiglione, a navigable river; and on the other it is encompassed with most pleasant*

risings, which look like a very great theatre, and all are cultivated, and
abound with most excellent fruits, and most exquisite vines: and there-
fore, as it enjoys from every part most beautiful views, some of which are
limited, some more extended, and some that terminate with the horizon,
there are loggias made in all the four fronts; under the floor of which, and
of the hall, are the rooms for the conveniency and use of the family. The
hall is in the middle, is round, and receives its light from above.

The Rotonda was one of Palladio's most influential buildings, a model, for instance, for Lord Burlington's Chiswick House. The interior was shown to advantage in Joseph Losey's 1979 film of Mozart's *Don Giovanni*.

Verona

Verona, not more than two hours from Venice by train, less by car, presents an ideal contrast to it. There are hills, a rushing Alpine river "from whose shore the rocks rise in a great crescent, dark with cypress, and misty with olive" (Ruskin), and the main thing missing from Venice: impressive, still standing Roman structures. The huge amphitheater (c. AD 100), with its forty-four tiers of seating (often renewed since the sixteenth century) once held 22,000 spectators. On the route down from the Brenner Pass into Italy, this was the first major town and building encountered by many northern invaders and visitors. Goethe, thirsting for the classical, had his first direct encounter with it in the arena. His excitement did not prevent him from analyzing, where most of us might just wander about and stare, how this great round developed and what effect it had on those who gathered there, how it is designed "to impress the people with itself, to make them feel at their best." Makeshift arrangements where the people at the back stand on benches, barrels, or carts, lead on to stands being put up. The architect then satisfies the "universal need" by creating "as plain a crater as possible":

… the public itself supplies its decoration. Crowded together, its members
are astonished at themselves. They are accustomed at other times to see
each other running hither and thither in confusion, bustling about
without order or discipline. Now this many-headed, many-minded,

fickle, blundering monster suddenly sees itself united as one noble assembly, wielded into one mass, a single body animated by a single spirit.
This "single body" has watched Roman gladiators and lions, such "great shows... as running at tilt, and other noble exercises, especially upon their carnival day" (Coryat), and in modern times the flourishing annual opera season.

As in many Roman towns, the most obvious site is only one among many; the lack of signs of ancient settlement in the lagoon underlines how usefully remote it was from life on the mainland. The Porta Borsari and a number of other arches survive, strikingly white in a town so full of pink and variegated marble. The Ponte Pietra (a modern version of the original, which was badly damaged in Second World War bombing) spans the charging blue-green Adige near the Roman Theater. This structure, begun perhaps a century before the amphitheater, was largely built over in the Middle Ages. It was unearthed in a good state of preservation in the nineteenth century and restored sufficiently for an annual drama festival to be established in 1962. As a result, some details, including what is left of the ancient marble floor of the *orchestra*, in front of the stage, are obscured in summer by modern stage-sets and seating. But watching actors rehearsing or scene-painters at work, remote though their practice and theory may be from Roman theater, probably takes us as close to it as contemplation of the empty stage area.

The theater complex slopes up the hill in terraces, with, at one side, an overflow of Roman architectural fragments: capitals, unplaced building blocks, inscriptions, sculptured scenes, part of the seemingly inexhaustible litter of empire. From the theater you can go on up the hillside, by lift or steps, to the former convent of San Girolamo. From the high terraces, as the steps pass pink oleanders (among which I saw, on one visit, small, delicate, yellow-marked spiders), the view across the river steadily improves. From the windows of the convent you can look down at the theater and out at high pines, the Adige, and the roofs and towers of the city: the tower of Sant'Anastasia nearby, cranes and tower-blocks only in the far distance. The convent now houses a fine archaeological museum. Among the exhibits is a larger than life representation of an emperor in cuirass and cloak. Identification is made a little problematic by the absence of his head, but there is an impressive amount of attention to the decorative details of his armor, including small heads of rams, lions, and elephants. There is also a good range of figures endowed with heads, some with elaborate imperial hairdos, others with divine crowns or diadems, none perhaps really outstanding but enhanced, in many cases, by the fine quality of the white marble. Having crossed a small, peaceful Renaissance cloister (restored in the 1920s) with palm-trees, you come to a display of mosaics from various areas of the evidently prosperous Roman city.

Verona survived as one of the principal cities of Visigothic Italy. Later it was a medieval *comune* and then, in the thirteenth and fourteenth centuries, the headquarters of the dynasty known as the della Scala or Scaligeri. One of the main building periods followed an earthquake in 1117, when the earlier churches of San Lorenzo, San Zeno, and the Duomo were reconstructed. Later came Sant'Anastasia, begun in the late thirteenth century and mostly completed in the fifteenth (the façade remained unfinished), a large building like other Dominican preaching-centered churches, with three naves and imposing Verona marble columns. Pisanello's fresco of *St. George and the Princess* (1437–8) is in the Pellegrini Chapel in this church. The famous chivalric scene of golden-curled saint and princess with fashionably high round forehead, with its equally famous horses, is above and to the right of the arch. Across rough terrain, on the other side of the arch, is what is left of the land of the dragon. The damaged state of the fresco seems only to enhance the romantic effects. A less romantic note of warning, however, is sounded by the presence of two hanged men, who have presumably performed less noble needs than George. The same artist's *Annunciation* (1423–4) is in the church of San Fermo. Pisanello enthusiasts should also go, beyond the confines of this book, to the Ducal Palace in Mantua, where substantial fragments of his Arthurian fresco cycle—knights, mêlées, ladies, a great castle—were uncovered in 1968.

Perhaps the best-known medieval monuments in Verona are the tombs of the Scaligeri, in the walled and railed enclosure outside the church of Santa Maria Antica. A blue-shirted official looks out suspiciously from the entrance, like a latter-day henchman of the proud lords within, for people who haven't purchased a ticket at the Torre dei Lamberti. The tombs—Cangrande (d. 1329), Dante's protector, above the church, Mastino II (d. 1351) and Cansignorio (d. 1375) in the enclosure—almost dwarf the church, raised up on platforms, thrusting upwards to the point of Mastino's sword or Cansignorio's lance. Some figures are winged. And the last of the tombs, with its decorative excrescences, seeks to move outward as well as upward. Altogether the Scaligeri wish to leave no doubt as to their status and aspirations—unfulfillable though their straining, piled high monuments seem to say that these were.

Cangrande's memorial is a copy. The original figure, and parts of its sword, are in the Castelvecchio museum. This was long the town's main fortress and palace, and as late as January 1944 it was here that Mussolini's son-in-law and former foreign minister, Count Galeazzo Ciano, and five others were tried and condemned for treason. Here the architect Carlo Scarpa designed one of the most imaginative and radiant of modern Italian museums, skillfully incorporating parts of the old buildings and walls into the new galleries and viewing spaces. Cangrande is dramatically displayed, more visibly than in the rather cramped churchyard. The large collection also includes frescoes (with some fragments still in place from the museum's days as a palace) and sinopie (chalk sketches beneath the frescoes themselves), paintings, and, in the first gallery, some striking medieval statues. Those of Santa Marta, once in the church of San Fermo (early fourteenth century) and San Bartolomeo (later fourteenth century), both Veronese work, their paint mostly intact, are the most approachable, less simply hieratic than the others. Bartholomew particularly seems to tremble on the verge of speech, the verge of a more modern, humane communication, while retaining something of his saintly distance, his "medievalness." Reflecting this transitional state, his eyes are painted black, but full individuality is not quite achieved because the pupils remain undifferentiated. One hand, which either blessed the viewer or carried an attribute, is missing. With the other he holds a Latin scroll proclaiming himself, commandingly but reassuringly, banisher of demons, destroyer of idols, and *omnium protector*.

The list of Verona's riches could go on: the many interesting and elegant buildings of Piazza delle Erbe and Piazza dei Signori, especially the Renaissance Loggia del Consiglio, its façade, above the slim columns of the arcade, deep yellow, frescoed, and with small statues of such Veronese or allegedly Veronese worthies as Catullus and Vitruvius; the Giardino Giusti, a sixteenth-century garden where "huge cypresses soar into the air like awls" (Goethe); and the fine medieval house and tomb romantically associated with Shakespeare's Juliet, despite the fact that she lived in Siena in the first version of the story. But perhaps the best way to conclude a visit to Verona is to return, refreshed by contrast, to Venice. Goethe, escaping joyously from the political and social responsibilities of his life on the other side of the Alps, found much of interest in his autumn journey through Verona, Vicenza, and Padua and, between them, the vineyards, the views of hills, "a profusion of flowers and fruits, hanging down from the trees and over the hedges and walls," roofs "laden with pumpkins, and the strangest-looking cucumbers hung from poles and trellises." But his real sense of occasion is reserved for Venice:

> It was written, then, on my page in the Book of Fate that at five in the afternoon of the twenty-eighth day of September in the year 1786, I should see Venice for the first time as I entered this beautiful island-city, this beaver-republic. So now, thank God, Venice is no longer a mere word to me, an empty name, a state of mind which has so often alarmed me who am the mortal enemy of mere words.

Readers tempted to mock the pomposity even of the mighty man of letters may prefer to hear his first example of how the city became real for him. When a gondola came alongside the boat in which he had traveled along the Brenta, he suddenly remembered the model gondola that his father had brought back from Venice and with which he was sometimes allowed to play. And so "when the gondolas appeared their shining steel-sheeted prows and black cages greeted me like old friends."

Appendix
A Selection of Other Places in Venice

Ca' da Mosto. Thirteenth-century palazzo on the Grand Canal (after Rio dei Santi Apostoli, before Rio di San Giovanni Grisostomo) which became a well-known inn, the Albergo del Leon Bianco, between the fifteenth and eighteenth centuries. Among the guests was William Beckford, who watched from his balcony, in the cool of evening, "the variety of figures shooting by in their gondolas":

> ... *every boat had its lantern, and the gondolas moving rapidly along were followed by tracks of light, which gleamed and played on the waters. I was gazing at these dancing fires, when the sounds of music were wafted along the canals, and, as they grew louder and louder, an illuminated barge, filled with musicians, issued from the Rialto, and stopping under one of the palaces, began a serenade.*

Conversation in the galleries and porticos was stilled. And then, as the barge rowed away, "the gondoliers, catching the air, imitated its cadences, and were answered by others at a distance, whose voices, echoed by the arch of the bridge, acquired a plaintive and interesting tone."

Fondaco dei Turchi. Early thirteenth-century palazzo on the Grand Canal. Turkish merchants used it between the seventeenth and nineteenth centuries. Restoration (from 1858) followed agitation by Ruskin, but was unimaginatively carried out. The building now houses a good natural history collection, including the skeleton of a large Ouranosaurus.

Gesuati. Rococo church on the Zattere, built by Giorgio Massari between the late 1720s and early 1740s. Officially this is Santa Maria del Rosario; the popular name comes from the earlier owners of the site, the order famous for its members' continual invocation of the name of Jesus. In the first chapel on the right is the *echt* Tiepolo *Virgin and Child with SS. Catherine of Siena, Rosa, and Agnese*. Tiepolo also painted the ceiling with *The Institution of the Rosary* and other scenes associated with St. Dominic. Vigorous statues of biblical figures in the nave include Moses bearing the tablets, robes fluttering as he descends hotfoot to deliver the Ten Commandments.

Gesuiti. Jesuit church on the Fondamenta Nuove, built in 1714-29, famous for its spectacular Baroque interior in which almost everything, including what at first may appear to be more conventional curtains and tapestries, is green-and-white marble. Titian's *Martyrdom of St. Lawrence*, in the first chapel on the left, survives from an earlier church on the site. It is hailed by Hugh Honour as "apart from a fresco by Raphael in the Vatican... the first successful nocturne in the history of art."

Museo Archeologico. Museum in the Piazza, near the Museo Correr. It houses one of the finest collections of Greek and Roman sculpture in northern Italy. Many of the works were bequeathed or given in the sixteenth century by Cardinal Domenico Grimani and his nephew Giovanni Grimani, Patriarch of Aquileia.

Museo Fortuny. Display, in the fifteenth-century Palazzo Pesaro degli Orfei, of work by or associated with Mariano Fortuny y de Madrazo (1871-1949), the Spanish designer and painter who lived here. His exotic fabrics were often inspired by Venetian examples from earlier centuries as well as by Arab and eastern designs, and used some of the same techniques. They were used both in the theater and for clothing. His best-known fictional customer is Proust's Albertine.

Museo di Palazzo Mocenigo. In Palazzo Mocenigo a San Stae, as it is called to avoid confusion with its namesake on the Grand Canal, an interesting collection of art and artifacts, mainly eighteenth-century, some from the days of Mocenigo ownership. Among the paintings of dignitaries is one of Procurator Giulio Contarini, whose daughter married a Mocenigo. The sitter, in rich red robe and gray wig, is perhaps less noticeable than the extravagant gilded frame, by Antonio Corradini or his workshop, with its bold flourishes, trumpeting Fame, Justice, spears, standards, and final upward sweep to the high crown. Larger paintings include Antonio Strom's canvas of the future Doge Alvise II Mocenigo arriving as ambassador in Constantinople and in a London which looks at least in part Venetian. Cannons smoke in salute, hats are doffed and hands extended, and the republic, in spite of its real lack of power, continues to cut a fine diplomatic figure. The museum also houses the Center for the Study of the History of Textiles and Costume. Selections from the collection are displayed in rotation; at the time of writing the selection includes fans, floral hats and waistcoats, and samples of Rococo fashion.

San Francesco della Vigna. A vineyard on this site was given to the Franciscans in 1253. Jacopo Sansovino began the present large, rather forbidding building in 1534 and Palladio added the façade in the 1560s. Among the paintings in the church are a triptych probably by Antonio Vivarini (c. 1415-76), a Virgin and Child by Antonio da Negroponte of about 1450-65, a resurrection possibly by Veronese and *The Holy Family with St. John the Baptist, St. Anthony Abbot, and St. Catherine* definitely by him. The fine altarpiece in one of the chapels on the left of the nave is by Alessandro Vittoria.

San Giobbe. Fifteenth-century church in Cannaregio. Pietro Lombardo carved the statues on the façade. He and his workshop also worked on the doorway and the Sanctuary (which includes the tomb of Doge Cristoforo Moro, d. 1471) and gave the interior essentially its present appearance.

San Pietro di Castello. The cathedral of Venice until 1807, a church on an island at the eastern end of the city. Most of the present structure is late sixteenth-century. The separate campanile is fifteenth-century with a later cupola. Inside, the "Throne of St. Peter" came originally from Antioch. Outside is a pleasant grassy area with oleanders, geraniums, and plane trees.

San Polo. Medieval church (largely rebuilt in 1804), near the Frari. In its Oratory of the Crucifix is a Stations of the Cross sequence by Giandomenico Tiepolo (1749).

San Salvatore (or San Salvador). Three-domed, sixteenth- and seventeenth-century church. Inside are Sansovino's tomb for Doge

Francesco Venier of 1556-61, Bernardino Contino's for Caterina Cornaro (see p.212) of 1580-4, showing her giving Cyprus to the doge, and Titian's late (1560s) *Transfiguration* and *Annunciation*.

San Sebastiano. Paolo Veronese's parish church, to which he and his brother, Benedetto Caliari, contributed many paintings and frescoes. The brothers' tombs are in the Lando chapel.

San Stae. Church on the Grand Canal with Baroque exterior by Domenico Rossi (1709-10) and contrasting light, airy, interior. There are paintings by Tiepolo and his contemporary Piazzetta. The Foscarini chapel, the third on the left, contains busts of four Foscarini worthies (ambassadors, procurators), one of them luxuriantly bewigged.

Santa Maria Zobenigo. This is the familiar name of Santa Maria del Giglio. Giuseppe Sardi's façade, commissioned by Antonio Barbaro, celebrates the deeds of the Barbaro family so extensively that Ruskin referred to its "insolent atheism."

Scuola Grande dei Carmini. Built probably by Longhena in 1668. The upper hall has ceiling paintings (1739-49) by Tiepolo. Most of the scenes show the Virtues. One, more strikingly, shows a white-clad Virgin, celestial but physical, almost sensual, appearing to a holy medieval Englishman, Blessed Simon Stock. Beneath the kneeling Simon are the skulls, sufferers and darkness of Purgatory, but the Virgin—or an angel on her behalf—brings him a scapular, the pieces of cloth which were believed to provide at least some relief from the tortures of Purgatory and which were associated with the Carmelite order.

Vittorio Cini Collection. In Palazzo Cini, near the Accademia and the Peggy Guggenheim: paintings, drawings, illuminated manuscripts, and books belonging to Cini (1884-1977), prominent politician, business-man, and patron. Tuscan artists are particularly well represented, among them Botticelli, Piero di Cosimo, and Filippo Lippi. (The Cini is open only between June and October.)

Further Reading

1. History

Paul Ginsborg, *Daniele Manin and the Venetian Revolution of 1848–9.* Cambridge: Cambridge University Press, 1979.

Christopher Hibbert, *Venice: the Biography of a City.* London: Grafton, 1988.

Frederick C. Lane, *Venice: a Maritime Republic.* Baltimore: Johns Hopkins University Press, 1973.

Donald M. Nicol, *Byzantium and Venice: a Study in Diplomatic and Cultural Relations.* Cambridge: Cambridge University Press, 1988.

John Julius Norwich, *A History of Venice.* London: Penguin, 1983.

David Wootton, *Paolo Sarpi: Between Renaissance and Enlightenment.* Cambridge: Cambridge University Press, 1983.

2. Guides and Travel Writing

Roberta Curiel and Bernard Dov Cooperman, *The Ghetto of Venice.* London: Tauris Parke, 1990.

Johann Wolfgang von Goethe, *Italian Journey.* Trans. W.H. Auden and Elizabeth Mayer. London: Penguin, 1970.

Hugh Honour, *The Companion Guide to Venice.* London: Companion Guides, 1997.

Henry James, *Italian Hours.* Ed. John Aucher. London: Penguin, 1995.

Alta Macadam, *Blue Guide: Venice.* New York/London: W.W. Norton/A.& C. Black, 1998.

Jan Morris, *Venice.* London: Faber & Faber, 1983.

3. Literature

Martin Garrett, *Traveller's Literary Companion to Italy.* Brighton: In Print, 1998.

Ian Littlewood, *Venice: a Literary Companion.* London: John Murray, 1991.

John Julius Norwich, ed., *Venice: a Traveller's Companion.* London: Constable, 1990.

John Pemble, *Venice Rediscovered.* Oxford: Oxford University Press, 1995.

Margaret F. Rosenthal, *The Honest Courtesan: Veronica Franco, Citizen and Writer in Sixteenth-Century Venice*. Chicago: University of Chicago Press, 1992.

Tony Tanner, *Venice Desired (Convergences)*. Ed. Edward W. Said. Cambridge MA: Harvard University Press, 1992.

4. Art and Architecture

Jeanne Clegg, *Ruskin and Venice*. London: Junction Books, 1981.

Richard Goy, *The House of Gold: Building a Palace in Medieval Venice*. Cambridge: Cambridge University Press, 1992.

——, *Venice: the City and its Architecture*. London: Phaidon, 1997.

Paul Holberton, *Palladio's Villas*. London: John Murray, 1991.

Deborah Howard, *The Architectural History of Venice*. London: Batsford, 1980.

Michael Levey, *Painting in Eighteenth-Century Venice*, New Haven CT: Yale University Press, 1994.

Peter Lauritzen, *Palaces of Venice*. London: Laurence King, 1992.

——, *Venice Preserved*. London: Michael Joseph, 1986.

——, *Venice: a Thousand Years of Culture and Civilisation*. London: Weidenfeld and Nicolson, 1978.

Giandomenico Romanelli, ed., *Venice: Art and Architecture*. London: Könemann, 1997.

David Rosand, *Painting in Sixteenth-Century Venice: Titian, Veronese, Tintoretto*. Cambridge: Cambridge University Press, 1997.

John Ruskin, *The Stones of Venice*. Ed. Jan Morris. London: Bellew Publishing, 1989.

Index of Literary
& Historical Names

Index of Places